Development and Social Change

j

11am

Sociology for a New Century

A PINE FORGE PRESS SERIES

Edited by Charles Ragin, Wendy Griswold, and Larry Griffin

Sociology for a New Century brings the best current scholarship to today's students in a series of short texts authored by leaders of a new generation of social scientists. Each book addresses its subject from a comparative, historical, and global perspective and, in doing so, connects social science to the wider concerns of students seeking to make sense of our dramatically changing world.

- *Global Inequalities* York Bradshaw and Michael Wallace
- *How Societies Change* Daniel Chirot
- *Cultures and Societies in a Changing World* Wendy Griswold
- *Crime and Disrepute* John Hagan
- *Gods in the Global Village: The World's Religions in Sociological Perspective* Lester R. Kurtz
- *Waves of Democracy: Social Movements and Political Change* John Markoff
- *Development and Social Change: A Global Perspective* Philip McMichael
- *Constructing Social Research* Charles C. Ragin
- *Women and Men at Work* Barbara Reskin and Irene Padavic
- *Cities in a World Economy* Saskia Sassen

Forthcoming:

- *Social Psychology and Social Institutions* Denise and William Bielby
- *Schools and Societies* Steven Brint
- *The Social Ecology of Natural Resources and Development* Stephen G. Bunker
- *Ethnic Dynamics in the Modern World* Stephen Cornell
- *The Sociology of Childhood* William A. Corsaro
- *Economy and Society* Mark Granovetter
- *People and Populations: Demography and the Human Experience* Dennis P. Hogan
- *Racism in the Modern World* Wilmot G. James
- *Health and Societies* Bernice Pescosolido
- *Organizations in a World Economy* Walter W. Powell

Development and Social Change

A Global Perspective

Philip McMichael
Cornell University

PINE FORGE PRESS
Thousand Oaks, California ✦ *London* ✦ *New Delhi*

For information, address:

 Pine Forge Press
A Sage Publications Company
2455 Teller Road
Thousand Oaks, California 91320
(805) 499-4224
E-mail: sales@pfp.sagepub.com

Sage Publications Ltd.
6 Bonhill Street
London EC2A 4PU
United Kingdom

Sage Publications India Pvt. Ltd.
M-32 Market
Greater Kailash I
New Delhi 110 048 India

Production: Rogue Valley Publications
Designer: Lisa S. Mirski
Typesetter: Scratchgravel Publishing Services
Cover: Lisa S. Mirski
Production Manager: Rebecca Holland

Printed in the United States of America

96 97 98 99 00 10 9 8 7 6 5 4 3 2 1

Library of Congress Cataloging-in-Publication Data

McMichael, Philip.
    Development and social change : a global perspective / Philip McMichael.
        p.   cm. — (Sociology for a new century)
    Includes bibliographical references and index.
    ISBN 0-8039-9066-9 (pbk. : alk. paper)
    1. Economic development projects—History. 2. Economic development—History. 3. Competition, International—History.
I. Title. II. Series.
HC79.E44M25   1996
306.3'09—dc20   95-20533
                                                              CIP

For Karen,
with love and gratitude

Contents

ABOUT THE AUTHOR

Philip McMichael grew up in Adelaide, South Australia, and he completed his undergraduate studies at the University of Adelaide. After traveling in India, Pakistan, Afghanistan, and Papua New Guinea, he pursued his doctorate in Sociology at the State University of New York at Binghamton. He has taught at the University of New England (New South Wales), Swarthmore College, and the University of Georgia and is presently Professor of Rural and Development Sociology at Cornell University. His book *Settlers and the Agrarian Question: Foundations of Capitalism in Colonial Australia* (1984) won the Social Science History Association's Allan Sharlin Memorial Award. He is the editor of *The Global Restructuring of Agro-Food Systems* (1994) and *Food and Agrarian Orders in the World Economy* (1995). He has served as director of Cornell University's International Political Economy Program and as chair of the American Sociological Association's Political Economy of the World-System Section. He and his wife, Karen Schachere, have two children, Rachel and Jonathan.

ABOUT THE PUBLISHER

Pine Forge Press is a new educational publisher, dedicated to publishing innovative books and software throughout the social sciences. On this and any other of our publications, we welcome your comments, ideas, and suggestions. Please call or write to:

Pine Forge Press
A Sage Publications Company
2455 Teller Road
Thousand Oaks, California 91320
(805) 499-4224
E-mail: sales@pfp.sagepub.com

Foreword

Sociology for a New Century offers the best of current sociological thinking to today's students. The goal of the series is to prepare students, and—in the long run—the informed public, for a world that has changed dramatically in the last three decades and one that continues to astonish.

This goal reflects important changes that have taken place in sociology. The discipline has become broader in orientation, with an ever growing interest in research that is comparative, historical, or transnational in orientation. Sociologists are less focused on "American" society as the pinnacle of human achievement and more sensitive to global processes and trends. They also have become less insulated from surrounding social forces. In the 1970s and 1980s, sociologists were so obsessed with constructing a science of society that they saw impenetrability as a sign of success. Today, there is a greater effort to connect sociology to the ongoing concerns and experiences of the informed public.

Each book in this series offers in some way a comparative, historical, transnational, or global perspective to help broaden students' vision. Students need to comprehend the diversity in today's world and to understand the sources of diversity. This knowledge can challenge the limitations of conventional ways of thinking about social life. At the same time, students need to understand that issues that may seem specifically "American" (for example, the women's movement, an aging population bringing a strained social security and health care system, racial conflict, national chauvinism, and so on) are shared by many other countries. Awareness of commonalities undercuts the tendency to view social issues and questions in narrowly American terms and encourages students to seek out the experiences of others for the lessons they offer. Finally, students need to grasp phenomena that transcend national boundaries—trends and processes that are supranational (for example, environmental degradation). Recognition of global processes stimulates student awareness of causal forces that transcend national boundaries, economies, and politics.

Reflecting the dramatic acceleration of the global economy, *Development and Social Change: A Global Perspective* explores the complex interplay between rich and poor countries over the post–World War II era. Its starting point is the view of international inequality predominant in the 1950s and 1960s. This thinking joined international organizations and Third World governments in a common ideology of state-managed economic and social change and championed the idea that, with a little help from rich countries and international organizations, poor countries could become developed countries, pulling themselves up by their own bootstraps. Reality, of course, fell far short of the vision that inspired development thinking, and this view, which McMichael calls the *development project*, gave way to *globalism*. Goals of integration with the world economy and openness to its forces supplanted goals of national development and "catching up with the West." McMichael's portrait of global interconnections at century's end spotlights the long reach of international markets and commodity chains and the many, often invisible, connections between producers and consumers worldwide.

Preface

The subject of development is difficult to teach. Living in relatively affluent surroundings, students understandably situate their society on the "high end" of a development continuum—at the pinnacle of human economic and technological achievement. And they often perceive both the development continuum and their favorable position on it as "natural"— a well-deserved reward for embracing the values of modernity. (This is likely to be the case also for students from the so-called Third World, although their experiences will be different.) It is difficult to put one's world in historical perspective from this vantage point. It is harder still to help students grasp a world perspective that goes beyond framing their history as a simple series of developmental or evolutionary stages—the inevitable march of progress.

In my experience, until students go beyond simple evolutionary views, they have difficulty valuing other cultures that do not potentially mirror their own. When they do go beyond the evolutionary perspective, they are better able to evaluate their own culture sociologically and to think reflexively about social change, development, and international inequality. This is the challenge.

The narrative that follows presents an overview of social change and development in the late twentieth century. It is not organized around competing theories of social change and development, nor does it adhere to a single, all-encompassing perspective. Rather, my narrative retraces the story of development as an increasingly global enterprise.

The tack this book takes is to introduce students to the global roots and dimensions of recent social changes and to the special role filled by the **development project**. It encourages them to think about development as a transnational project designed to integrate the world, and it helps them to see how this project is currrently undergoing dramatic revision via economic globalization. With these understandings in place, they will be better prepared for the many challenges that lie ahead.

Many of the available texts approach development through the lens of theory. Texts are usually organized around competing theories or perspectives (e.g., modernization versus dependency versus world-systems theory, liberal perspectives versus marxist perspectives, structuralism versus neo-liberalism, and so on). Students find themselves thrown into the task of evaluating abstract perspectives without proper grounding in knowledge of the post–World War II developmentalist era. While presenting competing theoretical perspectives is a fundamental part of teaching social change and development, students need a basic understanding of the context within which these competing theories arose and then collided.

The post–Cold War world that students live in today is very different from the world that gave rise to development theories. The rapid pace of social change makes the task of understanding this world akin to shooting at a moving target. The established units of sociological analysis (e.g., national societies and citizens, individual rational actors, and so on) are now surrounded by competing organizing principles—sub-national communities and supra-national regions, transnational webs of exchange and transnational communities, ethnic and cultural entities, expressive politics, and so on. It is even questionable whether development theory, as it is now known and debated, will survive the dramatic social changes of the post–Cold War world, as the ground is shifting—even degrading—under the development project.

This book has been designed with these new challenges in mind. My aim is to situate current changes historically, first presenting an overview of the development era (including its theoretical discourses) and then addressing its declining salience as a new global era emerges. Students who are already familiar with such social movements as feminism, grassroots activism, and rainforest protection, will find these issues here in the context of the shifting debates and challenges to the development project.

The text traces the steps in the gradual evolution of the development enterprise into an emerging **globalization project**, outlining the conditions under which the post–World War II managers of states and multilateral agencies institionalized development as a key organizing principle in the Cold War era. A series of case studies concentrate on the Third World countries' experience of the development project, individualizing this experience and showing how it differed across Third World countries and regions, while at the same time situating those individual experiences in a common process.

The common process of development itself has changed substantially. From the early 1970s, when new global trends begin to override the 1940s Bretton Woods development institutions, a new project of globalization began, gradually supplanting the development project, dramatized by the debt crisis of the 1980s. The text lays out the main features of this trend, including some of the major counter-mobilizations, such as the feminist and the environmental movements. New questions arise in a world that is simultaneously integrating and disintegrating and grappling with environmental problems on a global scale. The scale and style of politics are changing, and new issues of human rights have emerged in a world that is experiencing an increasingly rapid circulation of money, people, goods, electronic impulses, and ideas. All of these issues complicate our once tidy view of development and the problem of international inequality. The goal of this presentation is to offer students an integrated perspective on the forces that have changed how "development" is understood in the last quarter of the twentieth century.

By understanding the construction of the development era, students have a basis from which to begin to make sense of current trends of restructuring. These trends involve new discourses and new institutional developments, with a deep-rooted contention over the shape of the emerging world order.

Organization and Language

In examining the experiences of the development project, I have interwoven global and national issues, which helps to both situate situate current limits to nationally managed development and also helps to show how even national development strategies had intrinsic global dimensions. For example, Chapter 2's discussion of how Third World industrialization depended substantially on a system of food aid organized by the United States demonstrates how a global food system underwrote national developmentalism, instituting a classic developmentalist rural-urban exchange. Subsequent chapters link national agricultural modernization and rural depopulation in the Third World to global problems of growing political instability and international labor migration.

Finally, a word about language. It has become commonplace to note that the Third World and the Second World have ended as coherent entities, and I have tried to record this change during the narrative by adding the epithet "the former" to each of these terms. Although they certainly violate a heterogeneous reality as omnibus terms, they are useful as shorthand and certainly recognizable to most people. I stick with *First World* for no other reason than convenience. Similarly, in some instances I have used the terms *North* and *South* where these categories have a certain currency as political subdivisions of the contemporary world.

Acknowledgments

I have dedicated this book to my wife, Karen Schachere, for a multiplicity of wonderful reasons over and above her patience.

I also wish to express my thanks to the various people who have helped me along the way. I begin with my publisher and editor-in-chief, Steve Rutter, for his remarkable vision and his enthusiasm and faith in this project. Charles Ragin, the series editor, flew me out to Chicago for some early face-to-face discussions in which he convinced me to present a discussion of development as a narrative of the postwar world, to provide necessary background for post–baby boomers. He has been a close adviser, providing critical insights into the basic questions one confronts when bringing a textbook such as this to term. Elizabeth MacDonell performed the unenviable task of copyediting the first draft of the manuscript—she gave me invaluable advice on presentation of the text, and I hope I have lived up to it. Mary Douglas and Patterson Lamb performed their magic in copyediting the second draft of the manuscript, loosening and smoothing the prose, eliminating lapses in logic, and generally making it all presentable. Greg and Anne Draus, typesetters, created the pleasing illustrations and book pages. Rebecca Holland took care of more things behind the scenes in publication than I will ever know in her careful professional way. Two reviewers, Charles H. Wood of the University of Texas, Austin, and Valerie Gunter of the University of New Orleans, offered many useful hints on improving the presentation of ideas in this text. Le Padgett provided timely assistance at my office. And Linda Buttel gave invaluable advice and generous help on computer programming.

Finally, to my friends and supporters I am extremely grateful for your encouragement and insight. Fred Buttel pushed me to undertake this task, and he and Harriet Friedmann both went through the whole draft with a fine-tooth comb, helped me bring out the big picture, and rescued me from inconsistency and omission. Richard Williams offered me invaluable advice on meanings in the text and how to convey them to students. Michelle Adato steered me toward a richer understanding of social movements. Dale Tomich insisted that I be as didactic as possible—for me. Gary Gereffi straightened me out on the global production system. Heinzpeter Znoj challenged me on the question of the relevance of the nation-state. Shelley Feldman reviewed some early chapter drafts thoughtfully. I may not have succeeded in realizing all this good advice, but to all of you, my thanks.

A Timeline of Developmentalism and Globalism

WORLD FRAMEWORK	**Developmentalism (1940s–1970s)**
POLITICAL ECONOMY	State-Regulated Markets Keynesian Public Spending
SOCIAL GOALS	Social Entitlement and Welfare Uniform Citizenship
DEVELOPMENT [MODEL]	Industrial Replication National Economic Management [Brazil, Mexico, India]
MOBILIZING TOOL	Nationalism (Post-Colonialism)
MECHANISMS	Import-Substitution Industrialization (ISI) Public Investment (Infrastructure and Energy) Education Land Reform
VARIANTS	First World (Freedom of Enterprise) Second World (Central Planning) Third World (Modernization via Developmental Alliance)

MARKERS   Cold War Begins Korean War   Vietnam War
               (1946)   (1950–1953)   (1964–1973)

             Bretton Woods Marshall Plan   Alliance for Progress
               (1944)   (1946)   (1961)

          United Nations   Non-Aligned   U.N. Conference
            (1943)   Movement   on Trade Development
                           (1955)   Group of 77 (1964)

                              FIRST DEVELOPMENT SECOND DEVELOPMENT
                                DECADE   DECADE

– – – – – – ●————————●————————●————————●————————●
      1940   **1950**   **1960**   **1970**

INSTITUTIONAL   World Bank/IMF/GATT
DEVELOPMENTS   (1944)   (1944) (1947)

                  US$ as   PL-480 Program   Eurodollar/
             Reserve Currency   (1954)   Offshore $ Market

                  COMECON
                  (1947)

Globalism (1970s–)

Self-Regulating Markets (Monetarism)

Private Initiative via Free Markets
Identity Politics Versus Citizenship

Participation in the World Market
Comparative Advantage
[Chile, South Korea]

Efficiency (Post-Developmentalism)
Debt and Credit-Worthiness

Export-Oriented Industrialization (EOI)
Agro-Exporting
Privatization, Public and Majority-Class Austerity
Entrepreneurialism

National Structural Adjustment (Opening Economies)
Regional Free Trade Agreements
Global Economic and Environmental Management

Oil Crises	Cold War Ends	"New World	
(1973, 1979)	(1989)	Order" Begins	

Debt Regime
(Supervised State/Economy Restructuring)
(mid-1980s)

New International   Earth Summit (1992)
Economic Order Initiative
(1974)   Chiapas Revolt (1994)

Debt Crisis/
The "Lost Decade"

1970	1980	1990	2000

GATT   NAFTA (1994)
Uruguay Round   World Trade Organization
(1984)   (1995)

Offshore Banking   IMF/World Bank
Structural Adjustment Loans

Glasnost/Perestroika

Development and Social Change

Development and the Global Marketplace

To envision the global marketplace, think about the clothes you wear, the consumer goods you purchase, and the food you eat. Much of what you wear, use, and consume today has global origins. Even when a product has a "Made in USA" label, its journey to market probably combines components and labor from production and assembly sites around the world. Your athletic shoes could have been produced in China or Indonesia, your jeans assembled in the Philippines, your transistor radio or compact disk player put together in Singapore, your watch in Hong Kong. The fast food you eat may include chicken diced in Mexico or hamburger beef from cattle raised in Costa Rica. And, depending on your taste, your coffee is from Southeast Asia, Latin America, or Africa. You may not be a global citizen yet, but you *are* a global consumer.

The global marketplace is everywhere. The Japanese eat poultry fattened in Thailand with American corn, using chopsticks made with wood from Indonesian or Chilean forests. Canadians eat strawberries grown in Mexico with American fertilizer. Consumers on both sides of the Atlantic wear clothes assembled in Saipan with Chinese labor, drink orange juice from concentrate made with Brazilian oranges, and decorate their homes with flowers from Colombia. The British and French eat green beans from Kenya, and cocoa from Ghana finds its way into Swiss chocolate. Consumers everywhere are surrounded by world products.

Commodity Chains and Development

The global marketplace is a tapestry of commodity exchanges that bind producers and consumers across the world. The tapestry is a series of production stages, or networks of labor inputs, distributed globally among production sites. Sociologists call the series of production stages **commodity chains.*** When you eat, wear, or use a final product in a commodity chain, you participate in a global social process.

---

*All boldfaced terms are defined in the Glossary/Index.

Not everything you consume has such global origins, but the trend toward these worldwide supply networks is powerful. It is transforming the scale of economic development, reaching beyond regional and national boundaries. Some researchers have noted that the ingredients of a container of yogurt—from the strawberries and milk to the cardboard and ink for the carton—travel more than 6,000 miles to market in Germany, and yet all could be produced within a 50-mile radius.[1] As the supply networks expand, the scale and character of economic development are transformed. In the past, we understood **development** to be a process of economic growth organized nationally; but today, global economic integration is transforming development into a process of *globally organized economic growth.*

The role of the global marketplace in transforming the parameters of development is the theme of this book. Of course, the "global marketplace" is merely a metaphor for this transformation of development into a global process. Global trade networks have always been a part of the modern world. Sixteenth-century traders set in motion the Columbian exchange whereby European wheat crossed the Atlantic Ocean to the New World while American maize went to Europe and Africa. Today global exchanges are more intense in their scope and velocity; the ultimate measure is the trillions of dollars that circulate daily on international money markets—more money than any single country possesses.

Global Social Networks

In today's world, the interdependencies among people, communities, and nations are immediate. As an example, when you purchase a pair of athletic shoes, what does it mean to you? You are of course aware of the symbolic investment—you have a favorite basketball player who is a spokesman for the shoe company or a favorite athletic activity that is associated with the shoes. But you are also consuming materials and labor from many places in the global marketplace.

The *global labor force* is dispersed along production links of these commodity chains (see Figure 1). In the athletic shoe industry, the initial labor is related to the symbolic side of the shoe—design and marketing. This step remains primarily in the United States. Then there is the labor of producing the synthetic materials; of dyeing, cutting, and stitching; and of assembling, packing, and transporting. These forms of labor are all relatively unskilled and often performed by women, especially South Koreans, Taiwanese, Chinese, Indonesians, and Filipinos. Companies like Nike subcontract with such labor forces through local firms in the regional pro-

FIGURE 1

A Simple Representation of Commodity Chains Linking Global Production Sites with Global Consumers

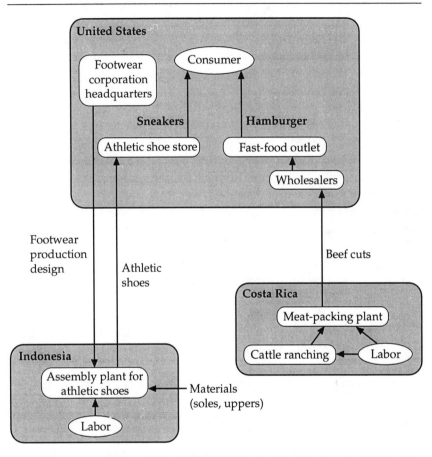

duction sites. South Korea and Taiwan are among the more reliable sites, generally having greater capacity and greater quality control than some other countries. But a shoe that costs Nike $20 on export from South Korea costs only $15 if made in Indonesia or China (1992 prices). Hence, in the early 1990s, Nike shifted a substantial part of its production to these lower-wage sites.[2]

Global job restructuring. Relocating production is a routine part of any competitive firm's operations today. As fashion and design change, so may production location. Labor costs and management patterns also affect location. Firms reroute the production chains to stay competitive. If you have shopped at The Gap recently, you know that this clothing retailer competes by changing its styles on a six-week cycle. The key to this kind of flexible organization is to use subcontractors who can be brought on line or let go as the market changes. The people who work with these subcontractors often have little security as one of the small links in this global commodity chain. Of course, job security varies by commodity, firm, and industry, but the employment insecurity all over the world reflects the uncertainties of the global market.

We hear a lot of discussion about whether the relocation of American jobs to Mexico is a short-term or a long-term trend. The topic raises questions. First, are "mature" economies, such as the United States, shedding their manufacturing jobs and becoming global centers of service industries (e.g., education, retailing, finance, insurance, marketing)? Second, do those jobs that shift south remain in Mexico, or do they shift further south to Central America or even to Southeast Asia, descending the wage ladder? We examine the connection between employment patterns and globalization in the chapters that follow. But our theme remains this: How does the redistribution of jobs on a global scale alter the meaning of development? To what extent is development now managed globally rather than nationally?

Global labor conditions. Another example from the global marketplace concerns *conditions of work,* illustrated in the global food industry. More and more fruits and vegetables are being grown under corporate contract by peasants and agricultural laborers around the world. Chile exports grapes, apples, pears, apricots, cherries, peaches, and avocados to the United States during the winter months. Caribbean nations produce bananas, citrus fruits, and frozen vegetables, and Mexico supplies American supermarkets with tomatoes, broccoli, bell peppers, cucumbers, and cantaloupes. Thailand grows pineapples and asparagus for the Japanese market, and Kenya exports strawberries, mangoes, and chilies to Europe. In short, the global fruit and salad bowl is bottomless. In an era when much of this production is now organized by huge food companies that subcontract with growers and sell in consumer markets across the world, these growers face new conditions of work.

As discussed in Chapter 1, non-Europeans have been producing specialized agricultural products for export for some time, but the scale and profitability of export food production have expanded greatly in recent decades as the number and concentration of world consumers have grown. Firms must remain flexible to compete in the global marketplace. Not only does this need for flexibility bring growers across the world into competition with one another as firms seek to keep costs down, but it also means that the produce itself must meet high standards of quality and consistency. Growers find that their work is defined by the needs of the umbrella firm to maintain its market image and a predictable supply of products desirable to consumers across the world. So not only is the job insecure; its very performance is determined by the requirements of the global market.

Again, most contract growing of fruits and vegetables is done by women. Women are considered more reliable as workers than men; they can be trained to monitor plant health and growth and to handle fruit and work efficiently. Employers presume that women are more suited to the seasonal and intermittent employment practices (e.g., harvesting, processing, and packing) necessary to mount a flexible operation.[3] In sum, the requirements of the global marketplace shape work and livelihood conditions at the community level.

The Social Web of the Global Market

We all experience economic globalization *locally*. That is why I began by asking you to think about your daily patterns of consumption and how they link you to the global marketplace. At a local level, it is difficult for us to conceptualize this marketplace as a continuously changing web of social networks across the world. We do not think about the global dimensions of the product we purchase at a supermarket or store. As long as we disregard these global links, the web appears to be the natural order of things. But we disregard these connections at our peril for several reasons.

For one, we can no longer understand the changes in our society without situating them within this global context. For another, we are likely to misinterpret social upheavals across the world if we ignore the contributions of global integration to political and economic instability. And finally, we cannot understand the consequences of disturbances in our complex biosphere without taking account of world-scale social transformations and stress on natural resources. The metaphor of the developing global marketplace helps us make these connections.

Along many of the commodity chains that sustain our lifestyle are people who experience globalization in quite different ways. Many are not consumers of commodities: four-fifths of the roughly 5 billion people in the world do not have access to consumer cash or credit.[4] Even so, they are often the producers of what we consume, and their societies are shaped as profoundly by the global marketplace as ours, if not more so. We seldom remember this. Also, it is difficult for us to perceive that the more extensive the global marketplace becomes, the greater its impact on societies in Latin America, Asia, and Africa.

For example, rain forest destruction is linked to the expanding global marketplace, although the connections are not always direct. Since the 1970s, Brazilian peasants have been displaced as their land has been taken for high-tech production of soybeans for export to feed Japanese livestock. These people have migrated en masse from the Brazilian southeast to the Amazon region to settle on rain forest land. Their dramatic slash-and-burn devastation of the forest captured the world's attention in the 1980s, forcing the industrialized world to see a link between poverty and environmental destruction. However, the precipitating connection between demand for animal protein in the Northern Hemisphere and rain forest destruction is less obvious. A further complication is our customary view of development as a *national* process, making it even more difficult for us to perceive in this episode a *world-scale* social process with particular local effects across the world. The case study of the "hamburger connection" outlines one such instance of world-scale social transformation with distinct local effects.

A brief examination of the footwear chain and the hamburger connection demonstrates how products that may be everyday items of consumption, particularly in the wealthier segments of the global market, may have considerable effects on producers and producing regions where they are made. Not only is there a spatial link between producers and consumers by way of the commodity chain, there is also a fundamental *social* link in the arrangements that are required to maintain the supply of the commodity.

Although we are just beginning to examine the social link, we can already see that it is quite tenuous and provisional. The more links that are made, the more interdependent become the fortunes of laborers, producers, and consumers across the world. A change in fashion can throw a whole community out of work. A footloose firm seeking lower wages can do the same thing. A new food preference in one part of the world will intensify export agriculture somewhere else. Intensification may offer the security of a contract to a grower community, but it may also increase that community's vulnerability to a more competitive producer elsewhere, given the variability of land fertility and wages and the mobility of firms. The intensification of beef exporting may displace not only a peasant community but also an economic culture built around local food production as local crops and livestock give way to scientifically prepared pastures and steers. It also may affect the economic priorities of a nation as well as that nation's (and the world's) resource base.

CASE STUDY

The Hamburger Connection

Between 1960 and 1990 forests disappeared at alarming rates in Central America. During this time, more than 25 percent of the Central American forest was converted to pasture for cattle that were in turn converted into hamburgers. Deforestation was linked, by way of the global marketplace, to an expanding fast-food industry in the United States. About one-tenth of American burgers use imported beef, much of it produced under contract for transnational food companies by Central American meat-packing plants. The Central American beef industry has had powerful institutional support through government loans assisted by the World Bank, the Agency for International Development (AID), and the Inter-American Development Bank (IADB). The plan was to tie the development of Central American societies to this valuable export earner.

Few people realized that consuming a hamburger might also involve consuming forest resources or that Central America's new beef industry would have vast environmental and social consequences. These consequences include the displacement of peasants from their land and forest dwellers from their habitat because more than half of Central American land was committed to grazing cattle. As less land was available for farming, the production of peasant staple foods declined. The Costa Rican government had to use beef export earnings to purchase basic grains on the world market to compensate for the declining local food supply and to feed the country's people. The global process of which the hamburger chain is part is thus linked to social and other changes in North and Central America.

Sources: Myers, 1981, p. 7; Place, 1985, pp. 290–295; Rifkin, 1992, pp. 192–193.

Dimensions of Social Change in the Global Marketplace

The changing contours and rhythms of the global marketplace, then, are metaphors for social change and development, revealing the interconnectedness of people across the world. Such interconnectedness has three dimensions. First, there is the integration of producers and consumers across *space* as commodities crisscross political boundaries. Second, this spatial integration brings in a new *time* dimension as the rhythms of the world market enter into and connect physically separate communities. For instance, a firm that establishes an export site in a community brings the new work disciplines required for production of global products. And third, once communities are integrated in the new time and space of the global marketplace, they are increasingly subject to decisions made by powerful market agencies such as governments, firms, and currency or commodity speculators. If oil prices rise significantly, for example, the effect is felt throughout the global economy in a variety of ways by a variety of social actors in the market—from farmers through petrochemical firms to travelers.

The continual reorganization of market conditions dramatically affects the livelihoods of people and their life trajectories. Today the global athletic shoe industry, turning footwear into fashion, generates new and evolving employment opportunities in the United States (specialty shoe stores, product design, and marketing) and in East and Southeast Asia (production and assembly). Capturing market shares by designing fashion and finding cheap labor sites is the name of the game. But this game continually reshuffles the employment deck and people's futures. And, although money makes this world go around, its accelerated circulation compresses people's lives into a unified social space (the global marketplace) and time (the shared upswings and downswings of the global economy).

Consider again the dynamics of the beef chain. Not only does rising hamburger consumption incorporate new grazing regions into the global marketplace, but this new space itself involves a new *social* time. In the United States, beef consumption developed and grew throughout the century-long process of settling the American (rural and urban) frontier. The current fast-food demand, however, compresses the modernization process for forest dwellers and Indian peasants, forcing them to adapt in a single generation, converting their habitats to pasture and displacing many of them to urban fringes. On the broader scale, the burning of forests and grazing of livestock intensify the threat to future generations of global warming. We are seeing the actions of humankind endangering the habitability of the planet. Here the long run, or rather our sense of it, is *reduced* by the finiteness of biospheric resources—perhaps the most dramatic effect of the compression of space and time.

Development as a Global Process

This introduction illustrates, through the examples of commodity chains and their social and environmental impacts, the global nature of economic activity. It may still be pursued by individual nation-states, but less and less does it resemble the old definition of development as *nationally organized economic growth*. In this book, you will examine the ways the world has moved from nationally organized growth toward *globally organized economic growth*. Let me emphasize here that development and economic growth are basically pursued goals. Historically this was not always so; we know this from observing still-existing communities of forest dwellers, who fashion their lives according to natural cycles. With the rise of modern European capitalism, state bureaucrats began to pursue economic growth to finance their military and administrative needs. But "development" as such was not yet a universal strategy. This phenomenon has occurred only in the post–World War II era as newly independent states joined the world community and the rush toward development, with quite varying success.

We are now in a period of rethinking development, given the evident failure of many countries to fulfill the promise of postwar development and the world's growing awareness of environmental limits. In this context *sustainability* has become a popular issue, forcing an evaluation of the total development enterprise. We shall trace the changing fortunes of development efforts, the shortcomings of which have produced two responses. One is to advocate a thoroughly global marketplace to expand trade and spread the wealth. The other is to reevaluate the purely economic emphasis and to recover a sense of cultural community. The "development debate" is re-forming around a conflict between the vision of the globalists and the culturalists: Do we continue expanding industry and wealth infinitely, or do we find a way that human communities (defined politically, ethnically, religiously) can recover social intimacy, healthy environments, and sustainable economic practices? Both visions are confronting a changing world, possibly a declining world, of which each is increasingly well aware.

The Global Perspective

I suggest that the terms of this development debate cannot be adequately understood or resolved without a global perspective. A worldwide perspective is necessary if we are to understand historical connections, such as those embedded in commodity chains. Clothing once made within the confines of a village from local materials with local labor for local use is now made in the global village from globally sourced materials with global labor for global consumption. But getting from the original village to the global village was not simply by passage of time or by economic integration: a series of historical processes was necessary to create the global village.

One such historical process was the construction of stable markets by modern states. This process not only encouraged international trade, but it also generated the idea of "development" as *organized social change* pursued by governments. Development was linked to state survival in a predatory and competitive international political environment. Without a global perspective, we cannot understand the developmental processes of either constructing markets or establishing a productive military-industrial power base for nations. And both of these processes contributed to the foundations of the global village.

The rest of the story involves understanding how the push toward development was institutionalized as an international operation, largely through the flurry of new state building in the mid-twentieth century as colonies gained independence. By that time, development had become a broad-based international endeavor to bring the non-European world into the (European) twentieth century by raising the living standards of all societies. Thus, development became the catchword in the succeeding decades as nations pursued the goal of raising living standards. Local villages were incorporated into the emerging national political and economic arena. But there was a trade-off: they gained technical and social assistance in return for their subordination to the state. At the same time, however, nation-states themselves were being incorporated into the emerging relations of the global village. On the way, they too made a trade-off: technical, social, and military assistance in return for their subordination to more powerful states, international agencies, and global firms.

To try to grasp these simultaneous dynamics, think of the Russian doll: when you twist each doll apart, you see another, smaller one nested inside it. This is a useful, preliminary way to gain a global perspective as it helps us to see how states, regions, and communities are interwoven. The Russian doll perspective ensures that what we observe *within* nation-states is understood in the context of what we can observe *among* nation-states, or indeed *across* them, where transnational firms roam.

Ultimately we need to see that local changes are simultaneously global changes and that changes with distinct patterns across different regions are globally connected.[5] That is, many local experiences and activities have global, and therefore shared, dimensions. Think again of how many of your individual consumption patterns are thoroughly "globalized" and replicated across the world. It is harder and harder to disentangle the local village from the global one. As we shall see, that is one dilemma the development debate is currently addressing.

Another dilemma addresses the tensions around the Western/Northern view and practice of development. Many social movements concerned with sustainability and social justice posit views of development that are quite different from the dominant Western goal of economic growth. Some exist within the West itself, where development patterns have undone and impoverished rural communities and generated urban blight. Consumer and producer cooperatives, farmers' markets, and organic farms are springing up as alternatives to developmentalism.

Western developmentalism takes its cue from an economic model driven by technology and market behavior rather than from existing cultures. The universal spread of developmentalism, therefore, will always generate cultural tensions where non-Western cultures are affected. The dilemma resides, partly, in the unequal power between Western states and firms and non-Western states, firms, and communities. This inequality is often expressed in the tension between the "haves" and the "have-nots," or between the North and the South (the majority of the populations of Africa, Latin America, and South and Southeast Asia). As we shall also see, this tension is amplified by the process of global integration; the pursuit of global management of economic, environmental, and political problems; and the cultural backlash against assumptions that West is best. The major thrust of this book is to make these tensions intelligible by situating them within a global, historical framework.

PART I

The Development Project
(Late 1940s to Early 1970s)

1

The Rise of the Development Project

We routinely refer to *development* as a way of organizing or motivating societies to change. It may mean developing ways of adapting to new environmental constraints or to changes in the size of a community. These are adaptive changes, concerned with maintaining a balance of human culture with nature. But such changes are not necessarily cumulative.

Our understanding of development has also come to mean *directional change*. Such change can be in the governing beliefs of societies (from religious to secular rule), in their social patterns (from rural to urban society), or in their material means (from animal to machine power). In all these dimensions there is a shift toward social arrangements that are familiar to the Western world. In other words, development is also associated with our lifestyle. This makes it appear almost natural.

If you reflect on this, you realize that development has come to be identified with a Western lifestyle. Most non-Western cultures have been exposed to this lifestyle, and many of their people (especially their social and political elites) have adopted Western styles of consumption. In addition, many non-Western societies have followed Western patterns in belief, in social patterns, and in material activities. This makes patterns of development that imitate the West appear to be even more natural.

Lately, however, countertrends have been emerging: some Islamic fundamentalists challenge Westernization; some environmentalists argue that our high-energy industrial consumer lifestyle cannot be sustained; growing numbers of people across the world inhabit "underground" or informal economies (on the margins of the formal political and economic system); and Western economies face a growing problem of unemployment. In other words, what might appear natural is not necessarily universally shared or permanent.

How can we untangle this puzzle? The most fruitful way is to think about the *historical context* in which development has evolved. History provides some answers to how development has come to assume a particular meaning—of cumulative change with a specific direction. Further, history allows us to understand how this conception of development has become almost universal.

Colonialism

Our appeal to history begins with a powerful simplification. It concerns the social psychology of European colonialism, built largely around stereotypes that have shaped perceptions and conflict for five centuries. (Colonialism is defined and explained in the following insert.) One such perception was the idea among Europeans that non-European native people or colonial subjects were "backward," or trapped in tradition. Colonial rule encouraged this idea, as European and non-European cultures were compared within a relationship in which Europe had the powerful military-industrial advantage. This comparison was interpreted, or misinterpreted, as European cultural superiority, or progress.

The broadly accepted misinterpretation of other cultures appears frequently in historical accounts. It is reflected in assumptions made by white settlers in North America and Australia about the indigenous people they encountered. In each case, the Europeans perceived the Indians and aborigines as people who did not work the land they inhabited. In other words, they had no right of "property"—a European concept. Their removal from their ancestral lands is a bloody reminder of the combined military power and moral fervor with which European colonization was pursued. It was buttressed by a process of cultural conquest, whereby Europeans systematically devalued and redefined non-European cultures in terms of European "superiority."

In precolonial Africa, as communities achieved stability within their environment, they developed rules for survival that were related to kinship patterns and supernatural belief systems. These rules were at once conservative and adaptive because, over time, African communities changed their composition, their scale, and their location in a long process of settlement and migration through the lands south of the equator. But European colonists in Africa saw these superstitious and traditional cultures as only occupying, rather than improving, the land. This perception ignored the complex social systems adapted first to African ecology and then to European occupation of that ecology.[1] Under these circumstances, the idea of the "white man's burden" emerged, a concept in which the West viewed itself as the bearer of civilization to the darker races. The ensuing colonial exchange was captured in the postcolonial African saying:

What Is Colonialism?

Colonialism is the subjugation by physical and psychological force of one culture by another—a colonizing power—through military conquest of territory. It predates the era of European expansion (fifteenth to twentieth centuries), extending, for example, to Japanese colonialism in the twentieth century and, more recently, Chinese colonization of Tibet. Colonialism has two forms: colonies of settlement, which often eliminate indigenous people (such as the Spanish destruction of the Aztec and Inca civilizations in the Americas), and colonies of rule, where colonial administrators reorganize existing cultures to facilitate their exploitation (such as the British use of local *zamindars* to rule the Indian subcontinent). The outcomes are, first, the cultural genocide or marginalization of indigenous people; second, the extraction of labor, cultural treasures, and resources to enrich the colonial power, its private interests, and public museums; and third, the elaboration of ideologies justifying colonial rule, including notions of racism and modernity.

"When the white man came he had the Bible and we had the land. When the white man left we had the Bible and he had the land." Under colonialism, non-Europeans lost control of many of their material resources, a condition that led to considerable social disorganization.

The non-European world appeared backward to the colonizers, who assumed that non-Europeans would and should emulate European social organization. Thus *modernity* came to be identified as the destiny of humankind. There was little acknowledgment of how non-Europeans were handicapped in this "ideal" endeavor. "Holding the Bible" became a metaphor for the state of non-Europeans who were left to pursue the European way without the resources to accomplish it.

Western secular and religious crusades in the forms of administration, education, and missionary efforts accompanied colonial rule to stimulate progress along the European path. The problem of course was that the ruling Europeans were unable to see the dynamics of the non-European cultures. Another problem was that Europeans ignored the paradox of bringing progress to colonized peoples whose sovereignty they systematically denied—a paradox experienced daily by the non-Europeans.

This paradox generated anticolonial movements seeking to wrest independence from Western occupation. But independence would occur in a changed world—a *post*colonial world. In this world, non-European cultures had either been destroyed or irrevocably changed through the colonial impact. Newly independent states emerged within a framework defined by the European conception of development. The adoption of the European model across the formerly colonial world was the underpinning of the post–World War II **development project**.

We continually evaluate the terms of the development project throughout this book, especially because (1) the project has been modified in various ways since the 1950s and (2) it is increasingly questioned as some of its expectations have failed to materialize. For the moment, it is important to emphasize that the founding assumptions and practices of the development project represented *historical choices* rather than an inevitable unfolding of human destiny. As we see in this chapter, the development project was an organized strategy to overcome the legacies of colonialism, several of which are discussed below.

The Colonial Division of Labor

From the sixteenth century, European colonists and traders traveled along African coasts to the New World and across the Indian Ocean and the China seas seeking fur, precious metals, slave labor, spices, tobacco, cacao, potatoes, sugar, and cotton. The European colonial powers—Spain, Portugal, Holland, France, and Britain—and their merchant companies exchanged manufactured goods such as cloth, guns, and implements for these products and for Africans taken into slavery and transported to the Americas. In the process, they reorganized the world.

The basic pattern was to establish in the colonies specialized production of raw materials and primary products that were unavailable in Europe. In turn, European manufacturing grew on the basis of these products as they became industrial inputs and foodstuffs for its industrial labor force. On a world scale, this specialization between European economies and their colonies came to be termed the **colonial**, or **international, division of labor**, illustrated in Figure 1.1.

This arrangement had two basic effects: it stimulated European industrialization, and it forced non-Europeans into primary commodity production. Such specialization disorganized non-European cultures, undermining local crafts and mixed-farming systems. In other words, not only did non-European cultures surrender their own handicraft industries in this exchange, but they were often forced to reduce their agriculture to an **export monoculture**, where local farmers became producers of a single crop for export. The disruption caused by this shift is made clear in the follow-

FIGURE 1.1

The "Colonial Division of Labor" Between European States and Their Colonial Empires

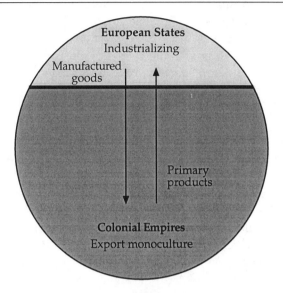

ing insert, which illustrates the interrelation and interdependence of all facets of a precolonial culture.

The destruction of non-European handicraft industries is well known. For example, in the East African kingdom of Buganda, British colonists found a thriving political culture with sophisticated craft production of barkcloth and pottery, neither of which was useful to Europe. Following the creation of the colonial state of Uganda in 1894, these crafts all but disappeared as Bugandan peasants were forced into producing cotton and coffee for export.[2]

Perhaps the best-known subjugation of native crafts occurred in the British conquest of India. Until the nineteenth century, Indian muslins and calicos were luxury imports into Europe (as were Chinese silks and satins). By that time, however, the East India Company (which ruled India for the British crown until 1858) undermined this Indian craft and, in its own words, "succeeded in converting India from a manufacturing country into a country exporting raw produce."[3] The company had convinced the British government to use tariffs of 70 to 80 percent against Indian finished goods and to permit virtually free entry of raw cotton

What Are Some Characteristics of Precolonial Cultures?

All precolonial cultures had their own ways of satisfying their material and spiritual needs. Cultures varied by the differentiation among their members or households according to their particular ecological endowments and social contact with other cultures. The variety ranged from small communities of subsistence producers (living off the land or the forest) to extensive kingdoms or states. Subsistence producers, organized by kin relations, usually subdivided social tasks between men, who hunted and cleared land for cultivation, and women, who cultivated and processed crops, harvested wild fruits and nuts, and performed household tasks. These cultures were highly skilled in resource management and production to satisfy their material needs. They generally did not produce a surplus beyond what was required for their immediate needs, and they organized cooperatively—a practice that often made them vulnerable to intruders because they were not prepared for self-defense. Unlike North American Indians, whose organization provided leadership for resistance, some aboriginal cultures, such as those of Australia and the Amazon, lacked leadership hierarchies and were more easily wiped out by settlers. By contrast, the Mogul empire in seventeenth-century India had a complex hierarchical organization based on local chiefdoms in which the chief presided over the village community and ensured that surpluses (monetary taxes and produce) were delivered to a prosperous central court and "high culture." Village and urban artisans produced a range of metal goods, pottery, and crafts, including sophisticated muslins and silks. Caste distinctions, linked to previous invasions, corresponded to divisions of labor, such as trading, weaving, cultivating, ruling, and performing unskilled labor. Colonizers typically adapted this social and political hierarchy to their own ends. (*Sources*: Rowley, 1974; Bujra, 1992)

into England. In turn, British traders flooded India with cheap cloth manufactured in Manchester. British-built railway systems moved Indian raw cotton to coastal ports for shipment to Liverpool, returning to the Indian countryside with machine-made products. In this way, British industrial technology (textile machinery and the steam engine) reinforced the colonial division of labor.

Social Reorganization Under Colonialism

This division of labor had a devastating effect on the social organization of craft production. In 1757, Robert Clive had described the textile city of Dacca as "extensive, populous, and rich as the city of London." Yet by 1840, Sir Charles Trevelyan testified before a British parliamentary committee that the population of Dacca "has fallen from 150,000 to 30,000, and the jungle and malaria are fast encroaching upon the town. . . . Dacca, the Manchester of India, has fallen off from a very flourishing town to a very poor and small town."[4]

Similarly, colonialism reorganized non-European agriculture to supply European consumers and industries. Plantations and other kinds of cash-cropping arrangements sprang up across the colonial world, dedicated to specialized tropical exports ranging from bananas to peanuts, depending on local agro-ecologies (see Table 1.1). In India, production of commercial crops such as cotton, jute, tea, peanuts, and sugar cane grew by 85 percent between the 1890s and the 1940s. In contrast, in that same period, local food crop production declined by 7 percent while the population grew by 40 percent, a shift that spread hunger and social unrest.[5]

TABLE 1.1

Selected Colonial Export Crops

Colony	Colonial Power	Export Crop
Australia	Britain	wool
Brazil	Portugal	sugar
Ceylon	Britain	tea
Egypt	Britain	cotton
Ghana	Britain	cocoa
Haiti	France	sugar
India	Britain	cotton, opium
Indochina	France	rubber, rice
Indonesia	Holland	rubber, tobacco
Ivory Coast	France	cocoa
Kenya	Britain	wool
Malaya	Britain	rubber, palm oil
Senegal	France	peanuts
South Africa	Britain	gold, diamonds

Colonial exports provided the raw materials of European capitalist civilization, while colonial labor was severed from its traditional agricultural patterns. The colonists induced their subjects to work in cash cropping, employing a variety of forcible methods such as enslavement, taxation, land grabbing, and recruitment for indentured labor contracts. In Africa and India, for example, new monetary taxes on households forced peasants to grow commercial crops to pay their taxes.

As European industry matured in the nineteenth century, colonial exports changed from luxury spices and silks to goods that could be consumed by the emerging urban masses—products such as sugar, coffee, tea, cocoa, tobacco, and vegetable oils. The expanding factories of Europe required new inputs of cotton, timber, rubber, and jute. Although the African slave trade subsided, the Europeans created other schemes of indentured labor. Impoverished Indian and Chinese peasants and handicraftsmen, many of whom found their livelihood undermined by colonial intervention or market competition from cheap textiles, were scattered to sugar plantations in the Caribbean, Fiji, Mauritius, and Natal; to rubber plantations in Malaya and Sumatra; and to British East Africa to build the Mombasa to Lake Victoria railway.

In the third quarter of the nineteenth century alone, more than one million contracted Indians went overseas. Today, Indians still outnumber native Fijians; they make up 50 percent of the Guyanese population and 40 percent of the residents of Trinidad. In the same period, 90,000 Chinese indentured laborers went to work in the Peruvian guano fields, while 200,000 went to California to work in the fruit industry, the goldfields, and the railways.[6]

This wholesale *reorganization of colonial labor* had five main effects:

1. Non-European societies were fundamentally transformed by the loss of their resources and craft traditions as their people became colonial subjects laboring in mines, fields, and plantations under a new regime of export production. A great deal of colonial labor was channeled away from reproducing local, non-European culture and into sustaining distant European urban and industrial needs. In other words, European development depended on the active disorganization of its colonies. Some observers refer to this disorganization as **underdevelopment**.

2. Labor reorganization required political change. Various systems of colonial rule anchored this new commercial regime. For example, a landed oligarchy (the *hacendados*) ruled South America before the

nineteenth century in the name of the Spanish and Portuguese monarchies. This kind of settler colonialism spread also to North America, Australasia, and Southern Africa, where settlers wrested land from the natives. As the nineteenth century wore on, colonialism became more bureaucratic and centrally organized. By the late nineteenth century, colonial administrations in Asia and Africa were self-financing systems, putting to use the loyalty of local princes and chiefs, bought with titles, land, or tax-farming privileges. Colonial subjects were forced into cash cropping to pay the taxes that financed the whole colonial enterprise.

3. The incorporation of male colonial subjects into cash cropping disrupted formerly complementary **gender roles** of men and women in traditional cultures. Women's traditional land-user rights were often displaced by new systems of private property, which put increasing pressure on food production, normally the responsibility of women. In Kenya, for example, the former interdependence between men and women in the Kikuyu culture was fragmented as the peasants' land was confiscated and the men migrated to work on European farms, reducing women's control over resources and lowering their status, wealth, and authority. [7]

4. European societies (especially the traders and manufacturers among them) reaped the benefits of a growing stream of products and profits from the colonial trade. Most important, European social organization was transformed as industrialization intensified. This was a single, *global* process, connecting social changes at each pole of the colonial division of labor. African slaves toiled in the New World and peasants toiled in Asia and Africa, in mines, on plantations, and in cash cropping for export to Europe. At the other pole, European peasantries were displaced from their lands into growing urban labor forces. Colonial subjects produced commodities such as sugar and cotton that were consumed by these new European labor forces in cheap, sugared foods and beverages and in inexpensive cotton clothing.

5. The removal of colonial people from their societies and their dispersion to resolve labor shortages elsewhere in the colonial world has had a lasting global effect—most notably in the African, Indian, and Chinese diasporas. The cultural mosaic that characterizes a number of world regions as well as some of today's ethnopolitical instability stems substantially from the worldwide movements of people during the colonial era.

Decolonization

At the same time that Europeans were attempting to "civilize" their colonies, colonial subjects across the Americas, Asia, and Africa began exploring the paradox of European colonialism—the European notion of rights and sovereignty juxtaposed against their own subjugation. For instance, in the French sugar colony of Haiti, the late-eighteenth-century Black Jacobin revolt powerfully exposed the double standard of European civilization. Turning French revolutionary rhetoric successfully against French colonialism at the turn of the nineteenth century, the slaves of the Haitian sugar plantations became the first to gain their independence, sending tremors throughout the slave-holding lands of the New World.[8]

This challenge to the colonial powers evolved across the next two centuries, from the early-nineteenth-century independence of the Latin American republics to the dismantling of South African apartheid in the early 1990s. Although **decolonization** has continued into the present day, the worldwide decolonization movement truly culminated in the collapse of European colonialism in the mid-twentieth century, when the second world war sapped the power of the French, Dutch, British, and Belgian states to withstand anticolonial struggles.

After the deployment of millions of colonial subjects in the Allied war effort for the Allied countries' self-determination, the returning colonial soldiers turned this ideal on their colonial masters in their final bid for independence. Veteran Nigerian anticolonialist and later president Nnamdi Azikiwe characterized African independence struggles by quoting Eleanor Roosevelt's description of the war effort: "We are fighting a war today so that individuals all over the world may have freedom. This means an equal chance for every man to have food and shelter and a minimum of such things as spell happiness. Otherwise we fight for nothing of real value."[9] Freedom was thus linked to overcoming the material deprivations of colonialism.

Colonial Liberation

Freedom also involved overcoming the social-psychological scars of colonialism. One profound legacy of colonialism is racism, a legacy that deeply penetrated the psyche of colonist and colonized and remains with us today. In 1957, at the height of African independence struggles, the Tunisian philosopher Albert Memmi wrote *The Colonizer and the Colonized*, dedicating the American edition to the (colonized) American Negro. In this work he claimed:

Racism . . . is the highest expression of the colonial system and one of the most significant features of the colonialist. Not only does it establish a fundamental discrimination between colonizer and colonized, a *sine qua non* of colonial life, but it also lays the foundation for the immutability of this life.[10]

To overcome this apparent immutability, West Indian psychiatrist Frantz Fanon, writing from Algeria, responded in 1963 with *The Wretched of the Earth*—a manifesto of liberation. It was a searing indictment of European colonialism and a call to people of the former colonies (the Third World) to transcend the mentality of enslavement and forge a new path for humanity. He wrote:

It is a question of the Third World starting a new history of Man, a history which will have regard to the sometimes prodigious theses which Europe has put forward, but which will also not forget Europe's crimes, of which the most horrible was committed in the heart of man, and consisted of the pathological tearing apart of his functions and the crumbling away of his unity. . . . On the immense scale of humanity, there were racial hatreds, slavery, exploitation and above all the bloodless genocide which consisted in the setting aside of fifteen thousand millions of men. . . . Humanity is waiting for something other from us than such an imitation, which would be almost an obscene caricature.[11]

Decolonization involved a liberatory upsurge, expressed in mass political movements of resistance. Most notably, the Indian independence leader Mahatma Gandhi kindled nonviolent forms of resistance that included wearing homespun cloth instead of machine-made goods and forswearing use of the English language. Other forms of resistance included tactics of terror against colonists, widespread colonial labor unrest, and eloquent appeals to justice in the language of rights and freedom in international forums. A new world order was in the making. From 1945 to 1981, 105 new states joined the United Nations as the colonial empires crumbled, swelling the ranks of the United Nations from 51 to 156. This global transformation, granting political sovereignty to millions of non-Europeans (more than half of humanity), ushered in the era of development.[12]

Decolonization and Development

The development era was intimately linked to decolonization. The link was through the idea of nations gaining political independence to pursue national economic growth strategies. There were models for this combination of political freedom and economic growth already, beginning with the revolt of the American colonies in the late eighteenth century. The mid-nineteenth-century U.S. Civil War confirmed this notion through eliminating the last vestige of colonialism in the slave plantation system of the Old South. The unified U.S. political and economic system represented the new *national model* of economic development, with a growing national integration between the agricultural and industrial sectors. The division of labor between industry and agriculture, which defined the global exchange between colonial powers and their colonies, now defined a dynamic *internal* exchange in the United States. Traders in Chicago, for instance, purchased midwestern farm products for processing, in turn selling machinery and manufactured goods to those farmers. The difference between the colonial and the national division between industry and agriculture is illustrated in Figure 1.2.

Latin America obtained its political independence in the 1820s as the Spanish and Portuguese empires declined. These empires began in the sixteenth century, at least a century before the emergence of other colonial powers, such as Holland, England, and France. Latin American commercial development centered on the prosperity gained through agricultural exports to Europe. Port cities like Rio de Janeiro and Buenos Aires grew as European immigrants came to Latin America to prosper from the commodity boom between 1870 and 1930. Sugar, bananas, and coffee from the tropical regions expanded alongside industrial crops such as cotton, sisal, and rubber, with wheat and livestock products coming from the *pampas* of

FIGURE 1.2

Distinguishing Between an International and a National Division of Labor

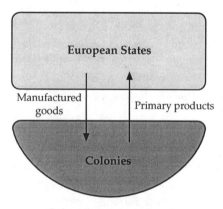

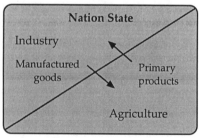

Colonial, or international,
division of labor

"Internal" division of labor,
between national economic sectors

CASE STUDY

Latin American Development: The Colombian Coffee Industry

The Latin American states, with their large European settlements and their early independence, had the opportunity, not available to other colonial regions, of developing a commercial culture around their lucrative export agriculture.

An example was the industrial reorganization of Colombian coffee growing, initiated through a particular combination of public and private enterprise. Coffee was Colombia's premier export crop from the late nineteenth century to the 1970s. It began as an estate crop, organized by large landowners. As international demand for coffee grew, small growers colonized the region of Antioquia in central Colombia. In 1928 a private, quasi-state organization, the National Federation of Coffee Growers of Colombia (FEDECAFE), was founded. The Colombian government ceded control of the country's coffee fund to FEDECAFE in return for its commitment to integrate the small growers into a modern production system based on new technologies such as modern fertilizers, hybrid seeds, and mechanization. Over time, coffee marketing and the provision of credit and banking services were organized through cooperatives and a new bank, Banco Cafetero. The region was integrated through transport systems, rural schools, health centers, and elaborate extension services to growers.

By 1931 the director of FEDECAFE articulated a national development culture, centered on a reorganized coffee industry:

> The coffee industry does not only represent the association of producers . . . rather, today and for many years to come [the industry] can say to the four winds: "I am fiscal equilibrium . . . I am external credit for the nation and the departments, I am the Bank of the Republic . . . I represent and on me depends a healthy monetary system based on the gold standard, exchange rate stability, the possibility of introducing to the country machinery, rails, scientific books, foreign professors, in a word, the civilization of Colombia from a material point of view."

In other words, coffee sustained an elaborate rationalization of Colombian agriculture and prosperity for the estate owners and the urban mercantile elites. As such it was identified as the basis of Colombian modernization.

Source: London, 1993.

Argentina and Uruguay. Because of the profitability of agro-exporting, Latin American political systems were dominated by powerful land-owning classes in coalitions with wealthy urban traders. In fact, in the pursuit of modern commercial development, the Latin American agro-export coalition was the national counterpart of the European industrial-financier coalition sponsoring European national development. Within the **international division of labor,** the mutual conditioning of these two economic poles was, again, a single global process.

The commercial development of Latin America distinguishes it from the rest of the colonial world that was under European rule until the mid-twentieth century. Although patterns of economic growth in Latin America reflect the legacy of an earlier colonial history (such as export agriculture and landed oligarchies), Latin America did embrace late-eighteenth-century French and U.S. ideologies of **liberal-nationalism,** coined in nineteenth-century Europe as modernity. Elsewhere in the non-European world, these ideologies would also flower with decolonization, but much later. The opportunity of one-and-a-half centuries of independence allowed a national political culture to express itself in agro-export-based development like that of Colombia. Indeed, in the early twentieth century, Argentina's gross national product per capita was similar to that of North America. But new Asian and African states formed at a historical time when development was organized internationally, as a *project.* Local cultures, long suppressed under colonialism, usually received short shrift in their move to imitate the Western model. The development project was rooted in an economic model driven by technology and market behavior rather than culture per se.

Postwar Decolonization and the Rise of the Third World

At the time of decolonization, the world was subdivided into three geo-political segments. These subdivisions came about after World War II (1939–1944) as the Cold War set in and Europe was divided between the capitalist Western (**First World**) and the communist Soviet (**Second World**) blocs. The term **Third World** arose in the 1950s and referred to those countries inhabited by non-Europeans that were poor and for the most part colonized by Europe (China, for example, was not fully colonized). There were stratifications across and within these subdivisions, and within their national units. The ways we divide the nations of the world are explained in the following insert.

How We Divide Up the World's Nations

Division of the nations of the world is quite complex and extensive, and it depends on the purpose of the dividing. The basic division made in the early postwar era was into Three Worlds: the First was essentially the capitalist world (the West plus Japan), the Second was basically the socialist world (the Soviet bloc), and the Third was the rest—mostly former European colonies. The core of the Third World was the group of nonaligned countries that tried to steer an independent path between the First and Second Worlds. These countries included Egypt, India, Indonesia, and Yugoslavia. In the 1980s a Fourth World was named to describe regions that were being marginalized internationally. Then there are the divisions used by the United Nations and other institutions of the development establishment: developed countries, developing countries, and least developed countries. Critics of the development establishment reconceptualized the division as one between the developed and the *under*developed worlds in the late 1960s. In the 1970s the oil-producing countries broke away and formed a producer cartel, becoming the Organization of Oil-Exporting Countries (OPEC). At the same time, a group of rapidly industrializing Third World countries became known officially as **newly industrializing countries (NICs)**—they represented a beacon to the rest of the Third World. Alongside this group and overlapping it are the **new agricultural countries (NACs)**—in which industrial agriculture for export had taken hold. Other groupings include the **G-7** states (the core of the First World) and the **G-77** states (the collective membership of the Third World that formed in the mid-1960s).

In the postwar era, the United States was the most powerful state—economically, militarily, and ideologically. Its superior standard of living (with a per capita income three times the average for Western Europe), its anticolonial heritage, and its commitment to liberalism in domestic and international relations gave it the trappings of an ideal society on the world stage. It was the undisputed leader of the First World, and it came to be the model of a developed society.

Ranged against the United States were the Soviet Union and an assortment of other communist states, primarily those of Eastern Europe. The Second World was considered the alternative to First World capitalism.

The Third World, the remaining half of humanity, was regarded as impoverished in standard economic terms (despite the fact that it had enormous numbers of people who grew their own food). Frantz Fanon added political and cultural dimensions to the notion of impoverishment. He termed these people the "wretched of the earth." Whereas the First World had 65 percent of world income with only 20 percent of the world's population, the Third World accounted for 67 percent of world population but only 18 percent of its income. Many observers believe that much of the gap in living standards between the First and Third Worlds derived from colonialism.[13]

This comparison of economic conditions between the First and Third Worlds generated the *vision of development* that would energize political and business elites in each world. Seizing the moment as leader of the First World, President Harry S. Truman included in a key speech on January 20, 1949, the following proclamation:

> We must embark on a bold new program for making the benefits of our scientific advances and industrial progress available for the improvement and growth of underdeveloped areas. The old imperialism—exploitation for foreign profit—has no place in our plans. What we envisage is a program of development based on the concepts of democratic fair dealing.[14]

The following year, a Nigerian nationalist echoed these sentiments:

> Self-government will not necessarily lead to a paradise overnight. . . . But it will have ended the rule of one race over another, with all the humiliation and exploitation which that implies. It can also pave the way for the internal social revolution that is required within each country.[15]

Despite the power differential between the United States and the African countries, the shared sentiments affirmed the connection between decolonization and development. For the Americans and their allies, this was the liberal vision writ large in the world—a vision of universal national opportunity to pursue economic growth. For the new states, self-government was the opportunity to put their houses in order to this end.

President Truman's proclamation offered a new paradigm for the postwar era: the division of humanity into the "developed" and the "underdeveloped" regions. The Mexican intellectual Gustavo Esteva commented:

> Underdevelopment began, then, on January 20, 1949. On that day, two billion people became underdeveloped. In a real sense, from that time on, they ceased being what they were, in all their diversity, and were transmogrified into an inverted mirror of others' reality: . . . a mirror that defines their identity . . . simply in the terms of a homogenizing and narrow minority.[16]

In other words, the proclamation by President Truman divided the world between those who were modern and "developed," and those who were not. *Modern* became the standard against which other societies were judged. This was a new way of looking at the world, a new paradigm. It assumed that colonialism was ending and that the underdeveloped world had only to follow the example of the modern world.

This new paradigm produced a strategy for improving the condition of the Third World. It is the premise for the development project. The division between the developed world and the underdeveloped world was generalized to be a matter of degree that could be set right by the project. First, no matter how diverse was the cultural heritage of Third World nations, the Western experience became the boilerplate model for their development. Second, conditions in the Third World were viewed as early stages on a universal path to modern society. Absent from this model was any acknowledgment that the colonies had made a contribution to European development or that the non-European societies had many intrinsic merits. In a postcolonial era, Third World states would be denied the opportunity to develop by exploiting the resources and labor of *other* societies. Development was modeled as a national process.

Ingredients of the Development Project

The linking of human development to national economic growth was a key historical event. This is why the term *development project* is useful. It was a political and intellectual response to the state of the world at the historical moment of decolonization. Under these conditions, development assumed a specific meaning. It imposed an economic understanding on social life. This meant that development was a process that could be universal and should be unimpeded by specific cultural patterns. Its two universal ingredients were the nation-state and economic change.

The Nation-State

The **nation-state** was to be the framework of the development project. Nation-states were territorially defined political systems based on the government/citizen relationship that emerged in nineteenth-century Europe. Use of this framework was a historical choice based on the West's experience, not on an inevitable unfolding of human destiny. The following insert illustrates the effects of these arbitrarily drawn boundaries, which continue to reverberate in world affairs of the present.

How Was Africa Divided Under Colonialism?

"The colonial powers inflicted profound damage on that continent, driving frontiers straight through the ancestral territories of
nations. For example, we drew a line through Somalia, separating
off part of the Somali people and placing them within Kenya. We
did the same by splitting the great Masai nation between Kenya
and Tanzania. Elsewhere, of course, we created the usual artificial
states. Nigeria consists of four principal nations: the Hausa, Igbo,
Yoruba and Fulani peoples. It has already suffered a terrible war
which killed hundreds of thousands of people and which settled
nothing. Sudan, Chad, Djibouti, the Senegal, Mali, Burundi and, of
course, Rwanda are among the many other states that are riven by
conflict." (*Source*: Goldsmith, 1994, p. 57)

During the 1950s, certain leading African anticolonialists doubted the
nation-state's appropriateness to postcolonial Africa. They knew that sophisticated systems of rule had evolved in Africa before colonialism. They
preferred an interterritorial, pan-African federalism that would transcend
the arbitrary borders drawn across Africa by colonialism. But these ideas,
and their pan-African movements, did not carry the day. Geopolitical decisions about postcolonial political arrangements were made in London
and Paris where colonial powers, looking to sustain spheres of influence,
insisted on the nation-state as the only appropriate political outcome of
decolonization. There was support for this outcome among African na-
tionalists, who formed an indigenous elite ready to assume power in the
newly independent states.

Pan-Africanism was short-lived; nevertheless, it did bear witness to an
alternative political and territorial logic. As historian Jean Suret-Canale
wrote in 1970:

> Like most frontiers in Africa today, those inherited by Guinea from the
> colonial partition are completely arbitrary. They do not reflect the limits of
> natural regions, nor the limits of separate ethnic groups. They were shaped in
> their detail by the chances of conquest or of compromise between colonial
> powers.[17]

In addition, some of Guinea's rural areas were in fact attached as hinterlands to urban centers in other states, such as Dakar in Senegal and
Abidjan in the Ivory Coast. Considerable cross-border smuggling today is
continuing testimony to these relationships. The pan-Africanists pro-

posed regional political systems in which colonial states would be subsumed within larger territorial groupings—such as an East African federation of Uganda, Kenya, and Tanganyika. To this end, in 1958, they organized a pan-African Freedom Movement of East and Central Africa, involving independence first, followed by federation.[18]

Fierce civil wars broke out in Nigeria in the 1960s and in Ethiopia in the 1970s, and states like Somalia and Rwanda collapsed in the early 1990s. These eruptions were all ethnic conflicts, rooted in social and regional disparities. Examined in retrospect, they show us that the pan-African intellectuals had considerable foresight. Furthermore, ideas about the limits to the nation-state organization resonate today in the growing macro-regional groupings around the world. These **macro-regions** involve states and firms that collectively reach beyond national boundaries to organize supranational markets. Examples include the **European Community (EC)**, the **North American Free Trade Association (NAFTA)**, and the **Asia-Pacific Economic Conference (APEC)**—regional groupings that are discussed in Chapter 5.

Economic Growth

The second ingredient of the development project was economic growth. Development planning was to focus on economic transformation. The emphasis on economic growth allowed the application of a *universal* standard to national development. The United Nations Charter of 1945 proclaimed "a rising standard of living" as the global objective. In national accounting terms, this "material well-being" indicator is measured in the commercial output of goods and services within a country. It is commonly associated with per capita gross national product (GNP) as a national average. Thus, per capita GNP, increasing annually at the rate of about 6 percent (assuming a lower rate of population growth), became the measure of successful development in the postwar era, in conjunction with increasing industrialization. Social scientist S. C. Dube commented: "Sights were set rather high when developing societies uncritically accepted the development theorists' assumption that life begins at $1,000 per capita and when an economic historian of Rostow's repute suggested that the test of development is one car for four persons in the society."[19]

Per capita income and commodity consumption, of course, were not deemed the sole measures of rising living standards. Other measures included health (e.g., rates of life expectancy and the incidence of doctors), literacy, and so forth. Nevertheless, the overriding criterion was movement up the economic scale toward the "good society," popularized by economist and U.S. presidential adviser Walt Rostow's idea of the advanced stage of "high mass consumption."[20]

In the minds of Western economists, development required a kind of jump start in the Third World. Cultural practices of wealth-sharing within communities—which dissipated individual wealth—were perceived as a *traditional* obstacle to making the transition. The solution was to introduce a market system based on private property and sustained investment. Rostow coined the term **take-off** for this transition, whereas economist W. Arthur Lewis argued that industrialization had a snowball effect. He said, "Once the snowball starts to move downhill, it will move of its own momentum, and will get bigger and bigger as it goes along. . . . You have, as it were, to begin by rolling your snowball up the mountain. Once you get it there, the rest is easy, but you cannot get it there without first making an initial effort."[21] Economic growth required a range of modern practices and institutions designed to sustain the development snowball, such as banking and rational accounting systems, education, private property, stock markets and legal systems, and public infrastructure (transport, power sources).

Limits of Economic Measures

As is becoming more and more apparent today, however, use of the *economic* yardstick of development is fraught with problems. Average indices such as per capita income obscure stratification between social groups and classes. Aggregate indices such as rising consumption levels, in and of themselves, are not accurate records of improvement in quality of life. In other words, hamburger consumption is not only a health risk; it also involves resource consumption—such as water, grain, and forest land—that may compromise the quality of life elsewhere or in the future. Additionally, economic statistics do not evaluate quality-of-life issues such as the desirability of industrialized and large-scale food systems. For example, between 1909 and 1957 the cost of U.S. food consumption, in constant prices, increased by 75 percent. Only 15 percent of this was because of physiological consumption; the remaining 80 percent or so of the statistical increase refers to greater transport and marketing costs.[22] Whether we need or want food produced and delivered under these energy-dependent and industrial conditions does not figure in the statistical representation of economic growth. On reflection, such prescriptions for economic development have key normative assumptions:

1. Living standards can be quantified, or measured, with a monetary index.

2. **Monetization** of a society is a common destiny, and an ever-expanding world of commodities is desirable.

3. Non-monetary, or non-commodified, social systems of activity (people growing their own food, performing unpaid household labor, doing community service) are "backward" and are not an appropriate basis of societal modernization.

4. Development policy should aim at reducing the living standards gap between the West and the Third World, with the West as the standard.

5. Each national society should pursue these goals individually (assisted with foreign aid).

These assumptions, which guided the development project, have been seriously questioned by Third World intellectuals. Environmental constraints and cultural revival have both played their part in stimulating the following kind of critique:

> The paradox and crisis of development arises from the mistaken identification of the culturally perceived poverty of earth-centred economies with the real material deprivation that occurs in market-centred economies, and the mistaken identification of the growth of commodity production with providing better human sustenance for all.[23]

We return to this critique in Chapter 7.

The Development Project Framed

Perhaps the most compelling aspect of the development project was a powerful perception by planners, governmental elites, and citizens alike that development was inevitable. Both Cold War blocs understood development in these terms, even if their respective paths of development were different. Each bloc took its cue from key nineteenth-century thinkers. The Western variant identified **free enterprise capitalism** as the high point of individual and societal development. This view was based in Jeremy Bentham's utilitarian philosophy of common good arising out of the pursuit of individual self-interest. The Communist variant, on the other hand, identified the abolition of private property and **central planning** as the goal of social development. The source for this was Karl Marx's collectivist dictum: "from each according to his ability, and to each according to his needs."

It is interesting that although the two political blocs subscribed to opposing representations of human destiny, they shared the same modernist paradigm. *National industrialization* would be the vehicle of development in each.

National Industrialization: Ideal and Reality

National industrialization had two key elements. First, it assumed that development involved the displacement of agrarian civilization by an urban-industrial society. For national development policy, this meant a deliberate shrinking of the size and share of the agricultural sector, as the manufacturing and service sectors grew. It also meant the *transfer of resources* such as food, raw materials, and redundant labor from the agrarian sector as agricultural productivity grew. Industrial growth would ideally feed back and technify agriculture. These two emerging national economic sectors would therefore condition each other's development, as in the post–Civil War U.S. case discussed earlier in this chapter and illustrated in Figure 1.2.

Second, the idea of national industrialization included the assumption of a *linear direction* of development. The goal of backward societies, therefore, was to play catch-up with the West. The Soviet Union's premier, Joseph Stalin, articulated this doctrine in the 1930s, proclaiming, "We are fifty or a hundred years behind the advanced countries. We must make good this distance in ten years. Either we do it or they crush us."[24] Stalin's resolve came from the pressures of military (and therefore economic) survival in a hostile, Cold War world. The Soviet Union industrialized in one generation, extracting a massive subsidy from the Soviet peasantry to finance urban-industrial development with cheap food.

The priority of industrialization is a legacy that shaped the thinking behind postwar developmentalism. Across the Cold War divide, industrialization was the symbol of success in each social system, and beyond the ideological rivalry each bloc shared the goals of the development project. Indeed, industrial development was pursued in each bloc for reasons of political legitimacy; the reasoning was that as living standards grew and people consumed more goods and services, they would subscribe to the prevailing philosophy behind the delivery of the goods and support their governments.

Cross-National Industrial Integration

Leaders of both the United States and the Soviet Union promoted opposing geopolitical spheres of capitalist and socialist development, respectively. Their political leadership strengthened as member states adopted their preferred industrial growth model. Adoption usually depended on obtaining access to U.S. or Soviet economic resources (aid, trade, and finance). In this way, patterns of economic and political interdependence emerged within the two blocs between the member nations. Very little exchange took place across the blocs.

In the Second World, the Soviet system of self-reliant industrialization and collectivized agriculture was extended to East Central Europe. The goal was to reduce Eastern Europe's traditional agricultural exports to Western Europe and to encourage industrial self-reliance. In 1947, the **Council for Mutual Economic Assistance (COMECON)** was established. It planned trade among the members of the East European bloc, exchanging primary goods for COMECON manufactured goods, and it also planned infrastructural energy projects for the bloc at large.[25]

In the First World, much of the postwar economic boom depended on *cross-national economic integration*. Integration came through export credits (where reconstruction loans were tied to imports of U.S. technology) and foreign direct investment. The U.S. emphasis on "freedom of enterprise" was the basis of postwar economic recovery and growth as firms outgrew national borders, investing in overseas production and managing international trade among countries in the First and Third Worlds.

Such economic integration under the banner of freedom of enterprise actually began to internationalize domestic economies as foreign ownership of economic sectors grew. Industries came to specialize in producing a part of a product, their output providing the input for the next plant downstream in the production line, which might cross national borders (as commodity chains). For example, French automobile plants assembled imported U.S. parts and sold the finished cars in England. Japanese livestock farmers produced beef cattle fed with imported soycakes from specialized soybean producers in Brazil and with corn products from specialized corn farmers in the United States. In other words, on a foundation of national economic growth, a global economy was reemerging, based on *intra-industry specialization* rather than simply on the exchange of products in a colonial-model division of labor (see Figure 1.3). As the development project matured, this new global pattern included the Third World, too, as we shall see.

The competitive—and legitimizing—dynamic of industrialization framed the development project across the Cold War divide and propelled member states in the same general direction. Third World states climbed on the bandwagon. The ultimate goal was to achieve Western levels of affluence. If some states chose to mix and match elements from either side of the Cold War divide, well and good. The game was still the same—catch-up. Ghanaian President Kwame Nkrumah claimed: "We in Ghana will do in ten years what it took others one hundred years to do."[26]

FIGURE 1.3

Intra-industry Specialization via International Integration

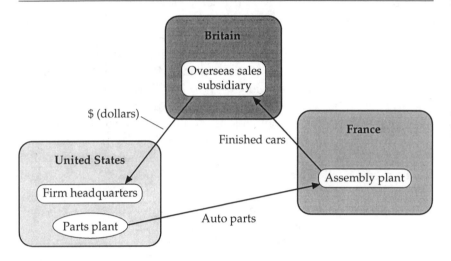

Intra-industry specialization in auto industry

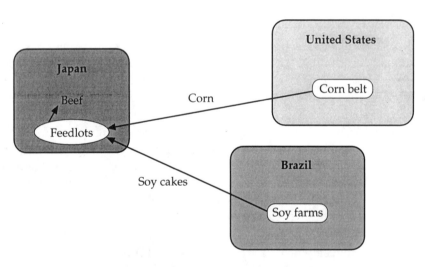

Intra-industry specialization in beef industry

Economic Nationalism

Decolonization encouraged a universal nationalist upsurge across the Third World. Such nationalism assumed many forms, depending on quite different configurations of social forces (peasant/landowner/professional/trading/manufacturing and labor classes) in each national political system. Nevertheless, the power of the development ideal was universal. It contributed to the establishment of relatively strong **developmentalist states** in most Third World countries, advocating variants of economic nationalism.

The developmentalist state was characteristic of **late starters** on the development path. Planning and public investment were necessary to the strategy of catching up. Three intersecting forces stood behind the developmentalist state:

1. Development economists encouraged state planning to overcome market inefficiencies in Third World countries (e.g., low literacy levels).

2. Post-colonial governments inherited a centralized administration from colonial patterns of rule.

3. Management of foreign assistance funds was centralized in the hands of the state, giving planning elites considerable leverage over their society. In fact, access to foreign aid often depended on a country's having a Western-style state with a bureaucracy composed of ministries, career civil servants, and the like.

Just as *political* nationalism sought to regain sovereignty for Third World populations, so *economic* nationalism sought to reverse the effects of the colonial division of labor. Third World governments were interested in correcting what they perceived as underdevelopment in their economic systems, especially through encouraging and protecting local industrialization efforts with tariffs and public subsidies.

Import-Substitution Industrialization

Economic nationalism in the Third World arose first among the Latin American states. It was associated with Raúl Prebisch, who was an adviser in the 1930s to the Argentine military government and then founding director of the Argentine Central Bank. During the 1930s, world depression, trade links weakened around the world. For Latin American states, landed interests lost political power as shrinking agro-export markets depleted their revenues. Prebisch seized the opportunity to implement import substitution. Import controls reduced expensive imports of manufactured goods from the West and shifted resources into domestic manufacturing.[27]

In 1951, Prebisch was elected executive secretary of the United Nations **Economic Commission for Latin America (ECLA)**. ECLA was central to the early formulation of a Third World posture on reform of the post–World War II global economy. ECLA argued that the impact of the United States on international trade was different from the impact the British economy had had in its nineteenth-century prime—when countries grew by trading with Britain. United States economic growth was, by contrast, much more "inner-directed." Arguing that the United States had less propensity to import primary products, ECLA advocated an "inner-directed" development strategy. This policy of **import-substitution industrialization (ISI)** became the new economic orthodoxy in the postwar era.[28] ECLA's view of import-substitution industrialization was in tension with the development project because it transformed the ideal of national economic growth into a potent form of economic nationalism. This threatened the notion of free enterprise that guided First World prescriptions regarding, for example, technological transfer, as we see in Chapter 2.

Promoters of ISI observed that primary goods exporters were paying more every year for imported manufactured goods. Manufacturing technology and unionized industrial labor were evidently more expensive over time, as productivity and wages grew. In fact, apart from the World War II boom, from 1870 to 1947 the **terms of trade** (purchasing power of primary exports in terms of manufactured imports) had declined steadily.[29] The prescription for reversing the discriminatory effects of the colonial division of labor was ISI.

Import-substitution industrialization largely framed initial economic development strategies in the Third World. Governments pursued ISI policies through exchange rate manipulation, import tariffs, and subsidization of "infant industries." The idea was to establish a cumulative process of domestic industrialization. For example, a domestic auto industry would generate parts manufacturing, road building, service stations, and so on, in addition to industries such as steel, rubber, aluminum, cement, and paint. In this way, a local industrial base would emerge.

Developmentalist Alliance

To secure an expanding industrial base, Third World governments constructed political coalitions of different social groups to support rapid industrialization. In Latin America, for example, this coalition-building formed a **developmentalist alliance**.[30] Its social constituency included commercial farmers, public employees, urban industrialists, merchants, and workers dependent on industrialization. Manufacturers' associations, labor unions, and neighborhood organizations signed on. Policy makers used price subsidies and public services such as health and education programs, cheap transport, and food subsidies to complement the earnings of urban dwellers and attract them to the cause of national industrialism. The developmentalist alliance was very much an urban-based politics because governments could more easily organize social benefits for urban than for rural dwellers. Providing these social services was a way of keeping the social peace through ensuring affordable food and establishing loyalty to the plan.

Ultimately, developmentalist states aimed at shifting Third World economic resources away from specialization in primary product exports. They redistributed private investment from export sectors to domestic production, although some states attempted to redistribute wealth at the same time. Brazil is often cited as a model of the former strategy, where public investment complemented private investment without much redistribution of wealth. The Brazilian state established a development bank to make loans to investors and state corporations in such central industries as petroleum and electric power generation.

Brazilian import substitution catered largely to the considerable demand of relatively affluent urban consumers as well as the growing industrial workforce with its more limited purchasing power. As local manufacturing of consumer products grew, the country for a time had to import manufacturing technologies. When the domestic market was sufficiently large, multinational corporations invested directly in the Brazilian economy—as they did elsewhere in Latin America during this period. Latin America in particular was characterized by relatively urbanized populations with expanding consumer markets.[31]

By contrast, the South Korean state directed national development, centralizing control and the distribution of industrial finance. South Korea had a more centrally planned private enterprise system, relying less on foreign investment than Brazil and more on export markets for the country's growing range of manufactured goods. South Korean developmentalism depended on a strategy in which the state channeled wealth into industrial investment, thereby reducing the economic inequality—among urban classes and eventually between urban and rural constituencies—that was characteristic of the Brazilian development pattern.

Whatever the form, the power of the development ideal was universal. Political elites embraced the development project, mobilizing the populace around an expectation of rising living standards. In turn, political elites expected economic growth to give them legitimacy in the eyes of their emerging citizenry.

In accounting for and evaluating the development project, this book gives greatest attention to the Western bloc. There are several reasons for this focus:

1. Western affluence was the universal standard.

2. The Western development trajectory in particular generated the concept of "modernity" and theories of "modernization" that became fashionable in the 1950s.

3. A large part of the Third World was fully exposed to the Western development project, and this is becoming true today of the countries that once belonged to the Second World.

4. The Western development project is being touted now, in the post–Cold War era, as the only real game in town.

Summary

The development project stemmed from a historical context in which the West offered a model for the future of economic growth along Western lines. This comparison began under colonialism, even though colonialism contradicted this ideal. Our brief examination showed that colonialism had a profoundly disorganizing impact on non-European societies through the reorganization of their labor systems around specialized export production. It also had a disorganizing social-psychological effect on these societies. Part of this impact included exposure of non-European intellectuals to the European liberal discourse on rights. Under these conditions anticolonial movements emerged, espousing the cause of independence as a liberating act.

The political independence of the colonial world was the key to the development project. Colonialism was increasingly condemned as individual countries sought their own place in the sun. And yet finding that place meant also accepting the terms of the development project. Those terms included a global consensus embedded in the postwar institutional structures that defined the world as an economic hierarchy. Third World states may have become individually independent, but they also came to be defined collectively as "underdeveloped."

Newly independent nations responded by playing the catch-up game—on an individual basis but, as the next chapter shows, within an international framework. The pursuit of rising living standards inevitably promoted westernization in political, economic, and cultural terms, as the non-European world emulated the European enterprise. The influential terms of the development project undercut Frantz Fanon's call for a non-European way, qualifying the sovereignty and diversity that often animated the movements for decolonization. It also rejected the pan-African insight into alternative political organization. Both of these ideas have re-emerged recently, and they have a growing audience.

Third World elites, once in power, had little choice but to industrialize. This was the measure of independence from the colonial division of labor. It was also the measure of their success as political elites. The mirrored image of the West was materializing.

The development project has come under increasing scrutiny in the 1990s, losing considerable credibility among members of Third World (now Southern) states. It has had quite mixed success, and there is a growing reaction to its homogenizing thrust. Ethnic or cultural identity movements have begun to reassert their political claims in some parts of the world. Also, there is a growing movement to develop alternative livelihood strategies beyond formal economic relations—to explore new ways of community living or simply to recover older ways of life that preceded the specializing thrust of modern commercial systems. These movements express a loss of faith in the ideals of the development project.

The remainder of this book explores how these ideals have worked out in practice, how they have been reformulated, and how a new Project has emerged out of these changes. The next chapter examines the development project in action.

2

The Development Project in Action

When countries became independent nation-states, they joined the development project, pursuing a strategy of national economic growth. This move led to their entering into the international economic cooperation associated with the **Bretton Woods** institutions. National economic growth depended on the stimulus of these new international economic arrangements. In addition, during the postwar period, the United Nations (U.N.) declared the 1960s and 1970s "Development Decades," during which the international community would cooperate in negotiating and integrating various development initiatives designed to strengthen development at the national level. In this chapter, we examine the construction of the Bretton Woods system and how its multilateral arrangements shaped the parameters of national development. We then look closely at the ways the development project affected and reshaped the international division of labor, especially in reorganizing agriculture across the world.

The International Framework of the Development Project

The pursuit of national economic growth by countries across the globe required international supports. These supports were an essential part of the development project. Foreign aid, technology imports, stable currency exchange, robust international trade—all were deemed necessary to sustain national development policies.

The first order of business was to revive and stabilize the world economy. International trade had fallen by 65 percent during the Depression of the 1930s as countries withdrew from trade. This withdrawal continued during a devastating second world war (1939–1945). Under these circumstances, the United States spearheaded two initiatives to reconstruct the world economy: the **Marshall Plan** and the Bretton Woods program. The former was a *bilateral initiative* because it involved agreements between two states on state-to-state activities; the latter was considered **multilateralism** as it involved collective agreements by a series of member states. The development project emerged within the **bilateralism** of the Marshall Plan and became formalized under the terms of the Bretton Woods program. It did not become a full-fledged operation until the 1950s, as newly independent states began forming. To understand its origins, we next look briefly at the Marshall Plan.

U.S. Bilateralism: The Marshall Plan

In the post–World War II years, the United States was overwhelmingly concerned with the reconstruction of Europe as the key to stabilizing the Western world. European grain harvests in 1946 were expected to reach only 60 percent of prewar levels. Scarcity of labor skills and certain goods depleted transport and communication networks, and countless refugees posed enormous problems. There was also a growing popular desire for social reform.[1] On returning from Europe in 1947, U.S. Assistant Secretary of State for Economic Affairs Will Clayton stated in a memorandum:

> Communist movements are threatening established governments in every part of the globe. These movements, directed by Moscow, feed on economic and political weakness. . . . The United States is faced with a world-wide challenge to human freedom. The only way to meet this challenge is by a vast new programme of assistance given directly by the United States itself.[2]

In these political circumstances, the United States hoped to use financial aid to stabilize populations and rekindle economic growth in strategic parts of the world. The other side of this strategy was to head off, and contain, communism—primarily in Europe where the Soviet Union had laid claim to territories east of Berlin, but also in the Far East where communism had gained ground first in China and then in North Korea. The United States sought to gain nations' allegiance to the Western free enterprise system by promoting their economic growth through financial assistance. In 1950, Secretary of State Dean Acheson stressed the urgency of concentrating such assistance in Western Europe, as a counterpoint to the consolidation of Eastern Europe under Soviet rule: "We cannot scatter our shots equally all over the world. We just haven't got enough shots to do that. . . . If anything happens in Western Europe the whole business goes to pieces."[3]

Meanwhile, since its founding in 1943, the United Nations had organized a collective, multilateral program of international relief. U.S. bilateral initiatives—assuming increasing importance in the context of the

Cold War—complemented and sometimes conflicted with these multilateral initiatives. For example, U.S. policy favoring bilateral initiatives overrode the proposals of two multilateral agencies established in 1943: the Food and Agricultural Organization (FAO) and the United Nations Relief and Rehabilitation Administration (UNRRA). When these agencies proposed a World Food Board in 1946 to organize reserves and regulate international trade in food, President Harry S. Truman's administration declined support. It chose instead to pursue bilateral programs in which the U.S. government retained control of assistance. In the Far East, U.S. food aid replaced UNRRA aid in an effort to bolster Chiang Kai-shek's anticommunist forces in China. And in Europe, UNRRA aid was replaced by the Marshall Plan.[4]

The Marshall Plan was a vast, bilateral transfer of billions of dollars to European states and Japan aimed at fulfilling U.S. geopolitical goals in the Cold War. The Plan restored trade, price stability, and rising production levels there. It aimed at securing private enterprise in these regions to undercut socialist movements and labor militancy. Dollar exports, allowing recipients to purchase American goods, closely integrated these countries' economies with that of the United States, solidifying their political loyalty to the Free World—the Western bloc of the Cold War world.

U.S. bilateral strategy aimed to consolidate this Western bloc under American leadership. The U.S. State Department considered the economic integration gained through dollar exports a way to stem the Western European trend toward economic self-reliance. The Europeans desired social peace and full employment, to be achieved through closely regulated national economies, but the United States government wanted an open world economy. The Marshall Plan solved this dilemma by offering an alternative way of stimulating national economic growth in Western Europe. Bilateral aid would facilitate international trade and investment arrangements in national economies.

Because Europe ran a serious trade deficit with the United States (which imported little from Europe), an ingenious *triangular trade system* was set in place to enable Europe to finance imported American technology and consumer goods. Through this arrangement, the United States obtained economic access to formerly protected European colonial territories. Raw materials exported from these territories to the United States produced dollar deposits in European colonial accounts in London banks. From these accounts, Western European states could finance their imports from the United States. In turn, U.S. investments in the colonial and postcolonial territories stimulated demand for European manufactured goods. And so the triangle was complete (see Figure 2.1).[5]

FIGURE 2.1

The Postwar Triangular Trade System Enabled Europe to Purchase American Technology and Goods

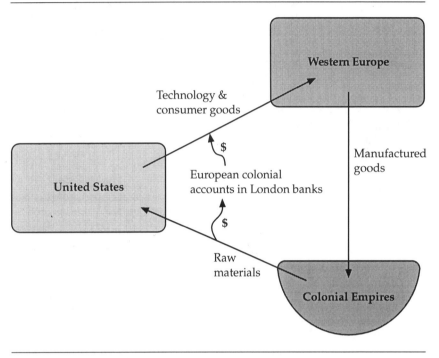

By 1953, the Marshall Plan had transferred $41.3 billion to the First World economies and had sent $3 billion in bilateral aid to the Third World. Post–World War II global economic reconstruction meant containment of communism first, spearheaded by the United States. Military and economic aid complemented each other. With containment in place, further reconstruction would be accomplished by a complex multilateral arrangement whereby infusions of American dollars would stimulate the world economy.

Multilateralism: The Bretton Woods System

The idea for an international bank was part of the plan to reconstruct the world economy in the 1940s. Trade was to be restored by using credit to revitalize regions devastated by war or colonialism. Through a global banking operation, funds would be redistributed to these regions to stimulate new production. The famous July 1944 conference of 44 financial ministers at Bretton Woods, New Hampshire, provided the opportunity to create such an international banking system. Here, the United States Treasury steered the conference toward chartering the foundation of the "twin sisters": the **World Bank** and the **International Monetary Fund (IMF)**.

Each institution was based on member subscriptions. The World Bank would match these subscriptions by borrowing money in international capital markets to raise money for development. The IMF was to disburse credit where needed to stabilize currency exchanges. Once the ministers approved formation of these Bretton Woods institutions, the conference president, Henry Morgenthau, foresaw the

> creation of a dynamic world economy in which the peoples of every nation will be able to realize their potentialities in peace . . . and enjoy, increasingly, the fruits of material progress on an earth infinitely blessed with natural riches. This is the indispensable cornerstone of freedom and security. All else must be built upon this. For freedom of opportunity is the foundation for all other freedoms.[6]

These were the key sentiments of the development project: multinational universalism, viewing natural bounty as unlimited, and a liberal belief in freedom of opportunity as the basis of political development. Human satisfaction was linked to rising living standards. Indeed, on delivering the "Resolution of Thanks" at the conference, the Brazilian delegate, Souza Costa, proclaimed that the Bretton Woods institutions were "inspired by a single ideal—that happiness be distributed throughout the face of the earth."[7]

Goals of the Bretton Woods agencies. The Bretton Woods agencies had these roles:

1. To stabilize national finances and revitalize international trade
2. To underwrite national economic growth by funding Third World imports of First World infrastructural technologies
3. To expand Third World primary exports to earn foreign currency for purchasing First World exports (for example, industrial technology and consumer goods)

The World Bank's mandate was to make large-scale loans to states for national infrastructural projects such as dams, highways, and power plants. These projects undergirded national economic integration and growth, complementing smaller-scale private and public investments. In the first 20 years of its operation, two-thirds of the Bank's lending was concentrated in purchasing inputs to build new transportation and electric power systems. Indeed, the World Bank's *Eleventh Annual Report* stated: "Most of the Bank's loans are for basic utilities . . . which are an essential condition for the growth of private enterprise." At the same time, the Bank invested in large-scale cash crop agriculture, such as cacao, rubber, and livestock.[8]

Meanwhile, the IMF provided short-term credits to stabilize national economies in balance-of-payment difficulties. A country in such difficulties typically owed more on imports than it earned on exports. A persistent deficit would put pressure on its currency to devalue, realigning its value downward relative to other currencies—making exports cheaper and imports dearer but risking domestic inflation. The IMF could extend short-term financial relief, in foreign currency, to a country faced with this dilemma, allowing it to cover its deficits while it balanced its exchanges with the rest of the world.

The Bretton Woods institutions lubricated the world economy by moving funds to regions that needed purchasing power. Expanded trade stimulated economic growth across the First World/Third World divide. At the same time, these agencies disseminated the development project, tempting Third World states to adopt the industrial and capital-intensive technologies of the West. Whereas Europe had taken several centuries to industrialize, Third World elites expected to industrialize rapidly through multilateral lending and so reduce their specialization in primary goods exporting. This shift would necessitate a change from labor-intensive to capital-intensive methods; the difference between these is explained in the following insert.

Capital-Intensive Versus Labor-Intensive Production

The difference between capital- and labor-intensive activities has to do with the ratio of labor to capital or to tools. The latter lighten labor's load. Ancient pyramid building was a labor-intensive activity, as the proportion of slaves to tools was high. Modern dam building tends to be capital-intensive because it uses explosives and earth-moving machinery rather than armies of diggers, although large amounts of labor may be used for certain parts of the project—such as erecting scaffolding. In general, as production processes are mechanized, they become capital-intensive; that is, they substitute capital for labor.

Biases of the Bretton Woods agencies. The Bretton Woods system was un- veiled as a universal and multilateral attempt to promote rising living standards on a global scale. Of the 44 nations in attendance at Bretton Woods, 27 were from the Third World. Nevertheless, for a number of rea- sons, the system had a definite First World bias. First, control of the Bank was skewed toward the five biggest (First World) shareholders—begin- ning with the United States, whose representatives appointed their own executive directors to the Board. The remaining seven directors repre- sented the 37 other member states. This asymmetry still exists; in 1993, the 10 richest industrial states controlled 52 percent of the votes, and 45 Afri- can countries controlled just 4 percent of the votes. Second, the president of the World Bank is customarily an American, just as the head of the IMF is customarily a European. Third, the Bank's procedure is to finance only foreign exchange costs of approved projects, thereby introducing a bias toward import dependence (in capital-intensive technologies) in develop- ment priorities. Finally, the IMF adopted a "conditionality" requirement, which required applicants to have economic policies that met certain cri- teria in order for them to obtain loans. International banks and other lend- ers inevitably adopted IMF conditionality as their own criterion for loans to Third World countries. In this way, Third World development priorities were tailored toward outside, that is, First World, evaluation.[9]

World Bank priorities. World Bank lending, however effective in its own terms, reflected these First World priorities. It emphasized what were con- sidered to be productive investments, such as energy and export agricul- ture, rather than social investments, such as education, health services, water and sanitation facilities, and housing. In addition, as a global opera- tion, the Bank found it more convenient to invest in large-scale, capital- intensive projects that might, for example, have common technological in- puts and similar appraisal mechanisms.[10] In this way, early Bank lending priorities established large-scale technologies as the basis for borrower countries to be incorporated into the development project.

Not only has the Bank heavily sponsored Western **technological trans- fer**; it has also established an *institutional presence* in Third World coun- tries.[11] When the Bank finances infrastructural projects, it sometimes ad- ministers these through agencies with semi-autonomous financial and political power within host countries. For example, in the late 1950s as a condition for further power loans the Bank insisted that the Thai govern- ment establish the Electrical Generating Authority of Thailand (EGAT). This agency then supervised a series of loans for large-scale dams, from 1964 (the Bhumibol hydroelectricity project) through the 1970s and 1980s.

Thousands of Thai peasants were displaced and resettled under the terms of the dam project, often on poorer lands than those they gave up and at considerable cost to their livelihood.

Given EGAT's semi-autonomous status, however, the agency was immune to demands by these displaced peasants for compensation. This status allowed development programs to be removed from direct political scrutiny. Under political pressure, in 1980 the Bank instructed borrowers to conduct social impact assessments to learn when projects would adversely affect people, who would then need help in resettling. The results, as one may imagine when whole communities are displaced, have been quite mixed. EGAT was only one of several such agencies established within Thailand with World Bank loans. Others include the Industrial Finance Corporation of Thailand (IFCT), the Thai Board of Investment (BOI), and the National Economic and Social Development Board (NESDB). Semi-autonomous agencies such as these, called **parastatals**, often override domestic political processes in the name of technical efficiency.

In spite of the likelihood that World Bank projects would short-circuit the political process, Third World elites embraced them in the interest of development. For instance, India's first prime minister, Jawarharlal Nehru, referred to the Rihand dam project as one of "the temples of modern India," especially in generating power for the Singrauli region, India's "Switzerland." The Bank was a leading donor in this project, funding the National Thermal Power Corporation (NTPC) as an alternative to India's infamously inefficient government bureaucracy.

In Malaysia, a similar parastatal agency called the Federal Land Development Authority (FELDA) was created by the Bank to administer three loans between 1968 and 1973. The purpose of the loans was to finance the clearing of sections of tropical rain forest and the resettling of 9,600 families who would grow oil palms and rubber trees. By 1982, by the Bank's own account, FELDA had developed 1.3 million acres (6.5 percent of Malaysian forest cover in the 1970s) and resettled 72,600 families. And in Colombia, between 1949 and 1972, over 70 percent of Bank loans supported such autonomous development agencies. These agencies allowed the Bank to gain an institutional footing within the recipient countries from which it administers the use of the funds.

In examining how the development project issued from the Bretton Woods institutions, we have focused on the World Bank as the key multilateral agency responsible for underwriting Third World development. First, in addition to its influence through the parastatals, the Bank exerted a considerable impact in framing development priorities through its on-site project agencies and its encouragement of large-scale power generation and transport projects; such projects brought about industrialization on a Western scale, often paid for through private investments, increasingly made by foreign corporations and complemented by Bank funds. Second, the Bank channeled loans into *intensive agriculture,* requiring fossil fuel, energy-dependent technical inputs such as fertilizers, pesticides, and hybrid seeds. And third, it catalyzed the central ideas of the development project. For example, it created the Economic Development Institute in 1956, which trained Third World officials (soon to be prime ministers or ministers of planning or finance in their own countries) in the theory and practice of development as understood in the First World.[12]

Finally, Bank lending became a model for other multilateral banks and aid agencies (such as the Food and Agricultural Organization) as they determined priorities for assistance. That is, multilateralism was more an ideal than a reality in the practice of the development project; in reality, Bank policy set the parameters. Third World elites by and large embraced this development path. Arguably, they were hardly in a position to present an alternative blueprint. When individual governments did experiment with socialist alternatives, loan funds rapidly dried up. Multilateral funding was committed to extending the realm of free enterprise.

Interstate Politics in the Postwar World Order

As the realm of free enterprise expanded, the political dynamics of the Cold War deepened. These dynamics had two aspects: the competition between the U.S.-led (First World) bloc and the Soviet (Second World) bloc for spheres of influence, and attempts by the Third World to avoid becoming pawns in this geopolitical game. While the United States and the Soviet Union were busy dividing the world, the countries of the Third World came together to assert their own presence in the international system. We explore the interplay of all these forces in the next sections.

Foreign aid. When we examine the patterns of Western foreign aid in the postwar era, we see that the universalist ideals of the development project were contradicted by the actual patterns of development assistance. All states could not be equal, as some were more significant players than others in the maintenance of order in the world market system. Western aid concentrated on undercutting competition from states or political movements that espoused rival (that is, socialist) ideologies of development. Its priority was to use funds and trade deals to stabilize geopolitical regions through regionally powerful states like South Korea, Brazil, Israel, South Africa, and Iran. These states functioned as military outposts in securing the perimeters of the so-called free world and in preventing a "domino effect" of defections to the Soviet bloc.

As a result, the rivalry across the Cold War divide governed a significant part of the political geography of the development project. In the 1950s, the Soviet Union appeared to be gaining on, if not outstripping, the United States in military and space technology. When the Soviet spacecraft *Sputnik* flew into outer space in 1957, followed by manned Soviet space flights, Second World industrial rivalry gained credibility in both the First and Third Worlds. At the same time, the Soviet Union was expanding economic and political relations with Third World states, especially newly independent states in Asia and Africa. The inherent political rivalry was dramatized in 1956, when the Soviet Union financed and built the Aswan Dam in Egypt. This Soviet initiative followed U.S. pressure on the World Bank not to fund the project, in opposition to the "Arab socialism" of Egypt's new leader, Gamal Abdel Nasser.

By 1964, the Soviet Union had extended export credits to about 30 such states, even though most aid was concentrated among eight countries. Under the Soviet aid system, loans could be repaid in local currencies or in the form of traditional exports, a program·that benefited states short of foreign currency. Not only was the Soviet Union offering highly visible aid projects to key states like Indonesia and India, but in its aid policies it was clearly favoring states that were pursuing policies of central planning and public ownership in their development strategies.[13]

To the United States and its First World allies, then, the development project was doing more than providing the Third World with Western technology and economic institutions. So long as the Third World, the source of strategic raw materials and minerals, was under threat from an alternative political-economic vision such as socialism, the survival of the First World was at stake. In 1956, this view was articulated clearly by Walt Rostow, an influential development economist:

> The location, natural resources, and populations of the underdeveloped areas are such that, should they become effectively attached to the Communist bloc, the United States would become the second power in the world. . . . Indirectly, the evolution of the underdeveloped areas is likely to determine the fate of Western Europe and Japan, and therefore, the effectiveness of those industrialized regions in the free world alliance we are committed to lead. . . . In short, our military security and our way of life as well as the fate of Western Europe and Japan are at stake in·the evolution of the underdeveloped areas.[14]

United States foreign aid patterns between 1945 and 1967 confirm this view of the world. Yugoslavia, for instance, received considerable aid as the regional counterweight to the Soviet Union on the western perimeter of Eastern Europe. Elsewhere, aid to geopolitically strategic states (including Iran, Turkey, Israel, India, Pakistan, South Vietnam, Taiwan, South Korea, the Philippines, Thailand, and Laos) matched the total aid disbursement to all other Third World countries.[15]

The Non-Aligned Movement. Ranged against this particular world order was an emerging Third World perspective, which advocated a more independent vision. As decolonization proceeded, the composition of the United Nations shifted toward a majority of non-European member states. In 1955, the growing weight of the Third World in international politics produced the first conference of "nonaligned" Asian and African states at Bandung, Indonesia, forming the **Non-Aligned Movement (NAM)**. The NAM used its collective voice in international forums to forge a philosophy of noninterference in international relations. At a subsequent meeting of NAM, President Nyerere of Tanzania articulated this position in terms of economic self-reliance:

> By non-alignment we are saying to the Big Powers that we also belong to this planet. We are asserting the right of small, or militarily weaker, nations to determine their own policies in their own interests, and to have an influence on world affairs. . . . At every point . . . we find our real freedom to make economic, social and political choices is being jeopardised by our need for economic development.[16]

An immediate bone of contention was the paucity of multilateral loans. By 1959, the World Bank had lent more to the First World ($1.6 billion) than to the Third World ($1.3 billion). Also, loan terms were tough. Third World members of the United Nations pressed for expanded loans, with concessions built in, and proposed that a U.N. facility perform these multilateral development functions. Third World members expected to exert some control over a Special United Nations Fund for Economic Development (SUNFED). The First World's response was to channel this demand away from the United Nations and toward the World Bank. Here a new subsidiary, the **International Development Association (IDA)**, was established to make loans at highly discounted rates (called "soft loans") to low-income countries. Between 1961 and 1971, the IDA lent $3.4 billion, representing about one-quarter of total Bank lending. In addition, several regional banks modeled on the World Bank were established—including the Inter-American Development Bank (IDB) in 1959, the African Development Bank (AfDB) in 1964, and the Asian Development Bank (ADB) in 1966.[17]

The Group of 77. The next contentious issue was the organization of international trade. The **General Agreement on Tariffs and Trade (GATT)** had been founded in 1947 on the principle of states negotiating reciprocal trade concessions. Because this principle assumed a level playing field, speakers for the Third World regarded it as discriminatory, as many Third World states were economically unable to make such reciprocal concessions.[18] In fact, during the 1950s the Third World's share of world trade fell from one-third to almost one-fifth, with declining rates of export growth associated with declining terms of trade.[19] Pressure from the Third World, led by the Latin Americans, resulted in the convening of the **U.N. Conference on Trade and Development (UNCTAD)** in 1964.

UNCTAD was the first international forum at which Third World countries, formed into a caucus group called the **Group of 77 (G-77)**, collectively demanded economic reform in the world economy. They declared that reform should include stabilizing and improving primary commodity prices, opening First World markets for Third World manufactures, and expanding financial flows from First World to Third World. Not only did UNCTAD become a regular institution, but it also served as a vehicle for Third World views.

While UNCTAD had limited effect on world economic relations, its considerable number of scholars and planners from the Third World infused international agencies with a Third World perspective. Perhaps its most concrete influence was on the World Bank under the presidency of Robert McNamara (1968–1981), who reconceived the Bank's role in global Keynesian terms. This shift meant linking economic growth to social equity, that is, growth through redistribution of wealth. "Growth with equity" was the new catch-cry, and planners embraced for a while the idea of investing in "basic needs." Infrastructural lending continued, but new Bank funds were directed into poverty alleviation projects, with rural development and agricultural expenditure rising from 18.5 percent of Bank lending in 1968 to 33.1 percent in 1981.[20]

As we see in Chapter 4, the solidarity of the G-77 lasted to the mid-1970s. At this point the organization of the world economy changed drastically, unraveling the tidy subdivision of the international system into its Three Worlds. This was the beginning of the end of the *Third World* as a credible term for a region of the world sharing a common past and common condition. It was also a time when the isolation of the First World and Second World began breaking down. But until then, the development project framed national economic growth in the Third World through a close relationship between international institutions and national policies. We now take leave of the institutional side of the development project and examine its impact on global economic relations.

Remaking the International Division of Labor

If the development project was an initiative to promote industrialization in the Third World, then it certainly had an effect. The result, however, was quite uneven, and in some respects industrialization was quite incomplete. Nevertheless, by 1980 the international division of labor had been remade, if not reversed. The Third World's exports included more manufactured goods than raw materials, and the First World was exporting 36 percent more primary commodities than the Third World.[21] In the remainder of this chapter we examine the shift in the international division of labor and its parallel reorganization of the *world food system.*

If we look at manufacturing, the European First World lost its relative position as the core of world manufacturing as industrial production dispersed across the world. Japan and a middle-income group of Third World states improved their share of world manufacturing output, from 19 percent to 37 percent.[22] In the next chapter we examine the implications of this rising group of middle-income Third World states. Here we focus on the redivision of the world's labor.

From the perspective of agriculture, the Third World's share of world agricultural exports fell from 53 percent in 1950 to 31 percent in 1980, while the American "breadbasket" consolidated its role as the pivot of world agricultural trade.[23] By the 1980s, the United States produced 17 percent of the world's wheat, 63 percent of its corn, and 63 percent of its soybeans; the U.S. share of world exports was 36 percent in wheat, 70 percent in corn, and 59 percent in soybeans.[24] On the other side of the globe, between 1961 and 1975, Third World agricultural self-sufficiency declined everywhere except in centrally planned Asian countries (China, North Korea, and Vietnam). In all regions except Latin America, self-sufficiency dropped below 100 percent. Africa's self-sufficiency, for instance, declined from 98 percent in 1961 to 79 percent in 1978.[25]

Two questions arise: First, why did commercial agriculture concentrate in the First World, while manufacturing dispersed from the First World to the Third World? Second, is there a relation between these trends? The answer lies in some of the policies of the development project. For one thing, Third World import-substitution industrialization (ISI) protected "infant" industries. In addition, farm subsidies sustained First World agriculture's rising productivity. Finally, the General Agreement on Tariffs and Trade (GATT) *excluded* agriculture from a multilateral agreement to reduce tariffs and expand international trade.

These three policies complemented one another, substantially reshaping the international division of labor. In considering the impact of these intersecting policies on the remaking of the international division of labor, we focus on the shaping of the world food order. This is illustrated in the case of the South Korean "miracle" on pages 60 and 61.

The Food Regime and the Changing Division of World Labor

An international regime is simply a set of rules governing trade among nations. An **international food regime**, it follows, describes the political organization of food production and distribution on a world scale. It connects producers and consumers across the world within a stable trading arrangement.[26]

In the postwar era, the United States set up a *food aid program* that channeled food surpluses to Third World countries. The program intensified American farming productivity and subsidized Third World industrialization with cheap food. It was a massive transfer of agricultural resources to the growing urban-industrial sectors of the Third World. This food regime put into practice the prescriptions of the development economists (see Chapter 1), but with a difference: it operated on a global, rather than a national, scale (see Figure 2.2).

The mid-twentieth-century food regime originated in the industrial agriculture established on the American plains in the late nineteenth century. At that time, along with Australia, New Zealand, and Argentina, the United States exported grains and meat to Europe to feed its growing industrial labor forces. These settler regions were already acting as industrial Europe's breadbasket. Settler farming also fed domestic industrial labor forces; agriculture and industry grew together in a national economic dynamic. This was the "inner-directed" development pattern that became the model for post–World War II development strategies. As we shall see, the model was difficult to replicate, as global economic relations limited the viability of such developments in the Third World.

Although the "inner-directed" model grew out of the size and wealth of the U.S. national economy, it also depended on protectionist policies. In particular, U.S. farm subsidies protected producers who specialized in one or two commodities only (such as corn, rice, sugar, and dairy products). Subsidies allowed farmers to produce on a large scale because they set prices for farm goods above the price at which these goods were released on the world market. To ensure the continuation of this policy, the U.S. government established import controls—the reason that it excluded agriculture from trade liberalization measures in the GATT (1955).

FIGURE 2.2

International Food Regime

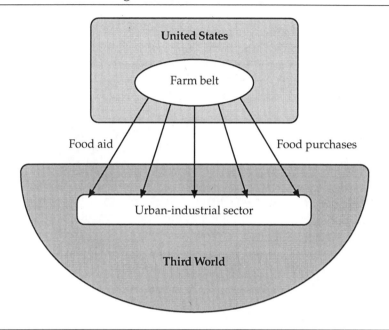

The Public Law 480 Program

Protected behind import controls and price subsidies, American farmers produced more than they could sell domestically. To dispose of these surpluses, the U.S. government instituted the **Public Law 480 Program (PL-480)** in 1954. It had three components: commercial sales on concessionary terms, such as discounted prices in local currency (Title I); famine relief (Title II); and food bartered for strategic raw materials (Title III). The stated goal of PL-480 was "to increase the consumption of U.S. agricultural commodities in foreign countries, to improve the foreign relations of the U.S. and for other purposes." By 1956, almost half of U.S. economic aid was in the form of food aid. In 1967, the U.S. Department of Agriculture reported: "One of the major objectives and an important measure of the success of foreign policy goals is the transition of countries from food aid to commercial trade."[27]

Title I sales under the U.S. PL-480 program anchored the food regime, accounting for 70 percent of world food aid (mostly wheat) between 1954 and 1977. By the mid-1960s, this food aid accounted for one-quarter of

South Korea in the Changing International Division of Labor

South Korea is arguably the most successful of the middle-income Newly Industrializing Countries (NICs). In the space of one generation, South Korea transformed its economy. In 1953 agriculture accounted for 47 percent of its gross national product (GNP), whereas manufacturing accounted for less than 9 percent. By 1981, these proportions had switched to 16 percent and 30 percent of GNP, respectively. At the same time, the contribution of heavy and chemical industries to total industrial output matured from 23 percent in 1953–1955, to 42 percent in 1974–1976. How did this happen?

South Korea was heavily dependent on injections of American dollars following the Korean War in the early 1950s, during which it pursued the ISI strategy. Initially, imports of cement, metals, chemicals, and fertilizers were banned to promote local production of these products. As the manufacturing base developed, this protection was extended to machinery and transport equipment. The Korean government's 1973 Heavy Industry and Chemicals Plan encouraged industrial maturity in shipbuilding, steel, machinery, and petrochemicals.

To keep industrial growth going, the South Korean government complemented ISI with an **export-oriented industrialization (EOI)** strategy, beginning with labor-intensive consumer goods such as textiles and garments. In the early 1960s, manufactured goods accounted for 17 percent of exports. This figure rose to 91 percent by the early 1980s as increasingly sophisticated electronics goods were added to the basket of exports. Thus, South Korean manufacturers, nurtured on ISI, gained access to foreign markets (especially the massive U.S. market) for their products.

South Korea exemplifies a developmentalist state whose industrial success depended on a rare flexibility in policy combined with the unusually repressive political system of military ruler Park Chung Hee (1961–1979). Koreans worked extremely long hours only to find their savings taxed away to support government investment policies. Industrial labor had no rights. Confucianism was a social cement; as an ethic promoting consensus and the authority of education and the bureaucratic elite, it provided a powerful mobilizing cultural myth. Being situated on the front line of the Cold War helped, as the United States opened its markets for Korean exports.

Wholesale changes were also apparent in the agricultural sector. Before 1960, virtually no Western-style bread was consumed in this relatively small country on the perimeter of the noncommunist world. The Korean culture cherishes rice, and at that time the country was self-sufficient in food. By 1975, however, South Korea was achieving only 60 percent of such self-sufficiency, and by 1978 it belonged to what the U.S. Department of Agriculture calls "the billion dollar club." That is, South Korea was now purchasing $2.5 billion worth of farm commodities from the United States, much of which was wheat. In addition, the South Korean government was providing free lunch bread to schoolchildren, and thousands of Korean housewives were attending sandwich-making classes, financed by U.S. funds.

Considering South Korea's history, this was indeed a dramatic transformation, not only in the country's diet and economic organization but also in its world economic relations, as South Korea began to import food and export manufactured goods. Under Japanese occupation, Korea had been turned into an industrial colony for the Japanese empire (1910–1945). After the 1945 partition of North and South Korea, the North had the heavy industry, and the South retained only a light industrial base. But the South included 70 percent of the Korean rice bowl, which was forced to supply 40 percent of its rice harvest to Japan during the war.

Even so, the South Korean farming population diminished by one-half as industrial expansion attracted rural migrants to the cities. This shift, however, was not because rice farming modernized. Recall that economic development is supposed to transfer labor from a modernizing agricultural sector to a maturing industrial sector. But South Korean rice farming remained extremely small scale, retaining an average farm size of 1 hectare (2.471 acres) during this time. In other words, while South Korean industry modernized dramatically, South Korean agriculture did not.

How did industry manage to modernize without the reciprocal modernization of the farm sector predicted in economic development theory? The answer is twofold. First, the South Korean government was unusually interventionist in economic planning, especially for agriculture, where it closely husbanded a small-scale farming system with farm credit and price supports. Second, this particular national economic strategy depended on the support of the international food order or regime, constructed by the United States in the postwar era.

Sources: Harris, 1987, pp. 31–36; Wessel, 1983, pp. 172–173.

world wheat exports, a quantity sufficient to stabilize the prices of traded food goods. The management of these food surpluses stabilized food prices, and this in turn stabilized two key parts of the development project: the American economy and its breadbasket, and Third World government industrial plans. Through market expansion, each came to depend on the other. The 1966 annual report on PL-480 to the U.S. Congress noted its positive impact on the U.S. balance of payments: "This increase in commercial sales is attributable in significant part to increased familiarity with our products through the concessional sales and donations programs. . . . [T]he economic development built into food aid programs measurably improves U.S. export sales opportunities."[28]

At this point, in 1966, 80 percent of U.S. wheat exports were in the form of food aid. During the 1960s, the U.S. share of world food aid was over 90 percent, although this fell to 59 percent by 1973.[29] By then aid had become increasingly *multilateral*, building on a supplementary system of food aid to needy countries that was established in the 1960s at the initiative of the United States. It was funded with financial pledges from the **Organization for Economic Cooperation and Development (OECD)** and administered by the United Nation's Food and Agricultural Organization (FAO).[30]

Food Importing

Under the aid program, wheat imports supplied burgeoning Third World urban populations. At the same time, Third World governments intervened in the pricing and marketing of food, establishing distribution programs to pass on the international subsidies to urban consumers (recall the discussion in Chapter 1 of the "developmentalist alliance," composed of manufacturers, labor unions, urban professionals, and middle classes). Cheap food thus supported consumer purchasing power and subsidized the cost of labor, in both cases improving the Third World market environment for industrial investments.

Returning to the South Korean case, wheat imports in that country quadrupled between 1966 and 1977,[31] while rice consumption began a gradual but steady decline. Cheap imported food allowed the government to maintain low grain prices to hold down industrial wages. Low wages subsidized the industrial export strategy, beginning with labor-intensive manufactures of clothing items. Meanwhile, from 1957 to 1982 more than 12 million people migrated from the rural sector to work in industrial cities such as Seoul and Pusan.[32] Thus, rapid industrialization in South Korea, fueled by labor transfers from the countryside, depended on a cheap food policy underwritten by food aid.[33] In this way, the food regime sponsored economic development in one of the "showcase" countries of the Cold War.

The impact of food aid varied elsewhere in the world, depending on the resources of particular countries and their development policies. The Korean case was a success story largely because the government centralized management of its rice culture and its industrial development (balancing establishment of an industrial base with export manufacturing) as well as the supply of labor to the industrial centers.

By contrast, urbanization in Colombia stemmed from the collapse of significant parts of the country's agriculture under the impact of food aid, followed by commercial sales of wheat. Unlike the government of South Korea, the Colombian government did not protect its farmers. Stimulated by the food aid program, imports of wheat grew tenfold between the early 1950s and 1971. Cheap food imports cut by half the prices obtained by Colombian farmers. They reduced their wheat production by about two-thirds, and other food crops, such as potatoes and barley, virtually disappeared. The displaced peasants entered the casual labor force, contributing to the characteristic low-wage economy of Third World countries.[34]

Between 1954 and 1974, the major recipients of U.S. food aid were India, South Korea, Brazil, Morocco, Yugoslavia, South Vietnam, Egypt, Tunisia, Israel, Pakistan, Indonesia, Taiwan, and the Philippines. In most cases, it was cheaper and easier for these governments to import wheat and wheat flour to feed their growing urban populations than to bankroll long-term improvements in the production, transportation, and distribution of local foods.[35] Food aid allowed governments to purchase food without depleting their scarce foreign currency.

Shipments of food were paid for in counterpart funds, that is, local currency placed in U.S. accounts in local banks by the recipient government. These funds could be spent only by U.S. agencies within the recipient country. They financed a range of development activities, such as infrastructural projects, supplies for military bases, loans to U.S. companies (especially local agribusiness operations), locally produced goods and services, and trade fairs.

Counterpart funds were also used to promote *new diets* among Third World consumers in the form of school lunch programs and the promotion of bread substitutes. As U.S. Senator George McGovern predicted in 1964:

> The great food markets of the future are the very areas where vast numbers of people are learning through Food for Peace to eat American produce. The people we assist today will become our customers tomorrow. . . . An enormous market for American produce of all kinds will come into being if India can achieve even half the productivity of Canada.[36]

In this way, as the food aid program wound down in the early 1970s, commercial sales of American farm commodities often continued, not only because Third World consumers had become dependent on such foods but also because they were mostly newly urbanized consumers. In the case of South Korea, rice consumption per capita continues its annual decline as Koreans continue to shift to flour-based products and animal protein. In Colombia, where commercial sales were prominent earlier and production of local staples collapsed, imported wheat became the substitute staple food. As we shall see in Chapter 7, when governments can no longer afford such food dependency, and food supplies dwindle, their urban populations will tend to riot.

Food Dependency

Across the Third World in general (with the exception of Argentina), wheat importing rose from a base of practically zero in the mid-1950s to almost half of world food imports in 1971. By 1978, the Third World was receiving more than three-quarters of American wheat exports.[37] At the same time, Third World per capita consumption of wheat rose by almost two-thirds, with no change in First World wheat consumption patterns. And Third World per capita consumption of all cereals except wheat increased 20 percent while per capita consumption of traditional root crops declined by more than 20 percent.[38] In Asian and Latin American urban diets, wheat progressively replaced rice and corn. Wheat (and rice) imports displaced maize in Central America and parts of the Middle East, and millet and sorghum in West Africa. Subsidized grain imports also undercut the prices of traditional starches (potatoes, cassava, yams, and taro). Thus, "peasant foods" were replaced by the new "wage foods" of grains and processed foods consumed by urban workers.[39]

The rising consumption of imported wheat in Third World countries indicates two far-reaching changes in the Third World in this period: (1) regions of increasingly tenuous peasant agriculture, as subsidized wage foods outcompeted peasant foods because of government-organized urban food markets; and (2) the expansion of an industrial labor force, as small producers (outside the agro-export sector) left the land and sought low-wage jobs in the rapidly growing cities.

In the conventional economic development model, these social trends occur within a national framework. In reality, under the conditions of the development project, they assumed global dimensions as First World farmers supplied Third World industrial labor.

Green Power

By the 1970s, Third World reliance on imports for modernized diets was considerable. PL-480 contracts offered incentives to governments receiving food aid to eventually expand their commercial imports of food. The food aid program subsided in the early 1970s in part because Third World commercial imports were swelling. In fact, Third World cereal imports more than tripled during the 1970s. By 1980 the structure of the grain trade had significantly altered, with the Soviet bloc joining the Third World (including China) as the major importing regions, and the European Community becoming a major grain exporter, rivaling the American breadbasket.[40] This phase in the international food trade (1973 to the present) involved cutthroat competition for Third World markets among the grain exporting countries. Commercial exports of food replaced the concessional exports of the postwar food regime.

The centerpiece of this new commercial phase was the U.S. government strategy of **green power**, a strategy of aggressive agro-exporting to consolidate America's role as "breadbasket of the world."[41] The strategy was recommended to President Nixon in 1971 as a way of resolving America's growing balance of payments difficulties—as Western Europe and Japan were beginning to erode America's industrial edge in world markets. The Williams Commission recommended that the United States should specialize in high-technology manufactured goods (machinery, computers, armaments) and agriculture. And so the government removed constraints on the use of American farmland and encouraged export agriculture under the slogan of planting "hedgerow to hedgerow." The green power strategy envisioned a reorganized world agriculture, based in a simple division of agricultural labor: the United States would expand sales of cheap grain to the Third World, which would pay with exports of labor-intensive crops such as fruit, vegetables, and sugar.[42]

The green power strategy doubled the U.S. share of world trade in grains (peaking at 60 percent) through the 1970s. Between 1975 and 1989, the United States and the European Community used ever-increasing export subsidies to try to corner world grain markets, reducing world agricultural prices by 39 percent.[43] Such food dumping intensified Third World food dependency and destabilized international trade. It is not surprising that the GATT Uruguay Round, which began in 1984, focused on the attempt to establish new rules for agricultural commodity trade—in essence, a new food regime. To put this in perspective, we need first to examine how green power affected farming in the Third World.

Remaking Third World Agricultures

Given the emphasis in the development project on industrialization, food aid turned out to be quite fortuitous; by keeping food prices low, it subsidized Third World industrial strategies. Cheap food fed urban populations, leaving urban consumers more income to spend on products of the new industries springing up behind state protection. As we have seen, the intent of the U.S. PL-480 program was also to create future markets for commercial sales of U.S. grains as Third World consumers shifted to wheat-based diets.

Consumption of final products, however, was only part of the strategy. The other thrust of the food aid program was to expand consumption of other agricultural goods, such as feed grains and agricultural technology. Export of these products followed a logic similar to that of the food aid program: finding outlets for surplus products. Behind this stood the massive state-sponsored expansion in American agricultural productivity, which more than doubled that of manufacturing during the period of the postwar food regime (1950s-1970s). The management of agricultural overproduction made disposal of surpluses a matter of government policy.

The Global Livestock Complex

Surplus grain was sufficiently cheap and plentiful to encourage its use to feed livestock rather than people. In this section, we consider how expanding supplies of feed grains stimulated the growth of commodity chains linking specialized feed producers with specialized livestock operations elsewhere in the world. We have already seen how Third World consumers shifted to a wheat-based diet. Here we take that dietary change one step further, as consumers shifted up the food chain to animal protein (beef, poultry, and pork). It is generally the case that the shift from starch, through grain to fresh vegetables and animal protein, signifies dietary affluence or modernization. But what historical forces bring this about? If we examine the dynamics of the food regime we can see that such dietary modernization is as much the result of policy as it is the consequence of rising incomes.

Elaborate U.S. grain-processing industries grew in the 1950s as cattle moved from open range feeding to grain feeding, with 75 percent fed on grain by the early 1970s. The grain companies that had formerly sold and processed wheat diversified into the mass production of processed feeds (corn, barley, soybeans, alfalfa, oats, and sorghum) for cattle and hog feedlots as well as poultry motels. Consumption of animal protein became identified with "the American way of life," as meat came to account for one-quarter of the American food bill by 1965.[44]

Poultry consumption more than tripled between the 1930s and 1970, and beef consumption roughly doubled between the turn of the century and 1976.[45] Under the auspices of Marshall Plan export credits for U.S. agribusiness products, this agri-food model spread to Europe and Japan. The European *Common Agricultural Policy (CAP)* allowed free entry to feedstuff imports (cereal substitutes), and the Japanese livestock industry became almost completely dependent on feed grain imports.

Under the food aid program, exports of feed grains also flourished as animal protein consumption took hold among urban middle classes in the Third World. The U.S. Feed Grains Council routinely channeled counterpart funds into the development of local livestock and poultry industries. Loans were made to over 400 agribusiness firms to establish subsidiary operations in 31 countries as well as to finance trade fairs and educational programs introducing livestock feeds and feeding techniques. By 1966, feed grains were the biggest single earner of export dollars for food companies.[46]

In 1969, four South Korean firms entered joint ventures with U.S. agribusiness companies (including Ralston-Purina and Cargill) to acquire technical and marketing expertise. According to the PL-480 annual report of 1970, these enterprises would use counterpart funds "to finance construction and operation of modern livestock feed mixing and livestock and poultry production and processing facilities. As these facilities become fully operational, they will substantially expand the market for feedgrain and other feed ingredients." In 1972, the annual report concluded that

> . . . these firms were instrumental in accelerating the introduction of US technology and were a major factor in the rapid expansion of . . . the increase in Korea's imports of US corn, soybean meal, breeding stock and other supplies and equipment. For example, annual Korean corn imports increased from about 3,000 tons prior to the conclusion of the first PL 480 private trade agreement in 1967 to over 450,000 tons in fiscal 1972.[47]

With livestock production expanding throughout the Third World, specialized feed grain supply zones (primarily of maize and soybeans) concentrated in the First World and in "middle-income" countries like Brazil and Argentina. Between the late 1940s and 1988, world production of soybeans increased sixfold. At the same time, maize production was revolutionized as a specialized, capital-intensive agro-industry. In the late 1980s, the value of the maize trade was six times that of the world wheat trade.[48] In other words, livestocking came to be linked, through the grain

CASE STUDY

How Food Commodity Complexes Reveal Social Structuring

The growing feed-grains trade traces changing social diets and, therefore, the transformation of social structures. Animal protein consumption reflects rising affluence in the Third World as the people of these countries embraced First World diets beyond those staple (grain, primarily wheat) diets promoted directly through food aid. The German statistician Ernst Engel formulated a law correlating the dietary move from starch, to grain, to animal protein and fresh vegetables with rising incomes. But instead of reflecting individual choice and mobility, the difference in diets has to do with who holds the power to produce certain foods and how patterns of consumption are distributed among social classes.

An example of such intervention in shaping the food chain comes from Costa Rica, a Central American state with a history of government and multilateral support of beef production. Between 1963 and 1973, in Guanacaste province, cattle herds increased by 65 percent while peasant bean production fell 41 percent. Declining food security for the poorer segments of Costa Rica forced its government to use foreign exchange earnings from exported beef to purchase basic grains on the world market to feed its citizens. On the global level, Engel's Law may be in effect, as different classes of people dine on different parts of the food chain, but it is a *managed* effect. As wealthy (often foreign) consumers dine "up" on animal protein, local peasants, displaced by cattle pastures, face an increasingly tenuous low end of the food chain, typically depending on low-protein starchy diets.

Source: Place, 1985, pp. 293–295.

companies, with crop farming elsewhere in the world. Thus specialized agricultures were linked by chains of commodities organized in global complexes—a pattern common to both agriculture and manufacturing. Indeed, the livestock complex was as central to postwar development and consumption patterns as the automobile complex.

The Green Revolution

The other major contribution to the remaking of Third World agriculture was the **green revolution**. This was a "package" of plant-breeding agricultural technologies originally developed under the auspices of the Rockefeller Foundation (in Mexico in the 1940s) and then in a combined venture with the Ford Foundation (in the Philippines in the 1960s). Scientists focused on producing high-yielding varieties (HYVs) of seeds that allowed intensified cropping patterns. The new hybrid seeds were heavily dependent on disease- and pest-resisting chemical protections in the form of fungicides and pesticides. Intensive irrigation and fertilization were required to optimize yields, a practice that promoted weeds, which then had to be killed with herbicides. In other words, the HYVs came with a considerable package of chemical and infrastructural inputs. The differences between traditional and modern farming are explained in the following insert.

What a Farm Looks Like Under Traditional and Modern Agriculture

The major difference between traditional and modern agriculture is specialization. Traditional farming is mixed farming that complements crops with livestock that is used as a source of animal power, dung fuel, post-harvest stubble grazing, and various items of subsistence, such as milk, hides, and tallow. Family or village labor is usually the norm. In contrast, modern farms specialize in one or two particular crops or livestock activities. This practice was very pronounced in colonies, where sugar plantations or coffee farms would replace traditional agriculture. With specialization and increasing scale comes capital intensity, as producers add mechanical, biotechnical, and chemical inputs. Agriculture becomes industrialized and may depend on hired labor to complement farm machinery.

In an important trend, a growing number of farmers around the world are redefining modern agriculture along organic and diverse lines (still using some modern technology) because it is a more sustainable form of farming. A resurgence of traditional agricultural practices, such as crop rotation and South American raised bed agriculture, has also enhanced sustainability.

The expansion of green revolution agriculture in the Third World embodied the two sides of the development project: the national and the international. On the *national* side, governments sought to improve agricultural productivity and the delivery of maize, wheat, and rice to urban centers as an *import-substitution* strategy. The green revolution produced dramatic yields, but they have been highly concentrated in a few ecologically advantaged regions of the Third World. Asia and, to a much lesser degree, Latin America have captured the benefits from the new grain varieties, while Africa has charted few gains. Maize, emphasized early, was not a very successful green revolution crop. The major wheat-producing countries in the Third World—India, Argentina, Pakistan, Turkey, Mexico, and Brazil—planted the bulk of their wheat acreage in the new hybrid varieties, accounting for 86 percent of the total green revolution wheat area by the 1980s. Meanwhile, six Asian countries—India, Indonesia, the Philippines, Bangladesh, Burma, and Vietnam—were cultivating over 87 percent of the rice acreage attributed to the green revolution by the 1980s. Because little commercial wheat or rice is grown in much of Africa, the green revolution largely bypassed that continent. Stagnant food production in many African countries stimulated soaring imports of wheat destined largely for the growing urban classes.[49]

On the *international* side, the food aid program helped to spread green revolution technology. A reformulation of PL-480, in 1966, included provisions for "self-help" measures in the contract for food aid. Although varying by recipient, these provisions always included "creating a favorable environment for private enterprise and investment, . . . development of the agricultural chemical, farm machinery and equipment, transportation and other necessary industries, . . . [and use of] available technical know-how." Counterpart funds routinely promoted agribusiness and green revolution technologies, complemented with loans from institutions such as the **United States Agency for International Development (USAID)** and the World Bank.[50] These agencies aimed to weave First World agricultural technologies into Third World commercial farming.

At the same time that it increased crop yields, the green revolution increased rural income inequalities. In parts of Latin America, such as Mexico, Argentina, Brazil, and Venezuela, as well as in irrigated regions of India, this high-input agriculture nurtured a process of economic differentiation among, and often within, farming households. Within households, women typically have less access to commercial opportunity. The green revolution package of hybrid seeds and supporting inputs had to be purchased; to buy them, participants needed a regular supply of money or credit. Women, particularly poor women, usually found themselves "out of the loop"—not only because of the relative difficulty of obtaining financing but also because of institutional barriers in agricultural extension traditions of transferring technology to male heads of households. In Muslim cultures where the tradition of *purdah* keeps women confined, "male agents do not have easy access to the women farmers, and female agents are . . . difficult to recruit."[51]

Among farming households, the wealthier ones were more able to afford the package—and the risk—of introducing the new seed varieties. They also prospered from higher grain yields, often with easier access to government services than their poorer neighbors who lacked the political and economic resources to take full advantage of these technologies. The rising incomes and higher yields of the wealthier households gave them a competitive advantage over their poorer neighbors. Rising land values often hurt tenant farmers by inflating their rent payments. Some poor households were forced to rent their land to their richer neighbors, or lost it through foreclosure to creditors. Finally, the mechanical and chemical technologies associated with the green revolution either reduced farmhand employment opportunities for poor or landless peasants (where jobs were mechanized) or degraded working conditions where farmhands were exposed to toxic chemicals, such as herbicides.[52]

To the extent that we can generalize, the spread of agribusiness typically exacerbates social inequalities in Third World countries. These inequalities take a number of forms. At the village level, gender and household differentiation have occurred, deepening inequities that began with the privatization of formerly communal lands under colonialism. Private property distribution often favors males at the expense of women, whereas commercial agriculture exposes peasants to competitive and unpredictable market forces, often to the disadvantage of poorer, and therefore more vulnerable, households. At the regional level, yield disparities increase between irrigated and nonirrigated districts. Such disparities and the emphasis on marketing of wage foods for urban consumers discriminate against the production of rain-fed grains, beans, and root crops.[53] And at the national level, governments have often centralized their power over rural areas through their role in administering aid and development programs such as the green revolution. Indeed, when the Indian government tried to assume control of the Punjabi "breadbasket" in order to stabilize the national food system in the 1980s, a Sikh separatist movement generated violent clashes between the central government and the Punjab, an essentially Sikh state.[54]

Anti-Rural Biases of the Development Project
Within the framework of the development project, Third World governments wanted to feed growing urban populations cheaply, both to maintain their political support and to keep wages down. Indeed, the

term **urban bias** has been coined to refer to the systematic privileging of urban interests, from health and education services through employment schemes to the delivery of food aid.[55] This bias was central to the construction of developmentalist political coalitions in the postwar era. Such coalitions were firmly based in the cities of the Third World.

Attention to the urban areas, however, did not go unnoticed in the countryside, which was neither silent nor passive. Growing rural poverty, rural dissatisfaction with urban bias, and persistent peasant activism over the question of land distribution put land reform on the political agenda in Asia and Latin America. When the Cuban Revolution redistributed land to poor and landless peasants in 1959, land reforms swept Latin America. Between 1960 and 1964, Brazil, Chile, Costa Rica, the Dominican Republic, Ecuador, Guatemala, Nicaragua, Panama, Peru, and Venezuela all enacted land reforms. The **Alliance for Progress** (1961)—a program of nationally planned agrarian reform coordinated across Latin America—provided an opportunity for the United States to support land reforms as part of a strategy to undercut radical insurgents and stabilize rural populations. Land reforms attempted to reproduce the American family farm model, first introduced in the late 1940s in East Asia (Japan, South Korea, and Taiwan), which was at that time under occupation by U.S. military forces. These land reforms were a model in two senses: first, as interventions to quell peasant militancy, and second, as a method of reducing tenancy and promoting owner-occupancy on a smallholding basis.[56]

The land reform movement, however, focused on redistributing only the land that had not already been absorbed into the agribusiness complex. In effect, the reforms exempted farmland undergoing modernization and dealt with what was left, including frontier lands. Indeed, alongside the strengthening of the agribusiness sector, considerable "re-peasantization" occurred during this period. In Latin America, two-thirds of the additional food production between 1950 and 1980 came from frontier colonization, and the number of small farmers with an average of two hectares of land grew by 92 percent. Arable land overall increased by as much as 109 percent in Latin America and 30 percent in Asia, but possibly declined in Africa.[57] Resettlement schemes on frontiers, including forests, were typically financed by the World Bank, especially in Indonesia, Brazil, Malaysia, and India. These strategies sometimes simply relocated rural poverty and resembled "a war against the earth's rapidly dwindling tropical forests." In Brazil, for example, between 1960 and 1980, roughly 28 million small farmers were displaced from the land by the government's sponsorship of agro-industrialization to enhance foreign exchange earnings from agricultural exports, notably soy products. The displaced farmers spilled into the Amazon region, burning the forest to clear new, and often infertile, land.[58]

Persisting rural poverty through the 1960s drew attention to the urban bias of the development project's industrial priorities. At this point the World Bank, under President McNamara, devised a new poverty alleviation program. It was a multilateral scheme to channel credit to smallholding peasants, and purportedly to stabilize rural populations where previous agrarian reforms had failed or been insufficient. The Bank itself acknowledged that almost half of its 82 agricultural projects between 1975 and 1982 were unsuccessful in alleviating poverty. Instead, the outcomes included displacement of hundreds of millions of peasants throughout the Third World, leakage of credit funds to more powerful rural operators, and the incorporation of surviving peasant smallholders, via credit, into commercial cropping at the expense of basic food farming.[59]

The lesson we may draw from this episode of reform is that neither the resettlement of peasants nor their integration into monetary relations is always a sustainable substitute for leaving peasant cultures to adapt to their surrounding environment themselves. The dominant assumptions of the development project heavily discriminated against the survival of peasant culture, as materially impoverished as it may have seemed.

Through a combination of state neglect and competition in national and world markets, the long-term decline of Third World peasant agriculture, begun in the colonial era, has accelerated. Land reforms and land resettlement programs (mainly in Latin America and Asia) notwithstanding, these interventions typically have done little to halt the deterioration of the peasant economy.[60] The commercialization of agriculture undermines the viability of household food production as a livelihood strategy for peasant populations and a subsistence base for the rural poor. The environmental stress associated with population growth and land concentration steadily downgrades survival possibilities for the rural poor as common lands and forest timbers for fuel disappear. The result is a growing stream of peasants migrating to overcrowded metropolitan centers of Latin America, Asia, and Africa.

Summary

Like the previously used example of the Russian doll, the development project was a multilayered enterprise; its components are delineated in the following insert. National strategies of economic growth, extending all the way down to farming technology, dovetailed with international assistance. The Bretton Woods institutions complemented bilateral aid programs in providing the conditions for Third World countries to pursue a universal goal of "catch-up." Third World governments embraced national industrial growth as the key to raising living standards. Third Worldism came to mean correcting the distortions, or imbalances, of the colonial division of labor. The key was industrialization. In this way, the Third World as a whole was incorporated into a singular project, despite national and regional variations in available resources, starting point, and ideological orientation.

What Are the Ingredients of the Development Project?

The development project was an organized strategy for pursuing nationally managed economic growth. As colonialism collapsed, it was incorporated in the newly independent countries. The Western experience of economic growth provided the model, and an international institutional complex provided the scaffolding for national development across the world. Some ingredients, then, were (1) an organizing concept (development as catching up to Western living standards); (2) a national framework for economic growth; (3) an international framework of aid (military and economic) binding the developing world to the developed world; (4) a growth strategy that favored industrialization; (5) an agrarian reform strategy encouraging agro-industrialization; and (6) central state initiatives to stimulate and manage investment and mobilize multi-class political coalitions into a developmentalist alliance supporting industrial growth.

Aid programs bound Third World development to the overall enterprise of global reconstruction. Military and economic aid programs shaped the geopolitical contours of the "free world" by integrating countries into the Western orbit. They also shaped patterns of development through technological transfer and subsidies to industrialization programs. We have reviewed here the significance of food aid in securing geopolitical alliances as well as in reshaping the international division of labor. As development economists had predicted, Third World industrialization depended on the transfer of rural resources. But this transfer was not confined to national arenas. Indeed, exports of First World food and agricultural technology revealed a *global* rural-urban exchange.

This global dimension is as critical to our understanding of the development processes during the postwar era as is the variety of national forms. We cannot detail such variety here, and that is not the point of this story. Rather, we are interested in understanding how the development project set in motion a global dynamic that embedded national policies within an international institutional and ideological framework. The international framework was theoretically in the service of national economic growth policies. But when we look closer, we find that the reverse was also true. Social changes within Third World countries had their own local face; nevertheless, much of their stimulus derived from a common global process. This process linked changes in the First World to changes in the Third World. One could say that all change under these circumstances was conditioned by global relationships, especially international transfers of economic resources.

In this chapter, we have examined one such example of these transfers, and we have seen how they condition the rise of new social structures. Transfers included basic grains directly supplying working-class consumers, and feed grains indirectly supplying more affluent consumers through the livestock complex. In this way, First World agricultural expansion was linked with the rise of new social classes in the Third World. At the same time, the export of green revolution technology to Third World regions stimulated social differentiation among men and women, and among rural producers, laborers, and capitalist farmers. Those peasants who were unable to survive the combined competition of cheap foods (priced to subsidize urban consumers) and high-tech farming in the countryside commonly migrated to the cities, further depressing wages. Not surprisingly, this scenario stimulated a massive relocation of industrial tasks to the Third World, reshaping the international division of labor. This is the subject of Chapter 3.

PART II

The Development Project Unravels

3

A Global Production System

The development project was built on the idea of parallel national programs of economic development. Each nation would raise its standard of living by producing a "national product" with as coherent an industrial structure and cohesive an industry-agriculture partnership as possible. "Catch-up" meant raising living standards and emulating the U.S. model of balanced or "inner-directed" growth. Public resources and macroeconomic planning policies were considered legitimate partners of private enterprise, to be assisted by multilateral and bilateral assistance programs.

From an international standpoint, the development project involved reconstructing the world economy along particular lines. The initial formulation by President Franklin D. Roosevelt was of "one worldism." Global unity would be expressed politically in the United Nations and be organized economically through the Bretton Woods institutions. However, as the Cold War intensified in the late 1940s, "one worldism" yielded to "free worldism" under President Truman. With the focus now on containment of Soviet and Chinese power, the world economy and the development project came to rest on the twin foundations of freedom of enterprise and the U.S. dollar as the international currency. In this arrangement, bilateral disbursements of dollars wove together the principal national economies of the West and Japan. And, as the source of these dollars, the U.S. Federal Reserve System led those countries' central banks in regulating an international monetary system.[1]

Under these conditions, the former colonies pursued the universal project of development, though with a considerable array of political regimes—ranging from military dictatorship through one-party states to parliamentary rule. Nonetheless, the image was of a *convergent* world of independent states at different points along a single path of modernization. At the same time, divergent forces were at work. These included a growing, rather than diminishing, gap between First and Third World living standards and a substantial differentiation among states within the Third World as the newly industrializing countries shot ahead of the rest.

In this chapter we consider the link between differentiation within the Third World and the growing First World/Third World gap. These two indicators signaled a dramatic reorganization of the international economy as an emerging global production system spun a giant web across the world.

Divergent Developments

Between 1950 and 1980, the rate of Third World economic growth exceeded that of the First World. It also exceeded the rate of growth of European countries during their early, comparable phases of development. However, when we consider population growth rates and per capita income, the game of "catch-up" appears to have been only that: a game.

In the postwar era, the per capita income of the Third World, as a proportion of that of the First World, remained steady—about 7 percent to 8 percent—but the difference in GNP per capita between First and Third Worlds widened from $2,191 in 1950 to $4,839 in 1975 (in constant 1974 dollars).[2] In the mid-1970s, the official multilateral definition of the absolute poverty line was an annual income of $50. At the time, about 650 million people were estimated to be living in absolute poverty around the world, with another 300 million living in relative poverty—with annual incomes between $50 and $75. By 1980, the numbers of the world's absolute poor had increased to one billion, according to calculations for the Brandt Report, *North-South: A Programme for Survival*.

These estimates may overstate poverty because in subsistence regions of the Third World per capita income calculations fail to include alternative survival possibilities. In so doing, they misrepresent local culture. Nevertheless, they express the unequal global distribution of income as purchasing power, and, because purchasing power commands resources, such global inequality is cumulative.[3] This situation was demonstrated in the example in Chapter 2 of the greater market power of animal protein consumers, a circumstance in which the demand for higher-value meat and thus indirectly for feed crops outcompetes food crops, thereby depleting local food security. And this disparity is amplified on a world market scale.

Thus, the evidence in the late 1960s to early 1970s suggested that most Third World countries were running to stay increasingly behind. The wealth gap between First and Third Worlds was evidently enlarging despite the promise of the development project. Moreover, the figures cited earlier do not reveal the growing inequalities of income and access to resources *within* these countries.

Industrial growth fueled by international assistance often brought economic development that relied on imported capital-intensive techniques and neglect of food production. The typical social consequence of these patterns was that growing numbers of rural and urban poor were deprived of the benefits of economic growth. The severity of this pattern often depended on the character of the particular country's political regime.

The so-called Brazilian economic miracle followed the pattern described above, with the economy expanding at an annual rate of around 10 percent during the decade of military rule after 1964.[4] But there was also a *net loss* of industrial jobs, a rising share of the total income gained by the top 10 percent of the population, and a growing number of people living at or below the poverty line, variously estimated at 50 percent to 80 percent of the population.[5] It was Brazil's enormous population and resource endowments that fueled the miracle.

By contrast, South Korea, with a much smaller population (it had two-thirds fewer people than Brazil), followed a different course. The South Korean regime enlarged the domestic market and consumer purchasing power by controlling the differentiation of income between rich and poor, which was roughly one-quarter of the distributional spread of income in Brazil.[6] Although the South Korean regime was authoritarian, its pattern of industrialization depended on implementing a comprehensive land reform program, setting a floor on rural incomes, and enjoying preferential access to the U.S. market for manufactured exports.

Differentiation among Third World countries increased, too, as a select few played the catch-up game more successfully than others and sprinted ahead. The average growth rate for the Third World in the 1960s was 4.6 percent, with per capita growth rates of 1 percent or less; six Third World newly industrializing countries (NICs),[7] however, grew at rates of 7 percent to 10 percent, with per capita growth rates of 3 percent to 7.5 percent.[8] These six countries were Hong Kong, Singapore, Taiwan, South Korea, Brazil, and Mexico.

The rise of the NICs revealed two sides of the development project. On the one hand, NICs appeared to fulfill the expectation of upward mobility in the international system. The central tenet of the development project was that individual living standards in each country would be raised by industrialization. The NICs evidently succeeded in this task, lending legitimacy to the project. They belonged to a group of other middle-income Third World countries whose annual manufacturing growth rates, 7.6 percent in the 1960s and 6.8 percent in the 1970s, exceeded those of their low-income Third World associates (6.6 percent and 4.2 percent, respectively) as well as those of the First World (6.2 percent and 3.3 percent, respectively).[9]

The other middle-income countries—for example, Malaysia, Thailand, Indonesia, Argentina, and Chile—were expected to follow the same path.

On the other hand, the rise of the newly industrializing countries also demonstrated the selectivity of the forces released by the development project. In the first place, the newly industrializing countries cornered the bulk of private foreign investment.[10] Much of this was concentrated in developing export production facilities in textiles and electronics in South Korea, Taiwan, Mexico, and Brazil. In 1969, for instance, most of the foreign investment in electronic assembly centered in the Asian NICs—Hong Kong, South Korea, Taiwan, and Singapore.[11] Between 1967 and 1978, the share of foreign direct investment in tax havens (offshore banks) and NICs increased from 50.6 percent to 70 percent, and the share of manufactured exports from the NICs that were controlled by transnational corporations already ranged in the early 1970s from 20 percent in Taiwan through 43 percent in Brazil to 90 percent in Singapore.[12]

In addition, the distribution of industrial growth in the Third World was highly concentrated. Between 1966 and 1975, over 50 percent of the increase in value of Third World manufacturing occurred in only four countries, while about two-thirds of the increase was accounted for by only eight countries: Brazil, Mexico, Argentina, South Korea, India, Turkey, Iran, and Indonesia.[13]

On the global scale, there was considerable differentiation among Third World countries and regions in levels of industrialization (the measure of development). The manufacturing portion of GDP in 1975 was 5 percent in Africa, 16 percent in Asia, and 25 percent in Latin America and the Caribbean.[14] By 1972, the Organization for Economic Cooperation and Development (OECD) reported: "It has become more and more clear that measures designed to help developing countries as a group have not been effective for [the] least-developed countries. They face difficulties of a special kind and intensity; they need help specifically designed to deal with their problems."[15] The notion of a universal blueprint was fading.

Acknowledging the limits of standardized remedies in the development project was one thing. It was quite another to recognize that the newly industrializing countries were not simply an arbitrary grouping of middle-income states; there were, in fact, strong geopolitical forces contributing to their industrial success. All states may have been equal in the Bretton Woods system, but some states were more equal than others when it came to their global position.

Hong Kong and Singapore are peculiar because of their historic role as entrepôts (port cities) in South China and the Malaccan Straits, respectively. They have shared in the East Asian expansion of the last quarter of the twentieth century, serving as vital centers of marketing, financial, and producer services. In addition, they are coordinating centers of the ethnic Chinese entrepreneurial networks in the region.

Within the context of the Cold War, the other four states—Taiwan, South Korea, Mexico, and Brazil—held strategic geopolitical positions in the international order, namely as consequential states in their regions. Their higher rates of economic growth draw attention to this dimension of the development project that included the transfer of enormous amounts of direct and indirect economic assistance from the Western powers. Military aid and preferential access to the U.S. market helped sustain authoritarian regimes that stabilized economic growth conditions for a time through such measures as investment coordination and the political control of labor. During the period of maximum growth, Taiwan, South Korea, Mexico, Singapore, and Brazil were distinguished by one-party or military rule. South Korea and Taiwan garrisoned U.S. troops, given their proximity to North Korea and China, respectively.

The Newly Industrializing Country (NIC) Phase in Context

The rise of the newly industrializing countries is part of a new historical phase of industrialization, in many ways extending the passage from the first to the second industrial revolution. Britain was the point of origin of the first industrial revolution, manufacturing textiles and processed food and exporting them to the world. Its late-nineteenth-century rivals—Germany, France, the United States, and Japan—pursued a second industrial revolution, building an industrial base around the production of steel, chemicals, and machinery. The NICs continued this legacy, combining both phases.

Early Third World industrialization has been termed primary import-substitution industrialization (ISI).[16] In this phase, a country shifts from importing manufactured goods to local manufacturing of basic consumer goods such as textiles, clothing, footwear, and food processing. Secondary ISI enlarges local industrial capacity for consumer durables such as automobiles, intermediate goods such as petrochemicals and steel, and capital goods such as heavy machinery. Whereas the Latin American NICs (Mexico and Brazil) began primary ISI in the 1930s and graduated to the secondary phase in the 1950s, the Asian NICs (Taiwan and South Korea) began primary ISI in the 1950s and did not move to the next stage until the 1970s.

The Asian newly industrializing countries financed their import-substitution industrialization (ISI) with a phase of primary export-oriented industrialization (EOI) based on the export of labor-intensive products. They graduated to secondary EOI (exporting higher-value-added products) once their industrial base had matured. Asian NICs, lacking the resource base of the Latin American ones, made the shift to exporting manufactured goods earlier than did their Latin American counterparts, which displayed a more diversified export composition (from minerals to foodstuffs).

With the exception of Hong Kong, most of the newly industrializing countries had powerful governments that guided considerable public investment into infrastructure development and industrial ventures with private enterprise. The South Korean state, in particular, virtually dictated the investment patterns in that nation. Success in ISI depended on the size of a country's domestic market as well as a ready supply of foreign exchange that would allow the country to purchase from the First World the capital equipment technologies necessary to sustain the new industrialization.

The passage of second industrial revolution technology from First to Third World sites followed a pattern of "technological shedding," similar to the idea of the product cycle popularized by Raymond Vernon in 1971. That is, as First World firms and states moved up the technological ladder, they shifted their second industrial revolution industries (such as chemicals, steel, and shipbuilding) offshore to Third World sites. This kind of offshore movement occurs as firms upgrade technologically, or when their wage bill rises as workers organize and find a political voice, or when polluting industries come under scrutiny. Thus, Japanese chemical plants have moved to Southeast Asia, and U.S. chemical plants have moved to Puerto Rico.

The product cycle effect has been particularly true in East Asia, where the Japanese government has promoted the adoption of older Japanese technology by South Korea and Taiwan. For example, in their primary ISI phase, South Korea, Taiwan, and Southeast Asian states like Malaysia imported Japanese textile machinery as they developed their own textile production facilities. They then sold the resulting products in Japan and the United States. Metaphorically, this product cycle effect has been termed the *flying geese pattern*. Akamatsu Kaname likened the effect to "wild geese flying in orderly ranks forming an inverse V just as airplanes fly in formation."[17] In this particular context, Japan retains the lead in technological developments as mature technologies are passed down the line and adopted by follower states in a strategy of catch-up. This pattern is illustrated in Figure 3.1.

FIGURE 3.1

The Flying Geese Pattern of Technological Shedding, from Mature to Developing Economies

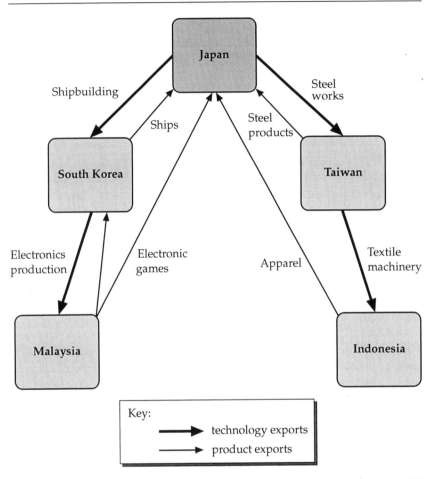

Key:
→ technology exports
→ product exports

Export-Oriented Industrialization (EOI) Displaces Import-Substitution Industrialization (ISI)

The ISI strategy emerged in the 1930s when international trade collapsed and independent Latin American states had the opportunity to build industrial capacity in the absence of foreign imports. But in the 1960s, international trade had begun expanding. In addition, Third

World industrialization based on import substitution, using First World technologies, led to a mounting foreign exchange bill and a saturation of domestic consumption markets—especially in Latin America. Under these constraints, exporting became an urgent next phase of industrialization for Latin states, the strategy now being to broaden markets and earn foreign exchange. The newly industrializing countries of East Asia were already selling in the United States, to which they had special access because of their geopolitical significance. For them, export orientation accompanied import substitution—within the flying geese framework as explained above.

Widespread export-oriented industrialization signaled a significant change in strategies of economic growth. The newly industrializing countries shifted their industrial orientation from supplying domestic markets to supplying foreign ones, using transnational corporation (TNC) investment and marketing networks. Industrial exporting had begun in the large states that had relatively mature industrial bases (Argentina, Brazil, Mexico, and India), starting with traditional labor-intensive manufactures—textiles and footwear, for example—and processing of local primary goods such as foodstuffs, tobacco, leather, and wood.[18] But the strategy behind export-oriented industrialization was really a process by which the First World shed the production of consumer goods, beginning with textiles and electronics items and graduating to machinery and computers.

The export-oriented industrialization strategy, in a world economy buoyed by rising First World consumer incomes, nurtured the phenomenon of the newly industrializing countries. In the 1950s, Hong Kong, an exceptional case, was already exporting manufactures, beginning with textiles and garments. From 1960 to 1978, as manufacturing grew in middle-income countries by about 7 percent annually, in the NICs the rate of growth was often twice that. And Third World manufacturing exports outpaced the growth in total world trade in manufactures during this period, increasing the Third World share of world trade from 6 percent in 1960 to over 10 percent in 1979. The bulk of this export growth was attributable to the newly industrializing countries, and its composition broadened from textiles, toys, footwear, and clothing in the 1960s to more sophisticated and competitive exports of electronics, steel, electrical goods, machinery, and transport equipment by the 1970s.[19]

The destination of these products diverged, however, with light manufactured exports (such as clothing and toys) going mostly to the First World (north) and heavy manufactured exports (such as steel and machinery) going to the Third World (south). There was also a significant subdivision among the Third World industrial exporters. The faster growth in manufactured exports occurred (from the late 1960s) in the East Asian states, which specialized in modern industrial products such as clothing, engineering goods, and light manufactures. The difference between these countries and the Latin American states is that the East Asian nations lack a natural resource base and have comparatively small domestic markets. Their success in export manufacturing was achieved by rooting their industrial base in the world economy. Thus,

> Mexico, Brazil, Argentina, and India . . . accounted for over 55% of all Third World industrial production but only about 25% of all Third World manufactured exports (narrowly defined). Hong Kong, Malaysia, Singapore and South Korea . . . were responsible for less than 10% of Third World production but 35% of all Third World manufactured exports (narrowly defined).[20]

The newly industrializing countries of Asia were quite exceptional in their export orientation for two primary reasons, both geopolitical. The first is that the East Asian perimeter of the Pacific Ocean was a strategic zone in the U.S. Cold War security system, and military alliances with these states were matched by economic concessions. The second is that Japan's historic trade and investment links with this region have become more robust as Japan itself has become a consequential world economic power. In each case, the Asian NICs have reaped the benefits of access to the insatiable markets of the United States and Japan. Global and regional context has been as influential in their growth as domestic policy measures and economic cultures.

The World Factory

The expanding belt of export industries in the Third World, led by the newly industrializing countries, provides a clue to a broader transformation occurring within the world economy at large. There was a new "fast track" in manufacturing exports, which was superseding the traditional track of exporting processed resources. This new export arrangement resembled a **world factory**. It involved production for world, rather than domestic, markets, through chains of production sites differentiated by their function in a global production system.[21]

The phenomenal growth of export manufacturing using labor-intensive methods in the East Asian region, as well as Mexico's border-industrial zone, signaled a reorganization of the world labor market. The Mexican Border Industrialization Program (BIP) dramatized this reorganization. In 1965, the Mexican government implemented the BIP to allow entirely foreign-owned corporations to establish labor-intensive assembly plants (known as **maquiladoras**) within a 12-mile strip south of the border. Concessions to firms, employing Mexican labor at a fraction of the U.S. wage and paying minimal taxes and import duties to the Mexican government, were part of a competitive world factory strategy. As reported in the *Wall Street Journal* of May 25, 1967, the Mexican minister of commerce stated: "Our idea is to offer an alternative to Hong Kong, Japan and Puerto Rico for free enterprise."

U.S. firms establishing assembly plants in the BIP concentrated on garments, electronics, and toys. By the early 1970s, 70 percent of the operations were in electronics, following a global trend of U.S. firms relocating electronic assembly operations to Southern Europe, South Korea, Taiwan, and Mexico, seeking low-cost labor in response to Japanese penetration of the transistor radio and television market. The 168 electronics plants established by 1973 on the Mexican border belonged to firms such as General Electric, Fairchild, Litton Industries, Texas Instruments, Zenith, RCA, Motorola, Bendix, and National Semiconductor. There were also 108 garment shops, sewing swimsuits, shirts, golf bags, and undergarments; some subsidiaries of large companies like Levi Strauss; and other small sweatshops (unregulated workplaces) subcontracted by the large retailers.[22]

The global proliferation of assembly plant industries (from Southeast Asia through Mexico and the Caribbean to Africa) marked the strategic use of export platforms in the Third World by competing transnational corporations (TNCs) in the United States, Europe, and Japan. As these companies sought lower-cost labor, the export platforms spread, driven by developments in the electronics industry. Thus, in pursuing their export-oriented industrialization strategy, the NICs sponsored the world factory system.

The Third Industrial Revolution

The world factory system is nourished by the technologies of the third industrial revolution. (See the following insert for an explanation of the three revolutions.) Especially important in the latest of these revolutions is the semiconductor industry. Semiconductors, in particular the integrated computer chip, are the key to the new information technologies that undergird the accelerating globalization of economic relations. Advances in telecommunications technologies enable firms, headquartered in New York or Tokyo, to coordinate production tasks distributed across sites in several countries. These technologies allow rapid circulation of production design blueprints among subsidiaries, instructing them in retooling their production. If a transnational corporation wants to redesign

Why Three Industrial Revolutions?

Subdividing patterns of world industrialization into three forms is a convenient way of typing them by timing and by their technologies. The first industrial revolution, associated with Britain, was based in the relatively simple mechanization of cotton spinning and weaving to form clothing and textiles for export. Also a part of this were the metal-working industries that produced iron goods, such as factory equipment and railway rolling stock. In this period, steam-driven machinery was improved, enabling advances in transportation.

The second industrial revolution involved steel and chemical technologies, with an emphasis on machine production rather than consumer items. Britain's rivals in this technology emerged at the close of the nineteenth century. The third industrial revolution, based in information technologies, underlies the global reach of transnational firms and banks and has depended on the proliferation of industrial assembly of electronic products in the newly industrializing countries.

its product to accommodate changing fashion, for example, it can instantaneously reorganize production methods in its offshore plants, using the new information-processing and telecommunication technologies.

The telecommunication technologies allow firms to organize along global lines, moving components and software among offshore sites and selling end-products in world markets. Thus we find "global assembly lines" stretching from California's Silicon Valley or Scotland's Silicon Glen to assembly sites in Taiwan, Singapore, Malaysia, or Sri Lanka.[23] These global assembly lines are extremely fluid commodity chains, as production organization among the links of the chains is centrally coordinated. That is, the pattern and content of these chains is determined continuously at the headquarters of transnational companies according to market conditions.

If we consider the spread of electronics assembly in the Third World from a national accounting perspective, it is just another indicator of export manufacturing expansion. But if we look at it from the perspective of the transnational firm, the electronics industry marked the rise of the globally integrated production system, where individual national production sites played the supporting role. This occurred for two reasons: first, electronics was itself a leading industry in establishing a world factory system, given the relative simplicity of electronic assembly operations and their global dispersion to export platforms across the world. Second, electronic components and products provide the technology of the third industrial revolution—an informational technology facilitating the global coordination of production and circulation in other industries, from banking to textiles to automobiles. In this way, the third industrial revolution globalized the conditions under which the first two industrial phases extend to the Third World.

The Global Production System

The consolidation of the world factory system spun a giant web of exchanges across the world. But it was by no means in the symmetrical pattern of a spider web. Economic globalization is not a uniform process. Global production systems are hierarchically ordered, and the hierarchies are fluid. Transnational corporations sometimes organize production hierarchies based on joint ventures with firms in other countries through capital investment or technological licensing. Firms may use joint ventures to gain access to technologies—for example, in the 1980s, Hyundai of South Korea moved into producing more sophisticated computer memory chips by way of a joint venture with Texas Instruments.[24] TNCs subdivide production sequences according to technological or labor skill levels. Moving labor-intensive activities to Third World export platforms is routine. Typically, high technologies remain monopolized by First World firms, with component processes (assembling, etching, and testing computer chips), component goods (pharmaceutical stock, engines, auto parts), and consumer goods (cameras, electronic games, TVs, and video-recorders) moved offshore for production in the Third World.

The global production system depends on a technological division of labor *within* industrial subsectors rather than a social division *between* economic sectors like industry and agriculture (see Figure 3.2). Under colonialism, economic relationships were ordered by the social division of labor—whether within the colonizing countries, or between them and their colonies. In the latter case, this colonial division of labor was in the form of a town/country relationship on a world scale, where colonies produced primary goods for European urban manufacturing centers.

This social division of labor continues under the contemporary global production system. Many Third World countries still depend significantly on agricultural commodities for export revenues—particularly in Africa and the Caribbean. But the technological division of labor associated with the hierarchies of the global production system now overlays the social

FIGURE 3.2

Technical Division of Labor Among Branches of a Transnational Firm Dispersed Across National Boundaries

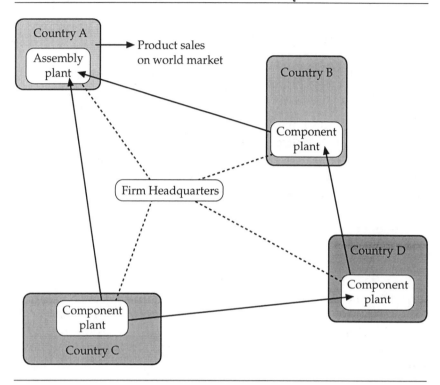

division. Instead of countries specializing in an export sector (manufacturing or agriculture), production sites in countries specialize in a constituent part of a production process spread across several countries.

As we saw in Chapter 2, industrial growth in the Third World complicated the international division of labor. Many Third World countries were no longer simply colonial producers and exporters of primary products. They made a range of manufacturing products, and some exported manufactured goods to the First World or to sites in a commodity chain en route to the world market. However, while the Third World accounted for 11 percent of world manufacturing exports at the end of the 1980s, these exports represented a shift during the 1970s and 1980s of only 1 percent to 2 percent of the First World's total consumption.[25] The composition of Third World exports may have changed significantly; however, their volume was still a relatively insignificant proportion of First World consumption (and the density of economic exchanges among First World countries). Nonetheless, the rise of export manufacturing registered an important world economic shift.

Export manufacturing, within the framework of the hierarchical commodity chains, dislodged production processes from national economic integration. This kind of globally linked specialization began in the 1960s in the First World with the transnational integration of the production of components of a final product. The change was essentially from producing a national product to producing a world product.[26] The following case study of the world car illustrates this development.

Dispersal of specialized production tasks across national borders, as demonstrated in the following case study, reflects the growing scale and reach of transnational corporations. As these companies have reorganized their operations for global sourcing of components and markets, they have dispersed their investments. The rise of the newly industrializing countries was dramatic testimony to the extension of global sourcing to some Third World sites. In the 1970s, 50 percent of all manufactured exports from U.S.-based TNCs were from Brazil, Mexico, Singapore, and Hong Kong.[27] For a decade from the end of the 1960s, there was a marked relocation of *industrial* investment from the First World to the Third World. Such industrial "decentralization" was the combined result of declining profitability on investments in the First World and deals made by Third World states to attract foreign investors to their export-oriented industrialization programs.

The Export Processing Zone

One such deal was the establishment of **export processing zones (EPZs)**—specialized industrial export estates that had minimal customs controls and were usually exempt from labor regulations and domestic taxes. EPZs served firms seeking lower wages and Third World governments seeking capital investment and foreign currency to be earned from exports. The first EPZ appeared at Shannon, Ireland, in 1958; India established the first Third World EPZ in 1965, and by the mid-1980s roughly 1.8 million workers were employed in a total of 173 EPZs around the world.[28]

At this point, the development project was no longer directing these dynamics. Governments were beginning to favor export market considerations over the development of domestic markets (local production and consumption). Export processing zones typically serve as enclaves—in social as well as economic terms. Often physically separate from the rest of the country, EPZs are built to receive imported raw ma-

CASE STUDY

The World Car: Brought to You by Ford and Mitsubishi

In the postwar era, the Ford Motor Company invested directly in a United Kingdom affiliate that produced the British Ford Cortina for local consumers; it had a British design and was assembled locally with British parts and components. At that time, no matter where the capital came from, supply linkages and marketing services were generated locally in import-substitution industrialization. In fact, governments pursuing import-substitution policies encouraged foreign investment in the domestic product.

However, this pattern has since changed. The Ford Cortina has now become the Ford Escort, the "world car" version of the original British "national car." Assembled in multiple national sites (including Britain), the Escort is geared to production for the world market. It uses parts and components from 14 other countries, including Germany, Switzerland, Spain, the United States, and Japan. Given the larger production run of a world car, Ford claimed a saving of 25 percent over the earlier method of building new cars separately for the North American and European markets.

Similarly, the Mitsubishi Motor Corporation, which is headquartered in Japan, has subsidiaries producing components in South Korea, Indonesia, Thailand, Malaysia, the Philippines, Australia, and even the United States (as joint ventures with the Chrysler Corporation and the Ford Motor Company). Mitsubishi cars, assembled in Thailand or Japan, are sold in the United States, Canada, the United Kingdom, New Zealand, and Papua New Guinea as Dodge or Plymouth Colts.

Sources: Jenkins, 1992, pp. 23–25; Stevenson, 1993, p. D1; Borthwick, 1992, p. 511; Sivanandan, 1989, p. 2.

terials or components and to export the output directly by sea or air. Workers are either bused in and out daily or inhabit the EPZ under a short-term labor contract. Inside the EPZ, whatever civil rights and working conditions that hold in the society at large are usually denied the work force. It is a work force assembled under conditions analogous to those of early European industrial history to enhance the profitability of modern, global corporations.

Much of the world's EPZ labor force is composed of women, usually denied the same respect as men.[29] In Mexico, roughly 85 percent of the work force of the *maquiladoras* is young women, supposedly more docile, agile, and reliable than men in routine assembly work—and certainly cheaper. When Motorola shifted its electronics plant 200 miles south from Phoenix to Nogales, its annual wage for assembly work fell from $5,350 to $1,060. The following description of a worker at an electronics *maquiladora* near Tijuana captures the conditions of this kind of labor: "Her job was to wind copper wire onto a spindle by hand. It was very small and there couldn't be any overlap, so she would get these terrible headaches. After a year some of the companies gave a bonus, but most of the girls didn't last that long, and those that did had to get glasses to help their failing eyes. It's so bad that there is constant turnover."[30]

Meanwhile, the transnational corporations that employ workers in export processing zones obtain other concessions, such as free trade for imports and exports, infrastructural support, tax exemption, and locational convenience for reexport. For example, for *maquila* investment in Sonora, one of the poorest border states, the Mexican government's most favorable offer was 100 percent tax exemption for the first 10 years, and 50 percent for the next 10.[31] In short, the EPZ is an island in its own society, separated from domestic laws and contributing little to domestic economic growth, other than some foreign currency earned on exports. It belongs instead to an archipelago of production sites dotted across the world, serving export markets.

The Transnational Corporation (TNC) Market

Export markets concentrate in the First World, where markets are a great deal denser than Third World markets. For example, the average proportion of the population owning a TV, car, or telephone is 0.1 percent in Asia (excluding Japan), 1 percent in Africa, and 6 percent in Latin America, but 60 percent in North America, 50 percent in Japan, 33 percent in Western Europe and Oceania, and 10 percent in the ex-Soviet Union.[32] Export, or world, markets are typically organized by TNCs.

Recent U.N. data reveal that much of world trade is now controlled by transnational corporations. The top five in each major market (such as jet aircraft, automobiles, microprocessors, and grains) typically account for between 35 and 70 percent of all world sales.[33] Further, much of world trade takes place inside the TNCs, as components move between foreign subsidiaries and parent corporations in the construction of a final product.

In the 1970s, the growth rate in the global trade of components came to match that of the global trade in final products.[34] And in 1991 for the first time, according to estimates from the U.N. Conference on Trade and Development, sales internal to transnationals exceeded their overall trade in final products, including services.[35]

At present, the combined sales of the largest 350 TNCs in the world total almost one-third of the combined GNPs of all industrialized countries and exceed the individual GNPs of all Third World countries. The majority of these firms are headquartered in the centers of the world economy: France, Germany, Japan, the United Kingdom, and the United States account for 70 percent of all transnational investment, and about 50 percent of all the companies themselves. The scale of the TNCs is enormous. For example, Pepsico, one of the largest beverage firms in the world, operates more than 500 plants with 335,000 workers in over 100 countries.[36]

The growing weight of transnational corporations in international trade has increased the pressure on other firms to go global. Firms do this either to reduce their labor costs or to expand sales by gaining access to broader markets. The revolution in communications and the development of transport and financial services has allowed firms to tap into the global labor force.

Manufacturing and the Global Labor Force

The formation of the global labor force had its roots in the development project. We have already seen that the urban bias of the project disadvantaged rural communities and actively expelled producers from the land. These phenomena occurred widely across the world and are the fundamental source of the global labor force. Historian Eric Hobsbawm observed: "Between 1950 and 1975 . . . in Europe, in the Americas, and in the western Islamic world—in fact everywhere except Continental South and East Asia and sub-Saharan Africa—peasants now form a minority of the population. And this process occurred with dramatic speed." [37]

For European societies, the process of depeasantization was spread over several centuries. Even then the pressure on the cities was relieved as people left them to emigrate to settler colonies in North America and Australasia. But, for Third World societies, this process has been compressed into a few generations, with only a little longer for Latin America. Rural migrants in many places have overwhelmed the cities.

These dispossessed people entered the global manufacturing work force as a cost-saving strategy for the major producers. Once First World firms developed technologies of mass production, they began relocating manufacturing to employ cheaper Third World labor. Mass production developed around large, routinized production runs that could be broken down and subdivided into specialized tasks. The assembly line that emerged in the automobile and meat-packing industries is a case in point. Each worker on the line did a simplified task that contributed to an overall production process. The simplification of specialized tasks is known as the deskilling of work.

Now, tasks deskilled through specialization—such as cutting and stitching in the garment or footwear industry, or assembly in the electrical, automobile, or computer chip industry—are often relocated to cheap labor regions. At the same time, the technologies to coordinate those tasks generate needs for new skilled labor, such as managerial, scientific, engineering, and technical labor.[38] This bifurcation of the labor force means that skilled labor concentrates in the First World, and unskilled labor is often consigned to the Third World. The coordination of both types of labor is the province of TNC enterprise, as detailed in the following description from the 1970s:

> Intel Corporation is located in the heart of California's "Silicon Valley." . . .
> When Intel's engineers develop a design for a new electronic circuit or process, technicians in the Santa Clara Valley, California, plant will build, test, and redesign the product. When all is ready for production of the new item, however, it doesn't go to a California factory. Instead, it is air freighted to Intel's plant in Penang, Malaysia. There, Intel's Malaysian workers, almost all young women, assemble the components in a tedious process involving hand soldering of fiber-thin wire leads. Once assembled, the components are flown back to California, this time for final testing and/or integration into a larger end product. And, finally, they're off to market, either in the United States, Europe, or back across the Pacific to Japan.[39]

In the 1970s, the relocation of deskilled tasks to lower-wage regions of the world was so prevalent that the concept of a **new international division of labor (NIDL)** was coined to describe this development. Briefly, NIDL referred to an apparent decentralization of industrial production from the First to the Third World, shown here in Figure 3.3. The conditions for this movement were defined as endless supplies of cheap Third World labor; the new technical possibility of relocating the unskilled portions of manufacturing processes to the Third World; and the development of transport, communications, and organizational technology, reducing the significance of distance in the coordination of activities by global firms.[40]

Skilled labor inputs concentrated in the North, except where enterprising states such as the newly industrializing countries of East Asia (South

FIGURE 3.3

The New International Division of Labor (NIDL)

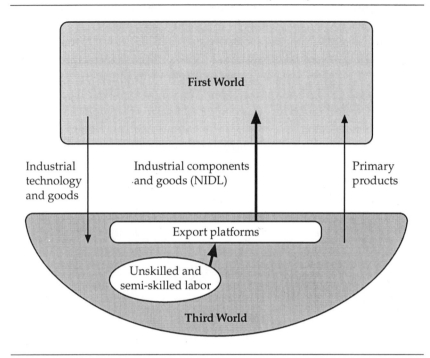

Korea, Taiwan, Singapore, and Hong Kong) used public investment to upgrade work-force skills. The upgrading was necessary as their wage levels were rising in relation to other countries that were embracing export production, such as Malaysia, Indonesia, and the Philippines. In 1975, if the hourly wage for electronics work in the United States was measured at 100, the relative value for equivalent work was 12 in Hong Kong and Singapore, 9 in Malaysia, 7 in Taiwan and South Korea, 6 in the Philippines, and 5 in Indonesia and Thailand.[41] This wage differentiation made the East Asian NICs' labor-intensive production less competitive, forcing them to upgrade their portion of the global labor force.

These Asian countries improved their competitiveness by specializing in more sophisticated types of export manufacturing for First World markets, using cheap skilled labor rather than cheap semi-skilled and unskilled labor. After upgrading their labor force, the NICs attracted skilled labor inputs to their countries as a regional growth strategy. As the skilled work came, these states became headquarters, or cores, of new regional divisions of labor patterned on the production hierarchy between Japan and its East and Southeast Asian neighbors. By 1985, the upgrading of this production hierarchy meant that an East Asian division of labor existed in the semiconductor industry for U.S. firms. Final testing of semiconductors (capital-intensive labor involving computers with lasers) and circuit design centers were located in Hong Kong, Singapore, and Taiwan; wafer fabrication in Malaysia; and assembly in Malaysia, Thailand, the Philippines, and Indonesia. Whereas in the 1970s semiconductors were assembled in Southeast Asia and then flown back to the United States for testing and distribution, by the 1980s Hong Kong imported semiconductors from South Korea and Malaysia to test them for reexport to the First World as well as for input in Hong Kong's fabled watch-assembly industry.[42]

Patterns of global and regional sourcing have recently mushroomed across the world, particularly under the stimulus of the electronics revolution. Firms establish either subsidiaries in other countries or extensive subcontracting arrangements—such as in labor-intensive consumer goods industries like garments, footwear, toys, household goods, and consumer electronics. For example, the Nike Corporation produces most of its athletic shoes through subcontracting arrangements in South Korea, China, Indonesia, and Thailand; product design and sales promotion are reserved for its U.S. headquarters, where the firm "promotes the symbolic nature of the shoe and appropriates the greater share of the value resulting from its sales."[43] U.S. retailers of every size also routinely use global subcontracting arrangements in the Asia-Pacific and the Caribbean regions to organize their supplies and reduce their costs, as illustrated in the following case study on Saipan.

The Saipan case study illustrates the dark side of subcontracting—a pattern of abuse commonly experienced by unprotected labor throughout the world. About 46 million children work for American firms in 19 different countries, with half this child labor in India alone. Many of these children work 14-hour days in crowded and unsafe workplaces.[44] Regardless of whether transnational corporations offer better conditions than local firms, the rise of global subcontracting permits little opportunity for regulation of employment conditions. The global labor force exists on such a broad scale across cultures, out of sight of regulators, that global working situations increasingly resemble the harsh conditions of early European industrial work before labor protections appeared. Some of today's global labor force has been generated by the expansion of agribusiness on a world scale, to which we now turn.

Global Subcontracting in Saipan

One of the production sites used over the past two decades as a supplier in global subcontracting is the tiny island of Saipan, in the Philippine Sea of the western Pacific. The commonwealth of Saipan has been a territory of the United States since the end of World War II, and the islanders are American citizens. In the early 1980s, new federal rules for the garment industry allowed duty free (and virtually quota free) imports from Saipan into the United States as well as liberal foreign investment conditions. Companies involved in garment production on Saipan include Arrow, The Gap, Montgomery Ward, Geoffrey Beene, Liz Claiborne, Eddie Bauer, and Levi Strauss. For certain of these companies, Saipan has strategic importance. Even though its exports make up only about 1 percent of all clothing imports into the United States, they account for roughly 20 percent of sales for some large American companies.

Saipan has a major advantage as a production site: although the "Made in USA" label can legitimately be put on any item produced there, the island was exempted from the federal minimum wage in 1976. The commonwealth government has maintained a minimum wage of $2.15 an hour since 1984 (compared with the federal minimum of $4.25 on Guam, another U.S. territory 120 miles to the south).

Saipan shipped about $279 million worth of wholesale garments to the United States in 1992, and, despite the label, more than half the labor force contributing to these exports is foreign—predominantly Chinese recruits. The clothing factories resemble sweatshops in their working conditions; they have recently attracted the attention of American labor unions and investigators from the U.S. Department of Labor and the Occupational Safety and Health Administration. These inspectors found Chinese workers whose passports had been confiscated and who were working 84-hour weeks at subminimum wages. One of the companies involved, Levi Strauss, responded by establishing new subcontract guidelines requiring improved conditions, which were also to be implemented in other sites in Myanmar and China.

Sources: Shenon, 1993, p. 10; Udesky, 1994; The Economist, June 3, 1995, p. 58.

Global Agribusiness

Just as the manufacturing transnational corporations use global sourcing strategies, so do agribusiness firms. The food trade is one of the fastest-growing industries in the world today, especially in processed foods like meat and flour products, and in fresh and processed fruits and vegetables. Food companies stretch across the world, organizing producers on plantations and farms to deliver products for sale in the higher-value markets of the First World. As we have seen, the livestock complex was one of the first segments of the food industry to internationalize. It is the basis of the following case study on the making of the "world steer."

CASE STUDY

Agribusiness Brings You the World Steer

The "world steer" resembles the "world car." It is produced in a variety of locations with global inputs (standardized genetic lines and growth patterns) for global sale (standardized packaging). Like the world car, the world steer is the logical extension of the mass production system that emerged in the post–World War II era, otherwise known as the "Development Decades" (1945–1970). These production systems are now global rather than national in scope, even though the consumers are still concentrated within the First World. The beef industry is subdivided into two branches: intensive feed-lotting for high-value specialty cuts and extensive cattle grazing for low-value, lean meat supplying fast-food outlets. We consider here the explosion of cattle ranching in Central America (Costa Rica, Nicaragua, Honduras, Guatemala, and El Salvador) as part of the North American hamburger connection.

   Cattle ranching expanded in Central America in the 1960s as the fast-food industry took off. Brahman bulls (or their semen) imported from Florida and Texas were crossed with native criollo and fed on imported African and South American pasture to produce a more pest-resistant, more heat-resistant, and beefier breed of steer. From conception to slaughter, the production of the steer is geared entirely to the demands of a global market. Animal health and the fattening process depend on medicines, antibiotics, chemical fertilizers, and herbicides supplied from around the world by transnational firms. In addition to these global inputs in the production of the world steer, there are the local conditions of beef production.

Postwar development strategies favored agro-exporting where possible so that a developing country could earn foreign currency for purchasing industrial technologies. Many Third World states continued to export tropical products they had begun producing in the colonial era. Central American states complemented their traditional exports (coffee and bananas) with beef. The cattle-ranching explosion in Central America began in the 1960s, when import restrictions on beef exports to the United States were eased by the Alliance for Progress (a hemispheric security project of economic reform sponsored by the United States). Governments entered into loan agreements with the World Bank, the Agency for International Development (AID), and the Inter-American Development Bank (IADB) to fund the expansion of pasture and transport facilities. Beef exporting from the region rose eightfold in 20 years, resulting from a 250 percent expansion of Central America's cattle herds. By 1978, Central American herds totaled 10 million head of cattle, supplying 250 million pounds of beef annually and accounting for 15 percent of U.S. beef imports. Among the foreign investors in this industry were large transnational companies such as International Foods, United Brands, Agrodiná mica Holding Company, and R. J. Reynolds.

World steer production has redistributed cattle holdings and open-range woodland from peasants to the ranchers supplying the export packers. More than half the rural population of Central America (35 million) is now landless or unable to survive as a peasantry. World steer production not only reinforces inequality in the producing regions but also threatens craftwork and food security.

Domesticated animals traditionally have provided food, fuel, fertilizer, transport, and clothing, in addition to grazing on and consuming crop stubble. In many ways, livestock have been the centerpiece of rural community survival over the centuries. Peasants have always used mixed farming as a sustainable form of social economy, hunting on common lands to supplement their local diets with additional protein. Elimination of woodlands reduces hunting possibilities, shrinks wood supplies for fuel, and destroys watershed ecologies. Also, development policies favoring other cattle breeds over the traditional criollo undermine traditional cattle raising and hence peasant self-provisioning.

Peasants forfeit their original meat and milk supplies and lose access to side products such as tallow for cooking oil and leather for clothing and footwear. In short, the spread of the world steer industry supplies distant mass consumer markets at the same time that it undermines local agro-ecologies. The world economy does not get something for nothing.

Sources: Sanderson, 1986b; Friedmann & McMichael, 1989; Williams, 1986, pp. 93–95; Rifkin, 1992, pp. 192–193.

Global sourcing also sustains the intensive form of livestock raising that requires feedlots. Three agribusiness firms headquartered in the United States operate meat-packing operations across the world, growing cattle, pigs, and poultry on feedstuffs supplied by their own grain marketing subsidiaries elsewhere in the world. Cargill, headquartered in Minnesota, is the largest grain trader in the world, operating in 49 countries with 800 offices or plants and more than 55,000 employees. It has established a joint venture with Nippon Meat Packers of Japan, called Sun Valley Thailand, from which it exports U.S. corn-fed poultry products to the Japanese market. ConAgra, headquartered in Nebraska, owns 56 companies and operates in 26 countries with 58,000 employees. It processes feed and animal protein products in the United States, Canada, Australia, Europe, the Far East, and Latin America. Tyson Foods, headquartered in Arkansas, runs a joint venture with the Japanese agribusiness firm C. Itoh, which produces poultry in Mexico for both local consumption and export to Japan. Tyson also cuts up chickens in the United States, using the breast meat for the fast-food industry and shipping leg quarters to Mexico for further processing (at one-tenth the cost of preparing them in this country) for the Japanese market.[45]

The New Agricultural Countries (NACs)

Despite the far-flung activities of these food companies, agribusiness investments have generally concentrated in select Third World countries such as Brazil, Mexico, Argentina, Chile, Hungary, and Thailand. Harriet Friedmann has called these countries the **new agricultural countries** (NACs).[46] They are analogous to the newly industrializing countries insofar as their governments promote agro-industrialization for urban and export markets. These agro-exports have been called nontraditional exports because they either replace or supplement the traditional tropical exports of the colonial era. Nontraditional exports comprise high-value foods such as animal protein products and fruits and vegetables. And, to carry the analogy further, the term the *new international division of labor* has been extended to these agro-exports because they supersede the exports associated with the colonial division of labor.[47] An example is Thailand, as illustrated in the following case study.

CASE STUDY

Thailand Becomes a New Agricultural Country (NAC)

Thailand's traditional role in the international division of labor as an exporter of rice, sugar, pineapples, and rubber has been complicated recently by its expanding array of nontraditional primary exports: cassava (feed grain), canned tuna, shrimp, poultry, processed meats, and fresh and processed fruits and vegetables. Former exports, corn and sorghum, are now mostly consumed domestically in the intensive livestock sector. Raw agricultural exports, which accounted for 80 percent of Thailand's exports in 1980, now represent 30 percent; processed food makes up 30 percent of manufactured exports. In other words, Thailand has become a new agricultural country.

Seen as Asia's supermarket, Thailand has rapidly expanded its food processing industry on a foundation of rural smallholders under contract to food processing firms. Food companies from Japan, Taiwan, the United States, and Europe use Thailand as a base for regional and global export-oriented production. In the 1970s, Japanese firms began investing in Thai agriculture to expand feed (soybeans and corn) and aquaculture supply zones for Japanese markets. Typically, Japanese food companies enter into joint ventures with Thai agribusinesses, providing high-technology production facilities and market access abroad.

Thai poultry production is organized around small growers who contract with large, vertically integrated firms. The Thai government established the Fourth Sector Co-operation Plan to Develop Agriculture and Agro-Industry in the mid-1980s, linking agribusiness firms, farmers, and financial institutions with state ministries to promote export contracts. In this way, the government has provided support with tax and other concessions to agribusinesses and, through the Bangkok Bank's Agricultural

Credit Development, has underwritten the distribution of land to landless farmers for contract growing and livestock farming. Thailand's mature feed industry, coupled with low-cost labor, makes its poultry producers very competitive with their counterparts in the United States, especially in the Japanese market, which is largely for deboned chicken. By 1987, this market was supplied equally by U.S. and Thai poultry exports, just one measure of Thailand's becoming a new agricultural country. Its agroexports are linked to the rich and growing markets in the Pacific Rim (especially those of Japan, South Korea, and Taiwan), accounting for over 60 percent of Thailand's foreign exchange reserves in the early 1990s.

Sources: McMichael, 1993b; Watts, 1994, pp. 52–53.

The Second Green Revolution

As we saw in Chapter 2, the green revolution encouraged agribusiness, deepening Third World agro-industrialism in the production of wage foods for urban consumers. Since then, agro-industrialism has spread from basic grains to other grains such as feedstuffs, to horticultural crops such as fresh fruits and vegetables, and, more recently, to feed-grain substitutes such as cassava, corn gluten feed, and citrus pellets as well as plant-derived biotechnology "feedstocks" for the chemical industry. This kind of agriculture depends on hybrid seeds, chemical fertilizers, pesticides, animal antibiotics and growth-inducing chemicals, specialty feeds, and so forth. In other words, it is a specialized, high-input agriculture, with high-value markets. It extends green revolution technology from basic to luxury foods and has been termed the second green revolution.[48]

The second green revolution is an indicator that high-income, consuming classes are increasing in the Third World, adopting the affluent diets associated with the First World. It involves, most notably, substituting feed crops for food crops, a move that further exacerbates social inequalities. In Mexico, for example, U.S. agribusiness firms promoted use of hybrid sorghum seeds among Mexican farmers in the late 1950s. In 1965, the government followed with a support price favoring sorghum over wheat and maize (products of the green revolution). As sorghum production doubled (supplying 74 percent of Mexican feedstuffs), wheat, maize, and even bean production began a long decline. Meanwhile, between 1972 and 1979, meat consumption rose among wealthier Mexicans, with increases of 65 percent in pork, 35 percent in poultry, and 32 percent in beef. At the same time, no kind of meat was available for about one-third of the population.[49]

The second green revolution also underlies the globalization of markets for high-value foods such as off-season fresh fruits and vegetables. This market is one of the most profitable for agribusinesses; high-value foods have become the locus of their growth. For example, as markets have deepened in the First World and transport technologies have grown alongside distribution systems, we now have "cool chains" that maintain chilled temperatures for moving fresh fruit and vegetables grown by Third World farmers to First World supermarket outlets. Firms such as Dole, Chiquita, and Del Monte have moved beyond their traditional commodities such as bananas and pineapples into other fresh fruits and vegetables. By coordinating producers scattered across different climatic zones, these firms are able to reduce the seasonality of fresh fruits and vegetables and thus create a global supermarket. Year-round produce availability is complemented with exotic fruits like breadfruit, cherimoya (custard apple), carambola (star fruit), feijoa (pineapple guava), lychee, kiwi, and passionfruit; vegetables such as bok choy, cassava, fava beans, and plantain; and salad greens like arugula, chicory, and baby vegetables.[50]

In this new division of world agricultural labor, transnational corporations typically subcontract with Third World peasants to produce specialty horticultural crops and off-season fruits and vegetables. They also process foods (such as fruit juices, canned fruits, frozen vegetables, boxed beef, and chicken pieces), often in export processing zones, for expanding consumer markets in Europe, North America, and Pacific-Asia.

Global Sourcing and Regionalism

Global sourcing is a strategy used by transnational corporations and host governments alike to improve their world market position and secure predictable supplies of inputs. But it is not where our understanding of global dynamics stops. Indeed, during the 1980s, there was a marked decline in the rate of TNC investment in the Third World,[51] which had become destabilized by debt stress (see Chapter 4). The decline of foreign investment also reflected a corporate restructuring trend in the First World. This decade of restructuring marked a new direction in firm marketing strategies: market segmentation.

The new direction represents a shift from standardized mass production to flexible production, using smaller and less specialized labor forces (as explained in the following insert). Whether flexible production

---

Mass and Flexible Production

The typical First World factory after World War II was organized along mass lines: a large work force performing mainly line work on an assembly line system of production. Mass consumer markets in consumer durables like cars and refrigerators were the target of this production system. As labor became unruly in the late 1960s and First World corporations faced declining profits, they relocated production—especially the unskilled assembly work—to sites in the Third World. Production decentralization complemented the industrial growth strategy of the newly industrializing countries. With modern computer technologies and automation, firms can pursue much more flexible production methods because product design can be more easily altered by computing, and production inventories can be reduced. The scale and specialization of the work force can be reduced and dispersed among several smaller sites—even though the overall production operation is closely coordinated by the new information/telecommunication technologies. Such coordination actually facilitates the global dispersion of some production, particularly of components. With smaller production runs and greater sensitivity to consumer desires, however, some high-tech products (like computers) are produced closer to their markets.

---

is actually replacing mass production is a matter of considerable debate. Flexible production is not yet universal, and between the two, mass production for market segments is more likely to be the order of the day. The balance depends largely on the size of the market segment.

The size of market segments is related to class-based income brackets. We have seen a considerable stratification of consumption over the past decade—in the broad quality range of cars and clothing items, and, as suggested above, in the segmentation of the beef market into high-value beefsteak and low-value hamburger. With a global market, firms are increasingly under pressure to respond to changing consumer preference as the life span of commodities declines (with rapidly changing fashion and/or technologies). The quick shifts in consumer tastes emphasize time as a strategic dimension of marketing, which means firms need to be more flexible in their production runs, in their use of inputs, in their use of inventory, and in their turnover of commodities on demand.

In the 1980s, the Toyota Company introduced the just-in-time (JIT) system of "destandardized or flexible mass production in which, at any given time, a wide variety of product types is being produced, and their character or configuration also changes rapidly and continually over time."[52] With JIT, simultaneous engineering replaces the sequential process of mass production—the "just-in-case" system in which materials are produced on inflexible assembly lines. Mass production generated massive inventories of inputs and finished products to supply standardized consumer markets. By contrast, simultaneous engineering makes possible quicker changes in direction of design and production, allowing a firm to respond to the pressures of rapid adjustment in volatile consumer markets. The Gap, for example, changes its inventory and "look" every six weeks. As the company's Far East vice president for offshore sourcing remarked, "The best retailers will be the ones who respond the quickest, the best . . . where the time between cash register and factory shipment is shorter."[53]

The JIT system concentrates these activities spatially for two reasons: (1) because automated technologies are less transferrable, and (2) because firms must respond quickly to local/regional market signals as fashions change.[54] Recent concentration of investment flows in the First World regions of the world market reflects this new corporate strategy. These are the regions with the largest markets, where an integrated production complex based on the JIT principle has the greatest chance to succeed. In other words, even if the commodity life cycle has quickened—and demanded greater production flexibility—mass consumption of such commodities still occurs. So firms will locate near the big markets.

The shift to flexible production encourages economic regionalism. Regionalism allows strategic countries to act as nodes in the trade and investment circuits reaching out from the key First World states. Thus, countries like Mexico and Malaysia become important investment sites precisely because of the new regional complexes of the North American Free Trade Agreement (NAFTA) and the Asia-Pacific Economic Conference (APEC).

In fact, the new industrial corridor in Mexico (from Mexico City north to Monterey) demonstrates this effect. U.S. and Japanese auto companies are currently expanding their operations there, with the North American market in mind. Car and light truck production in Mexico is projected to triple between 1989 and 2000. The city of Saltillo, which used to manufacture appliances and sinks, is building one of North America's larger auto-making complexes, including two General Motors plants, a new Chrysler assembly plant, a Chrysler engine plant, and several parts facilities.[55]

At the same time, U.S., Japanese, and European firms are rushing to invest in food processing operations in Mexico, consolidating its status as a new agricultural company supplying the North American market—similar to Thailand's new regional supermarket role. Firms such as Coca-Cola, Pepsico, General Foods, Kraft, Kellogg's, Campbell's, Bird's Eye, Green Giant, Tyson Foods, C. Itoh, Nestlé, and Unilever are investing in fruits and vegetables, meat, dairy products, and wheat milling to supply regional markets.[56] In fact, U.S. corporate investment in Mexican food processing, after declining 17 percent annually through the 1980s, rebounded by 81 percent in 1989, coinciding with Mexico's preparations to join NAFTA and with changes in the country's investment regulations allowing 100 percent foreign ownership of companies.[57]

New strategies of regional investment partly explain the repatterning of investment flows in the 1990s. As that decade began, foreign direct investment (FDI) in the Third World increased as global FDI declined.[58] In 1992, public and private funds flowing into the Third World surged 30 percent, exceeding aid to developing nations for the first time since 1983. Just as in the 1970s, when the newly industrializing countries were the locus of world economic expansion, the majority of this investment is now going to regionally significant states like China, Mexico, Indonesia, and South Korea. These states are significant because they have both large and growing domestic markets and/or they are located near other large, affluent markets, like those in East Asia and North America.

Although there may well be a trend toward flexible production systems, the age of mass production and consumption is by no means over. The commodity range is vast and consumer needs are endlessly differentiated, even if along predictable lines. Marketing strategies tend to segment consumers at the same time as they standardize these different consumer segments. We see this in the market segments in the car industry, ranging from luxury through various categories to basic styles.

Different kinds of firms have different kinds of strategies within the generic commodity-chain pattern, whether on a regional or global scale. In mid-1994, a *New York Times* article on growing corporate investment abroad illustrated these strategies. In the article, the Gillette Company, which manufactures razor blades especially for the European market, reported that proximity to the market is a priority, given the need to adjust rapidly to local competitors. Gillette has 62 factories in 28 countries, operating as regional companies and catering to specific cultural tastes. In the same report, a spokesman for the Wal-Mart Corporation, with broader consumer segments in mind, said, "With trade barriers coming down, the world is going to be one great big marketplace, and he who gets there first does the best."[59] Thus Gillette, the specialized producer, is geared to regional markets, while Wal-Mart, the retailer, sees the world as its oyster.

The world economy has tendencies toward both global and regional integration. Regional integration may anticipate world integration—especially as it promotes freedom of trade and investment flows among neighboring countries. But it also may reflect a defensive strategy by firms and states, who distrust the intentions of other firm/state clusters. At present, the world economy is subdivided into three macro-regions, centered on the United States, Japan, and Germany/Western Europe—each with hinterlands in Central and Latin America, Southeast Asia, and Eastern Europe/North Africa, respectively. But within those macro-regions there are smaller free trade agreements in operation, often based on greater economic affinity among the members in terms of their GNPs and wage levels. How the future will unfold—with global or regional integration as the dominant tendency—is not yet clear.

Summary

This chapter has examined the phenomenon of the newly industrializing countries from a global perspective, situating this series of national events in the rise of a global production system. In other words, the emergence of the NICs did not simply represent a possibility of upward mobility for individual states in the world economic hierarchy. It also altered the definition of "development." Until the 1970s, development was understood as primarily a national process of economic and social transformation. But by then two trends were becoming clear: (1) The First World was not waiting for the Third World to catch up. Indeed, the gap between these two world regions was expanding. (2) One strategy emerging among some Third World states was to attempt to reduce that gap by aggressive exporting of manufactured goods.

In the 1970s, "development" was redefined by the World Bank as successful "participation in the world market." The prescription was that Third World countries should now follow the example of the newly industrializing countries, pursuing a strategy of export-oriented industrialization. Specialization in the world economy, rather than specialization of economic activities within a national framework, was emerging as the criterion of "development."

Export expansion in the Third World can now be understood from two angles. On the one hand, it was part of a governmental strategy of export growth in both manufacturing and agricultural products. The successful governments have managed to convert liberalized policies regarding foreign investment into a recipe for what some term *upward mobility*. Indeed, the real exponents of this strategy, the Southeast Asian NICs (South Korea, Taiwan, Singapore, and now possibly Malaysia), have displayed an unusual capacity for a flexible form of state-capitalism, accompanied by considerable political authoritarianism, including labor repression. They were able to attract foreign capital with promises of stable political conditions and to anticipate industrial directions in the world economy. This ability permitted them to develop human and public capital and upgrade their export composition, in each case securing the benefits of riding the world economic curve. The result was a growing differentiation among Third World countries on the economic development index.

On the other hand, export expansion was part of a global strategy used by transnational corporations to "source" their far-flung activities. Certainly some middle-income Third World states converted domestic production into export production on their own as domestic markets became saturated; however, the transnational corporations were building a truly global economic system—in manufacturing, agriculture, and services. Global sourcing merged with the export-oriented strategy, especially as a result of the debt regime, as we see in Chapter 4. In effect, a new global economy was emerging. But it was no longer set in national economies. Now it was embedded in those parts of Third World societies that produced or consumed commodities that were marketed on a global scale. The global economy is largely organized around the web of transnational corporations, a web that is in constant flux because of competition. For any one state, the corporate-based global economic system is unstable and difficult to regulate. States attempt to address some of the labor and infrastructural needs of the global corporate economy—and their own foreign exchange needs—by organizing zones of export production.

As states have absorbed global economic activity into their internal organization, the Third World has subordinated its future to the global economy. Development has begun to shed its national identity and to change into a global enterprise in which individual states must participate—but tenuously.

4

A Global Infrastructure

The separation of the newly industrializing countries (NICs) from the rest of the Third World forced a reevaluation of the development project blueprint. The Third World was, of course, always quite heterogeneous—culturally, politically, and geopolitically as well as in its variety of resources and ecological endowments. The development project, however, had viewed the non-European world as homogeneous, classifying it as "undeveloped" and offering one model for its development. But this universal assumption began to unravel in the 1970s as a group of Third World states, defined by their rate of export-oriented industrialization, broke out of the pack. They were not merely pace setters for the rest to follow; their example served to recast the terms of the entire development enterprise. "Development," which had been defined as nationally managed economic growth, was redefined in the World Bank's *World Development Report 1980* as participation in the world market, as noted in Chapter 3.[1]

The redefinition prepared the way for superseding the nationally oriented development project. If development was no longer simply national economic growth but world market participation by producers and states, the world economy was emerging as the unit of development. States and even colonies had always participated in the world market. What was so different or significant, then, about the world economy from the 1970s on? That question is examined in this chapter as we look at the institutional changes in the world economy. We outline the rise of a global banking system, its overextended loans to state managers in the Third World in the 1970s, and the resulting debt crisis of the 1980s. That whole episode reframed development possibilities. States no longer looked inward for their development stimulus. They looked outward, where they found an institutional structure bent on managing a global economic system. The questions we explore in this chapter are whether and to what extent a global infrastructure is overriding national development possibilities. We begin by examining how a *new global infrastructure* came about.

What Is a Global Infrastructure?

A global infrastructure has been a key development in the late twentieth century. It is an institutional complex that organizes global economic activity. Just as nation-states began establishing a national infrastructure in the nineteenth century to coordinate economic growth, so a global infrastructure is now forming. The new infrastructure has several dimensions, both private and public/official. First there are the networks established by transnational corporations (TNCs) and transnational banks (TNBs) conveying commodities and money around the world; second, there are the multilateral financial institutions (the World Bank and the International Monetary Fund). Finally, there are bureaucratic entities—like states, regional **free trade agreements**, and the **World Trade Organization (WTO)**—that regulate the movement of goods, services, labor, and money through rules established in international forums.

Consider the private networks established by transnational corporations. The 1970s were a turning point in the organization of the world economy, largely because of the formation of a global production system. Already by 1971, the value of international production by transnationals exceeded the total exports of all market economies.[2] This trend toward globalization moved rapidly during the remainder of the decade, as transnational corporations established strings of foreign subsidiaries. The subdivision of labor among these subsidiary plants, where one plant supplied the next with its inputs and so on, expanded the networks of **intra-firm transfers**. (See Figure 3.2 on page 91.) These networks, or commodity chains, provide one part of the new global infrastructure.

The infrastructure shapes development possibilities as it organizes the world economy. Further, as it has grown in significance, it has also lent weight to those voices arguing for the successor to the development project, what I term the **globalization project**. This is a world order in which states implement rules of *global economic management*.

The process has already begun, and yet our frames of reference lag behind. Our present systems of economic accounting are nationally framed. That is, production, finance, and trade statistics are collected, recorded, and represented as national data. However, much international trade occurs between subsidiaries of global firms: "In 1990 more than half of America's exports and imports, by value, were simply the transfers of such goods and related services *within* global corporations."[3] Because such exchanges are internal to these firms, they are not strictly market transactions, even though they are recorded as such.

This observation is significant: when the proponents of the globalization project argue for free trade, they fail to point out that the transnational corporations eliminate market exchanges as they swallow up more and more economic activity around the world. Further, these intra-firm transfers and related cross-national commodity chains compromise national boundaries. As the cross-national interdependence of communities and regions grows, strengthened by the global infrastructure, national economic integration declines. That is, global networks of exchanges expand at the expense of national or local networks. This national situation is somewhat analogous to the fate of many small businesses in small towns as they disappear in the path of large national retail chains (such as Wal-Mart in the United States); the chains are able to link a series of towns and replace locally attuned services with standardized routines. If we continue to examine and measure change only on a national or local level, we will misunderstand its wider sources and directions.

The power of the global economic infrastructure appears most dramatically in the growing monetary value of the transnational corporations. By 1984, the world's top 200 TNCs had an annual turnover exceeding $3 trillion, which was equivalent to almost 30 percent of the gross world product.[4] Our patterns of consumption proclaim the standardized brand names and images of globalism. Global corporations attach their logos to national cultural symbols like soccer teams and various celebrities. Cultural icons are created by, or associated with, corporate sponsors and products, behind which stand the global networks that supply these giant firms.

As powerful as the transnational corporations have become in our lives, the **transnational banks (TNBs)** have had perhaps an even more profound impact. Their recent entry onto the global scene follows the rise of world financial markets in the 1970s. Global financial power challenges national sovereignty and thus the framework of the development project. Not only are the global financiers setting the new rules, but the states themselves are willingly accommodating the new requirements in order to establish their credit-worthiness with the global financial establishment, even when this comes at the expense of their integrity as self-governing nations.

Financial Globalization

Transnational or global banks (TNBs) formed in the 1970s. They were helped by the burgeoning *offshore capital market* that evaded the regulatory power of states. The TNBs were banks with deposits that were beyond

FIGURE 4.1

Representation of Offshore Banking

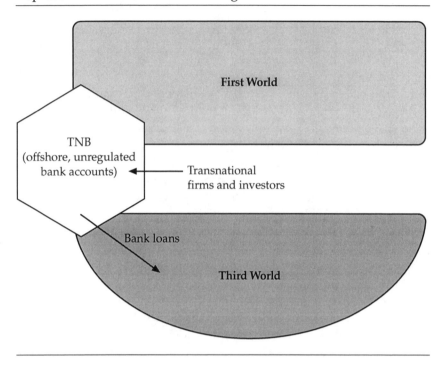

the jurisdiction or control of any government or deposits that were in a country that offered a haven from regulation, such as Switzerland, the Bahamas, or the Cayman Islands. TNBs used these deposits to make massive loans to Third World governments throughout the 1970s (as shown in Figure 4.1). International bank lending, at $2 billion in 1972, peaked in 1981 at $90 billion, then fell to $50 billion in 1985 as a debt crisis followed the orgy of overextended, or undersecured, loans.[5] To learn why this financial globalization occurred, we need to look at the dual nature of the Bretton Woods world order. Remember, under that world order national economic growth depended on the international circulation of American dollars.

The Bretton Woods arrangement maintained stable exchanges of currency between trading countries. To accomplish this stability, the American dollar was used as the international reserve currency, with the multilateral financial institutions (the World Bank and the IMF) and the U.S.

Federal Reserve Bank making disbursements in dollars. At the same time, fixed currency exchanges stabilized countries' domestic interest rates, which in turn stabilized the countries' economies. Governments could therefore implement macro-economic policy "without interference from the ebb and flow of international capital movements or flights of hot money," said J. M. Keynes, the architect of the postwar world economic order.[6] Within this stable monetary framework, Third World countries were able to pursue development programs with some predictability.

The Offshore Money Market

Foreign aid and investment, in the form of American dollars, underwrote national economic growth during the 1950s and 1960s. But it also bred a growing offshore dollar market. This was the so-called Eurocurrency market, initially centered in London's financial district. By depositing their earnings in this foreign currency market, transnational corporations evaded the central bank controls associated with the fixed exchanges of the Bretton Woods system. The Bretton Woods controls limited the movement of capital across national borders, constraining the global activity of the transnational companies.

Eurodollar deposits ballooned with the expansion of U.S. military and economic spending abroad during the Vietnam War. Between 1960 and 1970, they grew from $3 billion to $75 billion, rising to over $1 trillion by 1984. As overseas dollar holdings grew, dwarfing U.S. gold reserves, they became a liability to the U.S. government if cashed in for gold. With mounting pressure on the dollar, President Nixon burst the balloon by declaring the dollar nonconvertible in 1971. This was the end of the gold-dollar standard by which all currencies were *fixed* to a gold value through the American dollar. From now on, currencies would *float* in relative value, with the ubiquitous American dollar as the dominant (reserve) currency. That is, national currencies continued to be linked to a dollar standard, but this was more volatile than the gold standard had been as it fluctuated with changes in U.S. domestic and foreign policy. The termination of the Bretton Woods system of fixed currency exchanges was the opening wedge in breaking down the institutional structure of the development project and consolidating the global infrastructure.

The shift from fixed to floating currency exchanges ushered in an era of uncontrolled—and heightened—capital mobility as speculators anticipated variation in values by buying and selling different currencies. Financial markets, rather than trade, began to determine currency values, and speculation on floating currencies destabilized national finances. The new way of establishing monetary values has been a continuing problem in the absence of new monetary rules, especially with the magnitude of the international currency transactions. By the early 1990s, world financial markets traded roughly $1 trillion in various currencies daily, all beyond the control of national governments.[7] For example, the mid-1990s saw massive speculation in the Mexican *peso*, when investors expected NAFTA to strengthen the Mexican economy. When it didn't, traders tried to sell their *peso* holdings, a move that severely destabilized the Mexican economy and sent shudders through world financial markets, given Mexico's connection with the United States through NAFTA. The *peso* hemorrhage was so threatening to world financial markets that the United States stepped in to support the Mexican currency with billions of dollars of new loans. The bailout deal required Mexican oil revenues to be deposited in the U.S. Federal Reserve System; if Mexico defaulted, the United States would have access to those funds.

The dramatic loss of currency control by governments threatens nations' economic and political sovereignty. National planners cannot adequately regulate the value of their national currency because currency traders and financiers can influence policy just by moving funds around the world in search of financial profit. Global circulation of huge amounts of money causes national currencies to fluctuate in value. In 1992, the *New York Times* published an op-ed article in which the former chairman of Citicorp described the currency traders, facing 200,000 trading room monitors across the world, as conducting "a kind of global plebiscite on the monetary and fiscal policies of the governments issuing currency." He found this system to be "far more draconian than any previous arrangement, such as the gold standard or the Bretton Woods system, because there is no way for a nation to opt out."[8]

As we return to events of the 1970s, the next shock to the international financial system was the inflation of oil prices in 1973, as the 13 members of the **Organization of Petroleum Exporting Countries (OPEC)** formed a sellers' cartel and agreed on a common price for oil. Fueled by the dollars earned on rising oil prices in the mid-1970s, the offshore capital market grew from $315 billion in 1973 to $2,055 billion in 1982. The seven largest U.S. banks saw their overseas profits climb from 22 percent to 60 percent of their total profits in the same time period.[9] By the end of the 1970s, trade in foreign exchange was more than 11 times greater than the value of world commodity trade. This was a remarkable development! Because the circulation of money around the world continually altered profitability conditions by changing currency values, transnational corporations reduced their risk by diversifying their operations across the globe.[10]

By its effect on the transnational companies, the financial revolution accelerated the formation of a global production system. It also redistributed economic growth in the world economy. Oil-price inflation led to higher energy prices, which were passed on in higher prices for food and manufactures. This increase produced a severe downturn in the First World, and global economic growth fell by 50 percent in the mid-1970s. Meanwhile, the rise in oil prices greatly expanded the offshore money market, as OPEC states deposited their oil revenues (petrodollars) in the offshore banks. As the pools of offshore money mushroomed, so did the power of the global banks. With the First World in recession, the banks turned to Third World governments, eager to borrow and considered unlikely to default. By encouraging massive borrowing, the banks brokered the 1970s expansion in the middle-income Third World countries, which functioned now as the engine of growth of the world economy.

Banking on Development

The move by the banks into the Third World marked a *second* departure from the original institutional structure of the development project, as commercial bank lending effectively displaced official loans from bilateral and multilateral sources. With First World economic growth rates slowing and petrodollars flooding world financial markets, bankers looked to the Third World as a new source of income and began aggressively pursuing any and all takers. In the early 1970s, bank loans accounted for only 13 percent of Third World debt, while multilateral loans made up more than 33 percent and export credits accounted for 25 percent.[11] By the end of the decade, the composition of these figures had reversed, with banks holding about 60 percent of the debt. The various shifts from the original development model are summarized in the following insert.

The presence of willing private lenders was a golden opportunity for Third World states to exercise some autonomy from the official financial community. Until now, they had been beholden to powerful First World states for foreign aid and to multilateral agencies for funding of their development programs. The Latin American states especially had absorbed considerable foreign investment in their programs of import-substitution industrialization. Now, the money they borrowed from the global banks came not only with no strings attached but also with easy repayment terms because there was so much money to lend. Thus, the composition of Latin American borrowing shifted dramatically: official/public loans fell from 40 percent in 1966–1970 to 12 percent in 1976–1978, and private foreign direct investment fell from 34 percent in the late 1960s to 16 percent

---

Departures from the Development Model in the 1970s

The 1970s were the decade of transition away from the terms of the development project. One indication was that fixed currency exchanges ended when the dollar was removed from gold parity in 1971. Currencies now floated in value relative to each other rather than to a single standard. The currency instability was fueled through speculation, the instability undercutting possibilities for stable national macro-economic planning. Another indicator was the displacement of official, multilateral lending to Third World states by unregulated private bank lending. Because it was unregulated, the debt-financing system of the 1970s was unsound; too much money was lent on the assumption that countries could not go bankrupt. In a sense they did, however, and that is what the debt crisis was all about. Yet another indicator was the growing priority of producing manufactures and agricultural products for the world rather than the domestic market. During the 1970s, the G-77 countries attempted to reform the international economy, faced with the collapse of the Bretton Woods system. They tried unsuccessfully to revive ideas for public global economic management that had been introduced in the 1940s and rejected. Also, critics in the development establishment institutions began to reformulate ideas of development, with greater emphasis on poverty alleviation.

---

in the late 1970s; concurrently, foreign bank and bond financing rose from 7 percent in the early 1960s to 65 percent of all foreign financing in the late 1970s.[12]

With dramatic advances in telecommunications, global banking was a new option for national and, indeed, subnational banks, just as it was for firms competing for a share of an increasingly globalized marketplace. Regional banks from America's declining industrial heartland in Michigan, Ohio, and Pennsylvania, for example, established international portfolios as a surge in lending rose through the decade. The regional BancOhio, for one, expanded foreign lending from zero in 1979 to over $1 billion in 1983.[13]

With the collapse of the Bretton Woods monetary regime, financial regulation was practically nonexistent. Governments were even borrowing to finance short-term correction of their balance of payments following the oil shock. In this environment, commercial bank loans financed all manner of projects: meeting short-term liquidity needs, underwriting showcase modernization projects that legitimized governments by bank-rolling corrupt leaders and their cronies, and supporting legitimate industrial development. By 1984, all nine of the largest U.S. banks were lending over 100 percent of their shareholders' equity in loans to Mexico, Brazil, Argentina, and Venezuela, while Lloyds of London had lent a staggering 165 percent of its capital to these countries.[14]

The big borrowers—Brazil, Mexico, and Argentina—channeled funds into enlarging their industrial plant and energy production. Mexico claimed to have almost tripled its industrial facilities since 1970, and

> Brazil transformed itself from a country earning 70 percent of its export revenue from one commodity, coffee, into a major producer and exporter of a multiplicity of industrial goods including steel, pulp, aluminum, petrochemicals, cement, glass, armaments and aircraft, and of processed foodstuffs like orange juice and soybean meal. Rio de Janeiro and São Paulo have new subway systems, railroads have been built to take ore from huge mines deep in the interior to new ports on the coast, and major cities are linked by a modern telecommunications network.[15]

Much of this expansion was organized by public or *state-owned enterprises* (like the U.S. Postal Service), and much of it was designed to generate export earnings. Between 1970 and 1982, the average share of gross domestic investment in the public sector of 12 Latin American countries rose from 32 percent to 50 percent. State managers borrowed heavily to finance the expansion of public enterprise. Often this was done to establish a counterweight to the foreign investor presence in these economies, which accounted for about 50 percent of the Brazilian and 28 percent of the Mexican manufacturing sectors in 1970.[16] It was also done to improve the political standing, and private incomes, of state managers and military elites.

During the 1970s, public foreign debt grew twice as fast as private foreign debt in Latin America. In Mexico, state enterprises expanded from 39 in 1970 to 677 in 1982 under the rule of the Institutional Revolutionary Party (PRI). By 1978, foreign loans financed 43 percent of the Mexican government's budget deficit and 87 percent of state-owned companies. All across Latin America, public largesse supplemented and complemented foreign and local private investment and subsidized basic goods and services for the largely urban poor. Regarding the Argentine military's holding company, Fabricaciones Militares, an Argentine banker claimed: "No one really knows what businesses they are in. Steel, chemicals, mining, munitions, even a whore house, everything."[17]

As public foreign debt grew in the Third World, governments reached beyond the terms of the development project. Those terms centered on the management of private enterprise to build an industrial economy. In the 1970s, states borrowed heavily to make up lost ground. A great deal of the private enterprise involved unmanaged lending to governments by unmanageable global banks. Because it was so uncontrolled, this excessive debt financing inflated the foundations of the *developmentalist state*, the functions of which are explained in the following insert.

What Does a Developmentalist State Do?

The developmentalist state takes charge of organizing economic growth by mobilizing money and people. On the money end, it uses individual and corporate taxes, along with other government revenues such as export taxes and sales taxes, to finance public building of transport systems and state enterprises such as steel works and energy exploration. States also mobilize money by borrowing in private capital markets, competing with private borrowers. Where state enterprises (financed with public monies, but run on market criteria—such as the U.S. Postal Service) predominate, we have what is called *state capitalism.* Where they complement private enterprise, we simply have a form of state entrepreneurialism. On the people front, typically in postcolonial states, governments mobilized political coalitions of citizens from different social groupings—workers, capitalists, professionals, and small-business people. Political loyalty was obtained by the guarantee of certain kinds of social resources to these various groups: public services, price subsidies, easy credit terms to small businesses, tax exemption for capitalists, wage increases for workers, and so on. The developmentalist state used these coalitions to support its program of industrialization. When the government integrates labor unions and business into a three-way alliance with government economic programs designed to stimulate private enterprise, the result is a *corporatist* state.

For a time, public borrowing legitimized the idea of state capitalism, in actively complementing private investment. Third World developmentalist states appeared to be successfully in the driver's seat. There were of course variations: from the South Korean state's centralization of financial control over private investment patterns; through the Brazilian model of corporatism, in which nine of the ten largest firms were state enterprises and the state monitored financial investment; to the Mexican model of state entrepreneurship, which complemented private investment with productive public investment. The type of state capitalism practiced in Mexico was the more common kind, also practiced by Turkey, Peru, Venezuela, Indonesia, Tunisia, India, and Algeria. During the 1970s, state enterprises across the Third World enlarged their share of GDP by almost 50 percent. Needless to say, there was a high correlation between borrowing and public sector expansion.

State managers, driven by the promise of political glory and the financial spoils associated with economic growth, thus mortgaged the national patrimony. Borrowing in the Euromarkets was an effective counterweight to transnational corporation investment, even when it enabled states to insist on joint ventures with the transnationals.[18] But it also deepened the vulnerability of the developmentalist state to the banks and the global debt managers, who began appearing on the scene in the 1980s. Before we address the debt crisis, however, we must consider global political maneuvers in the 1970s, as they presaged the global politics of the 1980s.

The New International Economic Order (NIEO) Initiative and the Politics of Development

The surge of borrowing pursued privately what Third World states attempted to accomplish publicly in their formal demand for a **New International Economic Order (NIEO)**, made in the U.N. General Assembly in 1974.[19] These states demanded reform of the world economic system to improve their position in international trade and their access to technological and financial resources.

The political strategy behind the NIEO initiative was Third Worldist: it identified "underdevelopment" in the Third World as the result of historical conditions. Instead of blaming the victim, Third World spokespersons wanted the international community to acknowledge the inequality in the organization of the world economy. This strategy had its roots in the Third Worldism of the decolonization movement, where colonialism was blamed for global inequality. The legitimacy of Third Worldism rested on three other conditions.

First, the record of the development project was patchy at best, with some middle-income countries like Brazil and Mexico recording strong growth rates, and a failure at worst. Despite exceeding the growth target of 5 percent per annum (in aggregate) set by the United Nations for the second development decade of the 1960s, economic and social indices suggested that most Third World countries were not achieving the rising living standards promised by the development project. The World Bank reported in 1974:

> It is now clear that more than a decade of rapid growth in underdeveloped countries has been of little or no benefit to perhaps a third of their population. Paradoxically, while growth policies have succeeded beyond the expectations of the first development decade, the very idea of aggregate growth as a social objective has increasingly been called into question.[20]

Second, a theoretical literature termed the **dependency** school of thought was flourishing at the time. Taking their cue from the Prebisch thesis (see Chapter 1), dependency theorists argued that the unequal economic relationships of aid, trade, and investment in the postcolonial era between First and Third Worlds perpetuated the colonial legacy. In other words, the more the First World invested in and traded with the Third World, the more exploitive this North/South relation became. As an additional consequence, North/South inequality was reproduced within Third World countries, between growing "metropolitan" urban centers and stagnating "peripheral" rural hinterlands. The *dependista* solution, as Latin American scholars and activists referred to it, was protection, or withdrawal, from exploitive world economic relationships.[21]

Third, the multilateral and bilateral programs established through the development project were quite selective. Aid funds were unequally distributed across the world, with the smallest amounts reaching the neediest cases. The First World was not forthcoming with financial assistance for price stabilization measures for Third World primary exports such as tin, cocoa, and sugar. In addition, the *general system of preferences* (GSP) was quite skewed. GSPs were established under pressure from the U.N. Conference on Trade and Development to reduce tariffs on Third World exports of manufactured goods under the GATT agreements. The goods selected by the First World for reduced protection turned out to be those originating in industries controlled by transnational corporations, while those that were excluded tended to originate in domestic industries.[22] This finding lends weight to the observation in Chapter 3 that a global economy was forming alongside and across the set of national economies.

Responses to these conditions took two different directions. The first was a new strategy of development taken by the international aid community. This strategy, known as the **basic needs approach**, derived from writings by development scholars such as Dudley Seers. In 1969, Seers had redefined "development" as realizing the potential of human personality. In this formulation, "economic growth is for a poor country a necessary condition of reducing poverty. But it is not a sufficient condition."[23] Development was redefined here as targeting basic human needs rather than simply raising income levels.

This micro-level approach to development appeared in a World Bank report entitled *Redistribution with Growth* (1974), coinciding with Bank President McNamara's concern for improving bank access to the poorer segments of the Third World. It focused on alleviating rural poverty by promoting agrarian reforms in land tenure, credit opportunities for poor peasants, improved water delivery systems, agricultural extension services, and increased access to health and education. As a result, Bank lending shifted its focus toward rural development and agriculture, increasing its annual loan commitments to these areas from 18.5 percent to 31 percent between 1968 and 1981.[24]

The World Bank's "Assistance to the Rural Poor" scheme has been termed an intensification of "global central planning" insofar as it repeated the top-down technical relationship with rural communities.[25] While professing to assist 700 million smallholders (not the landless) with credit, the scheme's net effect tended to integrate subsistence farmers into the agricultures associated with the second green revolution. Furthermore, data from the Organization for Economic Cooperation and Development (OECD) demonstrate that the basic needs emphasis did not produce a fundamental redirection of aid flows in the 1970s, despite the International Development Association's greater attention to sub-Saharan Africa and increased bilateral aid to the poorest Third World countries.[26] Nevertheless, however ineffectual, the basic needs strategy had been articulated and has been refined since into an alternative to current globalist prescriptions.

The second, Third World, response to the aid community was to argue that focusing on inequalities within the Third World as the source of poverty neglected global inequalities. Of course, both relationships were responsible and mutually conditioning, but the interpretive stakes were high. As Honari Boumedienne, the Algerian president, told the U.N. General Assembly in 1974:

> Inasmuch as [the old order] is maintained and consolidated and therefore thrives by virtue of a process which continually impoverishes the poor and enriches the rich, this economic order constitutes the major obstacle standing in the way of any hope of development and progress for all the countries of the Third World.[27]

The Group of 77 nations within the U.N. Conference on Trade and Development (UNCTAD) duly prepared the statement regarding the New International Economic Order (NIEO). This was a charter of economic rights and duties of states, designed to codify reform of the global system along Keynesian lines. The NIEO charter demanded reform of international trade, the international monetary system (to liberalize development financing, debt relief, and increased financial aid), and technological assistance. In addition, it proclaimed the economic sovereignty of states and the right to collective self-reliance among Third World states.[28] Although the NIEO also embraced the Second World, the Soviet Union declined involvement on the grounds that the colonial legacy was a Western issue.

The First World's response was to affirm cooperation and to assist the Third World cause—where it strengthened the world economic order, that is. There were several parts to this response, including the World Bank's basic needs strategy. Among the provisions of the strategy were stabilization of rural populations and extension of commercial cropping; stabilization of the conditions of private foreign investment by improved coordination of economic policy across the North/South divide; and a U.S. strategy of buying time by trying to institutionalize the dialogue within forums such as the French-initiated Conference on International Economic Cooperation (1975–1977), which met several times but reached no agreement.[29]

The First World response combined moral themes with governance. But the master theme was really time; as it passed, so did the energy of the NIEO initiative. In the short term, the unity of the Third World fragmented as the prospering OPEC states and the newly industrializing countries (NICs) assumed a greater interest in *upward mobility* in the international order. In the long term, the redistributive goals of the NIEO would be overridden by the new doctrine of **monetarism** that ushered in the 1980s debt crisis through drastic restrictions in credit and, therefore, social spending by governments. An official of the U.S. National Security Council referred quite deliberately to the expectation that the differentiation among Third World states would promote a form of *embourgeoisement* as prospering states sought to distance themselves from their poorer neighbors.[30]

The moral of this story is that the Third World attempted to assert its political unity in the world at just the time when economic disunity was spreading, as middle-income states and poorer states diverged. The ease of debt financing by way of the offshore capital markets was a key incentive in promoting individual mobility and fracturing collective solutions among the Third World states. The First World's representatives had an interest in fostering the private solution, as expansion of the global production system was necessary to First World economic health. The idea of encouraging a country's participation in the world market as the new development strategy was already strongly rooted. In short, the First World managed to sidetrack the Third World's collective political initiative and assert the market solution to its developmental problems.

In the meantime, the goal of the NIEO in redistributing wealth from First to Third Worlds in some ways came to pass. Although much of the wealth was oil money, recycled through bank lending to the Third World, it nevertheless met the demands of Third World elites for development financing (in addition to financing rising costs of imported fuel as well as rising military expenditure, which contributed to about one-fifth of Third World borrowing). Much of this money was concentrated in the middle-income states and considerably undercut Third World political unity. The marked differentiation in growth patterns of countries intensified in the ensuing debt crisis of the 1980s. With the political context set, we return to the debt.

The Debt Regime

The 1980s debt crisis consolidated two distinct trends that had been emerging in the 1970s: (1) the undoing of the Third World as a collective entity, as economic growth rates diverged among states; and (2) global managerialism, in which the world economy was managed through coordinated, rule-based procedures—the **debt regime**. The break-up of the Third World enabled global elites in the Bretton Woods institutions and the First World to argue that the international economic order was not responsible for the crisis centered in Latin American and African states. They claimed that the experience of the newly industrializing countries proved this. In other words, debt stress and economic deterioration in the poorer zones of the world, they said, stemmed from a failure to copy the NICs' strategy of export diversification in the world market. As we know, however, the NICs, though held up as examples of market virtue, were in fact state-managed economies.

The export-led strategy informed the 1989 World Bank report *Sub-Saharan Africa: From Crisis to Sustainability*—regardless of whether the world market could absorb such a proliferation of exports:

> Declining export volumes, rather than declining export prices, account for Africa's poor export revenues. . . . If Africa's economies are to grow, they must earn foreign exchange to pay for essential imports. Thus it is vital that they increase their share of world markets. The prospects for most primary commodities are poor, so higher export earnings must come from increased output, diversification into new commodities and an aggressive export drive into the rapidly growing Asian markets.[31]

Debt was of course not new to these regions of the world. Between 1955 and 1970, several countries (including Argentina, Brazil, Chile, Ghana, Indonesia, Peru, and Turkey) had the terms of their debt rescheduled—

sometimes several times—to ease the conditions of payment. And debt servicing (paying off the interest) was consuming more than two-thirds of new lending in Latin America and Africa by the mid-1960s. The difference now was the combination in the 1970s of oil shocks and unsecured lending by the banks, which intensified debt. During the 1970s, an average of three countries a year rescheduled their debts, and after 1974 debt-servicing capacity declined.[32]

The real debt crisis began in 1980 when the U.S. Federal Reserve Board moved to stem the fall in the value of the dollar resulting from its overcirculation in the 1970s lending binge. The United States adopted a monetarist policy of reducing the money supply. This in turn restricted credit and raised interest rates as banks competed for dwindling funds. Lending to Third World countries slowed and shorter terms were issued— hastening the day of reckoning on considerably higher-cost loans. Some borrowing continued, nevertheless, partly because oil prices had risen sharply again in 1979. Higher oil prices actually accounted for more than 25 percent of the total debt of the Third World. Previous debt had to be paid off, too, especially the greater debt assumed by overconfident oil-producing states like Nigeria, Venezuela, and Mexico.[33]

Third World debt totaled $1 trillion by 1986. Even though this amount was only half the U.S. national debt in that year, it was a significant problem because countries were devoting new loans entirely to servicing previous loans.[34] Unlike the United States, which was cushioned by the dollar standard (the *de facto* international reserve currency that countries and traders preferred), Third World countries were not in a position to continue this debt servicing. There are several reasons for this dilemma. For one thing, real interest rates had grown 14 times between 1974–1978 and 1981–1982, meaning that the dollar reserves countries used for repayment had lost value against other currencies. In addition, the credit crunch in the early 1980s produced a recession in the First World, which therefore could not keep consuming Third World products at the same rate. Third World export revenues took a dive. On top of this, primary export commodity prices fell 17 percent (relative to First World industrial exports) during this period. The Third World lost about $28 billion in export revenues.[35] Finally, the Third World's share of world trade fell from 28 to 19 percent between 1980 and 1986.[36]

The World Bank estimated the combined average annual negative effect of these "external" shocks in 1981–1982 to be 19.1 percent of GDP in Kenya, 14.3 percent in Tanzania, 18.9 percent in the Ivory Coast, 8.3 percent in Brazil, 29 percent in Jamaica, and over 10 percent in the Philippines.[37] The result was that many Third World countries were suddenly mired in a *debt trap*: debt was choking their economies. And in order to repay the interest (at least), they would have to drastically curtail imports and drastically raise exports.

Reducing imports of technology would jeopardize economic growth. Expanding exports was also problematic, as commodity prices were at their lowest since World War II and would only slide further as world markets were flooded with more commodities. Some of these commodities were also losing markets to substitutes developed in the First World. Since the mid-1970s sugar price boom, the soft-drink industry, for example, had steadily replaced sugar with fructose corn syrup, a biotechnological substitute. (When you purchase a can of soda, notice that sugar is not listed anymore as an ingredient.) Other substitutes include glass fiber for copper in the new fiber-optic telecommunications technology, soy oils for tropical oils, and synthetic alternatives to rubber, jute, cotton, timber, coffee, and cocoa.[38] The market was not going to solve these problems alone.

Debt Management

The chosen course of action was debt management. The Bretton Woods institutions once again were in the driver's seat, even though around 60 percent of Third World debt was with private banks. The International Monetary Fund (IMF) took charge because it had originally been given the task of evaluating a country's financial condition for borrowing (even though this function had broken down in the 1970s). The IMF now had a supervisory status that individual banks did not have in the financial system at large.

Debt management took several forms, beginning with stabilization measures. Stabilization focused on financial management—such as cutting imports to resolve a country's imbalance of payments. **Structural adjustment** measures take a more comprehensive approach by restructuring production priorities and government programs in a debtor country—basically reorganizing the economy. In combination with the World Bank and its **structural adjustment loan (SAL)**, the IMF put restructuring conditions on borrowers to allow them to reschedule their loans and pay off their debt. By the mid-1980s, loan conditions demanded a *restructuring of economic policy*, the idea being that debtors should follow multilateral prescriptions for political and economic reforms to ensure economic growth and regular debt service.

Under this regime the responsibility for irredeemable debt fell on the borrowers, not the lenders–unlike U.S. bankruptcy law. Debt was defined as a liquidity problem (shortage of foreign currency) rather than a systemic problem.[39] With this perspective, the global managers placed the blame on the policies of the debtor countries rather than on the organization of the global financial system. This view was possible for two reasons. First, the International Monetary Fund was in a position to insist that debt rescheduling (including further official loans) was possible only if individual states submitted to IMF evaluation and stabilization measures, which included World Bank structural adjustment loans. Second, despite attempts at debt strikes (by Peru, among others), debtors collectively were in a weak bargaining position, especially because of the great differentiation among Third World countries—in growth rates and size of debt. In addition, an individual solution for debt rescheduling was often preferred by indebted governments to the uncertainty of a collective debtors' strike.[40]

In 1982, Mexico and Brazil became the first countries to reschedule their debt in this new way, signaling the start of the debt regime—when global management swung into gear. This new management drew on the example of the 1973 coup in Chile, where a military junta instituted the first experiments in monetarist policies by slashing social expenditures. The Mexican bailout institutionalized debt rescheduling, with new terms of repayment. Mexico was the first real "ticking bomb" in the global financial structure. By 1982, it was $80 billion in debt; more than three-quarters of this amount was owed to private banks, with U.S. banks having almost half their capital in Mexican loans. To effect the bailout, the IMF put up $1.3 billion, foreign governments $2 billion, and the banks $5 billion in "involuntary loans."[41] A global managerial group, including the banks, the multilateral financial community, and the First World governments, put together the bailout package.

The Mexican bailout became a model for other bailout programs, primarily because the Mexican government effectively implemented the stabilization measures the IMF demanded in return for debt rescheduling. Also, Mexico proved to be one of the states that undermined the possibility of a collective debtor strike. It was in fact rewarded for its refusal to participate in a regional effort to form a debtors' club in 1986. Mexico also engaged in **debt swapping**, whereby foreign investors purchased its debt at a discount in world financial markets in return for ownership of Mexican equity.[42]

Reversing the Development Project

As countries adopted the rules of the debt managers and restructured their economies, they reversed the path of the development project. These rules had two key effects. First, they institutionalized the new definition of development as participation in the world market. In particular, the debt managers pushed for export intensification as the first order of business—as we saw in the World Bank's 1989 report on sub-Saharan Africa above. Second, the rescheduling conditions brought dramatic adjustments in economic and social priorities within indebted countries. These adjustments tended to override the original development goal of managed national economic growth, substituting for it managed global economic growth. In effect, these actions stabilized indebted economies so they could at least service their debt—that is, repay the interest due the banks and the Bretton Woods financial institutions. Rescheduling bought time for debt repayment, but it also came at a heavy cost.

Adjustment measures included drastic reduction of public spending (especially on social programs, including food subsidies), currency devaluation (to inflate prices of imports and reduce export prices and thereby improve the balance of trade in the indebted country's favor), privatization of state enterprises, and reduction of wages to attract foreign investors and reduce export prices. Most of these measures fell hardest on the poorest and least powerful social classes—those dependent on wages and subsidies. While many businesses prospered, poverty rates climbed. Governments saw their developmentalist alliances crumble as they could no longer afford to subsidize urban social constituencies. The erosion of living standards across the former Third World is illustrated in the following case study of Mexico.

In Africa, the severity of the debt burden meant that Tanzania, the Sudan, and Zambia were using more than 100 percent of their export earnings to service debt in 1983. In Zambia, the ratio of outstanding debt to GNP increased from 16 percent to 56 percent in 1985. African economies were particularly vulnerable to the significant fall in commodity prices during the 1980s: copper accounted for 83 percent of Zambia's export earnings and 43 percent of Zaire's, coffee for 89 percent of Burundi's export earnings and 64 percent of Ethiopia's, cotton for 45 percent of Sudan's and 54 percent of Chad's export earnings, and cocoa for 63 percent of Ghana's total exports. As primary commodity prices fell while the cost of imported technology and manufactured goods rose, the terms of trade moved against Africa. During the 1980s, an African coffee exporter had to produce 30 percent more coffee to pay for one imported tractor, and then produce more coffee to pay for the oil to run it.

IMF/World Bank adjustment policies in Africa reduced food subsidies and public services, leading to urban demonstrations and riots in Tanzania, Ghana, Zambia, Morocco, Egypt, Tunisia, and Sudan. In Zambia, for example, the price of cornmeal—a staple—rose 120 percent in 1985 following

CASE STUDY

The Social Costs of Mexican Debt Rescheduling

According to the National Nutrition Institute, about 40 percent of the Mexican population is malnourished—their diets have little rice, eggs, fruit, vegetables, milk, and meat. As part of the IMF loan rescheduling conditions in 1986, food subsidies for basic foods such as tortillas, bread, beans, and rehydrated milk were eliminated. Malnourishment grew. Minimum wages fell 50 percent between 1983 and 1989, and purchasing power fell to two-thirds of the 1970 level. The number of Mexicans in poverty rose from 32.1 to 41.3 million, matching the absolute increase in population size during 1981 to 1987. By 1990, the basic needs of 41 million Mexicans were unsatisfied, and 17 million lived in extreme poverty.

Meanwhile, manufacturing growth rates plummeted, from 1.9 in 1980–1982 to 0.1 in 1985–1988, leading to a considerable decline in formal employment opportunities. Coupled with drastic cuts in social services, the reduction in manufacturing led to further deterioration of living standards. By 1987, 10 million people could not gain access to the health system, a situation that contributed to the "epidemiological polarization" among social classes and regions—such as the difference between the infant mortality rates of northern and southern Mexico, and between those of rural and urban areas and lower and upper classes.

Agriculture was also restructured as Mexico had assumed the role of a new agricultural country with extensive state-sponsored agro-industrialization. By 1986, Mexico was exporting to the United States more than $2 billion worth of fresh fruits, vegetables, and beef, but also importing from that country $1.5 billion in farm products, largely basic grains and oil seeds. IMF strictures made dependency on staple foods more expensive and reduced the government's role in subsidizing food staples. The loan conditions also deepened Mexico's agro-food exporting role by expanding the use of land for export agriculture and setting the stage for the early 1990s agrarian reform that has eroded the **ejido** system (small-farmer rural collectives).

Sources: George, 1988, pp. 139, 143; Barkin, 1990, pp. 101, 103; de la Rocha, 1994, pp. 270–271.

such an adjustment policy. School enrollments declined at the same time as skilled Africans migrated in droves. Between 1980 and 1986, average per capita income declined by 10 percent, and unemployment almost tripled.[43] In effect, all the "development" indicators, including infant mortality, took a downturn under the impact of adjustment policies. The greater impact on the poor, compared with higher-income groups, is borne out in an internal report of the International Monetary Fund on cost increases as a result of adjustment in Kenya. Relatively speaking, the poor shouldered an extra burden as the price of basic goods and services increased, from 10 percent for food to 95 percent for clothing and shoes.[44]

Oxfam reported in 1993 that World Bank adjustment programs in sub-Saharan Africa were largely responsible for reductions in public health spending and a 10 percent decline in primary school enrollment. In the late 1980s, UNICEF and the U.N. Commission for Africa reported that adjustment programs were largely the cause of reduced health, nutritional, and educational levels for tens of millions of children in Asia, Latin America, and Africa.[45]

Much has been written about the "lost decade" of the 1980s for the poorer regions of the world economy, meaning that the debt crisis set them back considerably. If we combine per capita GDP figures with changes in terms of trade and debt rescheduling, average per capita income is estimated to have fallen 15 percent in Latin America and 30 percent in Africa during the 1980s. But in South and East Asian countries, by contrast, per capita income rose. These Pacific Asian states were more in step with the global economy. Along with the South Asian states, they benefited from the oil boom in the Middle East, the most rapidly growing market at this time. The Pacific Asian states exported labor to the Middle Eastern countries, from which they received monetary remittances. One particular reason the Pacific Asian states were relatively immune to the "lost decade" was that the ratio of their debt service to exports was half that of the Latin American countries during the 1970s.[46] Besides their geopolitical advantage, they were less vulnerable to the contraction of credit in the new monetarist world economic order.

The debt crisis certainly exacerbated the demise of the Third World. It continued to lose collective political ground as governments yielded sovereignty to the global managers, and it fractured into several zones, including what some refer to as the emerging "Fourth World"—particularly impoverished regions, especially countries in sub-Saharan Africa. At the same time, the debt crisis enhanced the infrastructure of global management, to which we now turn.

Global Managerialism

Global managerialism refers to the relocation of the power of economic management from nation-states to global institutions. It may not be an absolute relocation, but neither is it a zero-sum game where "global" and "national" are mutually exclusive. Each folds into the other. Most important, national institutions embrace global goals. This is not clearly understood because nation-states still exist and their governments still make policy. It appears to the casual observer that because states exist, national projects must also. In this global context, that is not necessarily the case. Governments are quite often making policy on behalf of the **global managers**—officials of the multilateral institutions as well as executives of transnational corporations and global bankers.

The conditions laid down during the debt regime are an obvious example of this form of surrogate global management. Indebted states agreed to implement certain policy changes and restructuring of economic priorities in order to reestablish credit-worthiness in the eyes of the global financial community. When a state gives priority to export production over production of domestic goods to repay debt, for example, it appears to be putting the national financial house in order. This policy may affect the flow of money, but it also strengthens the hand of global management and further embeds the productive forces of that country in the global economy. Global managerialism does not necessarily come from the outside; it can be adopted into the very policies and procedures of states as they attempt to reposition their producers in the global economy.

Global managerialism embraces the whole world, not just the formerly colonial countries. Indeed, IMF debt-rescheduling measures were common in the First and Second Worlds. For example, Poland's massive debt and subsequent austerity programs had much to do with destabilizing the perimeter of the Second World, leading to the collapse of the Soviet bloc in the late 1980s. And from 1978 to 1992, more than 70 countries of the former Third World undertook 566 stabilization and structural adjustment programs imposed by the IMF and the World Bank to control their debt.[47] All this restructuring did not necessarily resolve the debt crisis. In fact, the debtor countries collectively entered the 1990s with 61 percent more debt than they had held in 1982.[48]

Privileging the Banks

As a consequence of growing debt, many countries found themselves under greater scrutiny by global managers. This circumstance put them in a position where they were surrendering greater amounts of their wealth to global agencies. 1984 was a turning point. In that year, the direction of

FIGURE 4.2

Net Transfers of Long-Term Loans to Third World States, 1980–1990

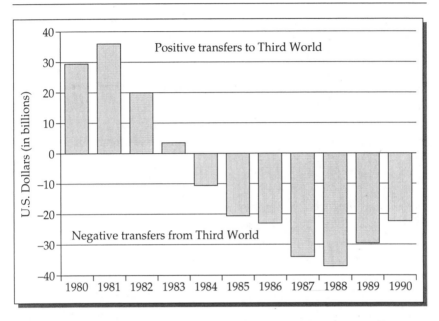

Source: United Nations Development Program. 1994. Human Development Report. Oxford: Oxford University Press, p. 64.

capital flows reversed—that is, the inflow of loan and investment capital into the former Third World was replaced by an *outflow* in the form of debt repayment (see Figure 4.2). The (net) extraction of financial resources from this poorer world zone during the 1980s exceeded $400 billion.[49] Massive bank debt had become public debt, the repayment of which now fell on the shoulders of the governments themselves.

The balance of power under this system of global management has been quite unequal. Indebtedness was addressed as an individual state's problem and, certainly, the banks wrote off some debt. But the banks were protected from complete debt loss by the First World governments, whose central bankers had agreed in 1974 to stand behind the commercial bank loans, as lenders of last resort.[50] In fact, the banks not only recovered some of their outstanding loans, but the recovery was managed for them by the global managers. As in the case of Mexico, a condominium of First World governments, Bretton Woods institutions, and global banks came together to determine debt rescheduling procedures on a case-by-case basis. The conditions were laid down by the IMF, in consultation with the World Bank. And the conditions forced a reshuffling of national priorities. This procedure was universal, but it had drastic effects in the poorer regions of the world economy.

An example of the universal impact of debt management policies concerns unemployment. The collapse of economies in the poorer zones drastically reduced the growth rate of exports from richer to poorer countries. Up to three million person-years of employment were lost in North America in the 1980s as a result of declining exports, and Great Britain lost exports equivalent to 49 percent in real terms in the early 1980s, thereby contracting jobs in its export sector. The debt crisis was handled primarily as a banking crisis, leaving national economies to respond however they could.[51]

Challenging the Developmentalist State

Treating the debt crisis as a banking crisis meant that global financial health overrode other considerations, including the viability of government management of national economies. Keynesian (state interventionist) policies had steadily eroded through the 1970s in the First World as the ideology of economic liberalism spread its message of giving the market a free rein. Public expenditure fell; so did wage levels as organized labor lost ground because firms were moving offshore and/or cheaper imports from the newly industrializing countries were flooding domestic markets.

Under the new monetarist doctrine in the 1980s, this trend was extended south. The debt regime directly challenged the developmentalist state. Debt managers demanded a *shrinking* of states of the former Third World, both through reduction in social spending and through the **privatization** of state enterprises. In order to reschedule their debt, governments sold off the public companies that had ballooned in the 1970s. As a result, the average number of privatizations in this region of the world expanded ten-fold across the decade.[52]

Although there is no doubt that developmentalist state elites had pursued excessive public financing, privatization accomplished two radical changes: (1) it reduced public capacity in developmental planning and implementation, thereby privileging private initiative; and (2) it extended the reach of foreign ownership of assets in the former Third World—precisely the condition that governments had tried to overcome in the 1970s. Between 1980 and 1992, the stock of international bank lending rose from 4 percent to 44 percent of the GDP of the Organization for Economic Cooperation and Development.[53] Rather than losing the money they had loaned in such excessive amounts, banks earned vast profits on the order of 40 percent per annum on Third World investments alone.[54] At the end of the decade, foreign investment in the Third World countered a global declining trend between 1989 and 1992, increasing from $29 to $40 billion (especially in Mexico, China, Malaysia, Argentina, and Thailand).[55] The restructured zones of the global economy were apparently now quite profitable for private investment: wages were low, governments were not competing in the private capital markets, and an export boom in manufactured goods and processed foods was under way.

The debt regime, in dealing with the problem of adjustment on a case-by-case basis, transformed the discourse of development in two distinct ways. First, the conditions imposed on debtors for renewal of credit enabled the debt managers to reframe the national project. There was no longer a question of pursuing the goals of the original development project; rather, wholesale restructuring (to compete in the global economy) was necessary to guarantee repayment of debt.[56] Second, austerity measures, privatization, and export expansion renewed the global economy rather than individual national economies. Austerity measures lowered wages to encourage foreign investment, privatization ensured the revival of the principle of the global freedom of enterprise, and export expansion sustained the flow of products to the wealthier zones of the global economy.

Each measure potentially undermined the coherence and sovereignty of national economies. Lowered wages reduced local purchasing power. Wage earners had to tighten their belts; as a result, the market for goods produced locally contracted. Privatization of public enterprises reduced the capacity of states. They were no longer in a position to enter into joint ventures with private firms and lay plans for production priorities. Reduction in public expenditure generally reduced states' capacity to coordinate national economic and social programs. Finally, export expansion often displaced local production systems—as we saw, for example, in the case study about the "world steer" in Chapter 3. The following case study of the Dominican Republic offers a parallel but different example of the challenge to state developmentalism under the conditions of the debt regime.

As parts of national economies became embedded more deeply in global enterprise through commodity chains, they weakened as national units and strengthened the reach of the global economy. This situation was not unique to the 1980s, but the mechanisms of the debt regime institutionalized the power and authority of global management within states' very organization and procedures. This was the turning point in the story of development.

CASE STUDY

Turning the Dominican Republic Inside Out

Historically, the Dominican Republic was a plantation economy established under Spanish colonialism. Ever since the country achieved independence in the nineteenth century, sugar exporting has been its overwhelming economic activity; other exports are coffee, cocoa, and tobacco. National economic development has depended centrally on the health of these exports. In the 1980s, the contribution of these primary commodity exports to the total export earnings fell from 58 percent to 33 percent. We know that sugar in particular was under threat from industrial substitutes manufactured in the First World as well as from First World protection of its domestic sugar beet producers. The Dominican government responded to this shortfall, under pressure from the International Monetary Fund, by instituting an *export-substitution strategy* to generate new sources of export revenues to service its substantial foreign debt. This strategy, encouraged by the 1980s U.S. Caribbean Basin Initiative (CBI) to promote foreign investment in agro-export sectors, was based in an export promotion law and an agro-industrial law passed in 1984. In addition to industrializing agriculture, the state was branching into nontraditional exports, which were anything other than the products previously exported. Nontraditional exports included tropical root crops such as yams and taro; vegetables and horticultural crops such as peppers, tomatoes, green beans, and eggplants; and tropical fruits such as melons, pineapples, and avocados. Beef products were the most significant agro-industrial export.

The adoption of this broad agricultural restructuring involved policy reversals that removed government supports for basic food production; these fell substantially, with the result that over 50 percent of the Dominican household food basket was now imported. In addition, social programs that redistributed some wealth were undermined in the rush to subsidize firms in the nontraditional agricultural sector.

As in most countries, domestic food production in the Dominican Republic depended on state support, restriction of imports, subsidized credit and technical assistance for small producers, and regulation of local markets and stabilized prices for the more vulnerable classes in Dominican society. In the country's structural adjustment, the global managers reorganized the national agricultural bank, reducing available credit for these social programs. Rice, produced under heavy state assistance with guaranteed prices, was "liberalized" in 1988, leading to the demise of the national rice crop and greater reliance on rice imports.

Meanwhile, the previous sugar plantation lands were leased by the state to transnational corporations such as Chiquita and Dole for the production of pineapples. These companies were given access to the land without having to invest in it. With plantations elsewhere—in Hawaii, Thailand, the Philippines, Guatemala, and Honduras—these transnationals are able to negotiate favorable conditions from host governments. Laura Raynolds observes that "most of the roughly 2,000 workers in the new pineapple plantations are casual day laborers who are unprotected by national labor legislation. These workers, many of whom are women, have no job security and are paid less than even the subminimum wage. Labor unions have either been crushed outright or co-opted by the combined forces of the state and the transnational corporations." Regarding the concessions made by the government to the TNCs to attract them to the Dominican Republic, she adds that "these concessions increase the likelihood that production will relocate if the state does not maintain a satisfactory level of subsidization. . . . [T]he Dominican state has forfeited direct control over critical national land resources and rural labor forces."

In short, the makeover of the Dominican state's national economic priorities was a combined operation, involving global institutions as well as new state initiatives. The outcome has been a considerable weakening of the state's capacity to pursue a viable and stable national economic plan in the interests of the majority of its citizenry, who depend on the government to redistribute economic opportunity and regulate domestic markets. If states undertake economic reforms to expand agro-industrial production to benefit their wealthier citizens, and expand exports to attract foreign investors, are they not pursuing short-term profits at the expense of long-term national stability?

Sources: Raynolds, 1994, pp. 218, 231–232; Raynolds et al., 1993, p. 1111.

Restructuring States

Internalizing the authority of global management involves two significant and related changes in the structure of power. First, the conditions of debt rescheduling actively reorganize states. Second, the reorganization has a profoundly unrepresentative character to it, as bureaucrats in the global agencies exert more and more influence on how states should conduct their economic affairs. Reform policies are routinely imposed by the global agencies with little or no scrutiny by the citizens of the state undergoing restructuring. Chapter 2 reported that the World Bank established local agencies to administer its projects as a matter of course. Under the debt regime, this practice blossomed under the pretext of shaking markets loose from government regulation. Giving the market free rein is arguably a euphemism for allowing such bureaucrats, global banks, and global firms a stronger hand in determining what should be produced, where, and for whom.

The power of the global managers is typically institutionalized through the administration of adjustment programs. Throughout the Bretton Woods era, the International Monetary Fund exerted considerable influence on the fiscal management of states by applying conditions to the loans it made to adjust short-term balance of payments.[57] But this influence involved merely financial stabilization measures. Structural adjustment loans, by contrast, restructure economic initiatives in debtor countries and redistribute power within the state. The most widespread restructuring redistributes power from program-oriented ministries (social services, agriculture, education) to the central bank and to trade and finance ministries.[58] The importance of this shift is the loss of resources to state agencies that support and regulate economic and social sectors affecting the majority of the citizenry, especially the poorer classes. These resources are shifted to the agencies more directly connected to global enterprise, where economic criteria replace the social criteria that define the national project. Perhaps the most dramatic example of state restructuring in recent years is illustrated in the following case study of Mexico.

CASE STUDY

Restructuring the Mexican State

In preparation for the implementation of the North American Free Trade Agreement (NAFTA) in the 1990s, Mexico undertook a major restructuring plan. For two decades, the Mexican state had been guiding agro-industrialization and regulating the basic grains sector. Centralized control over the production and sale of grain, of course, encouraged corruption and political patronage, especially with the country's one-party rule under the legendary Institutional Revolutionary Party (PRI). Although modernization priorities favored the development of irrigated commercial agriculture in the context of the two green revolutions, President Echeverría's 1971 revision of the agrarian reform code, under pressure from **campesinos** (peasants and farm workers) for greater participation, had renewed financial and institutional support for the *ejido* sector—community-controlled landholdings deriving from the Mexican Revolution of 1910. Basic grain prices were subsidized and various forms of agricultural credit assisted the small farm sector. In other words, the state managed both an extensive rural social system, based on *campesino* agriculture that supplied foods to domestic markets, and a profitable commercial agribusiness sector. But the government supported the *campesino* sector with multilateral loans rather than a national progressive tax. When Mexico's oil prices fell in 1981, the debt financing of the basic grains sector could no longer continue. Nor could the national food security system, a grain production and distribution scheme that had begun the previous year under the Lopéz Portillo government. These essential national institutions were scrapped.

Between 1980 and 1991, Mexico negotiated 13 adjustment loans with the World Bank, and six agreements with the IMF. The World Bank proposed an agricultural structural adjustment loan in 1986 to assist in the elimination of imported food subsidies, the privatization of rural parastatal agencies, the liberalization of trade and domestic food prices, "sound" public investment, and cutbacks in the size of the agricultural ministry. These were the conditions of the loan. Rural social services were subordinated to economic criteria that focused on agro-industrial priorities. This was a marked turnaround from the days of the Bank's basic needs strategy in the 1970s, which had supported a program of integrated rural development in Mexico. Equity concerns were giving way to the rush to open national economies to trade and investment, in the interests of stabilizing the global financial system.

In 1991, a follow-up sectoral adjustment loan for Mexican agriculture further liberalized food importing, privatized state-owned monopolies, and eliminated price guarantees on corn—a drastic step. The social repercussions were sufficiently severe that the Bank subsequently supported the government's Pronasol and

Procampo programs, which offered financial assistance to poor rural producers.

Overall, however, the country went through a decade of liberal reforms, mandated by the global managers and pursued by the Mexican government to maintain its creditworthiness—made essential by the prospect of joining NAFTA. The state abandoned its substantial role as manager and regulator of the enormous agricultural sector. It withdrew its financial support from the campesinos, shifting those funds into expanding agro-exports.

With this drastic shrinking of state involvement in the rural sector, the percentage of *campesinos* with access to official credit fell from 50 percent to less than 20 percent at the end of the 1980s. To fill the void left by the state, *campesino* organizations have mobilized to create new and locally controlled credit systems. Their dilemma is that now they must negotiate with the National Banking Commission (CNB), which regulates credit arrangements and is increasingly geared to the new principles of global competitiveness; these are quite different from the principles on which *campesino* communities run.

In sum, when states restructure, they may improve their financial standing and their export sectors, but the majority of citizens and poorer classes find their protections stripped away in the country's rush to participate in the world market.

Sources: Salinger & Dethier, 1989; McMichael & Myhre, 1991; Myhre, 1994; Barry, 1995, pp. 36, 43–44, 144.

In another part of the world, structural adjustment policies pursued by the multilateral agencies in Africa reveal a telling rethinking of the state's role in development. Initially, as presented in the World Bank's 1981 (Berg) report, the goal of "shrinking" the state was justified as a way to improve efficiency and reduce urban bias.[59] **Structural adjustment programs (SAPs)** directly challenged the political coalitions and goals of the national developmental state. At the same time, SAPs strengthened finance ministries in the policy-making process.[60] In other words, within the African countries, power moved from the developmental coalitions (urban planning, agriculture, education) to the financial group, which was most concerned with a country's ability to obtain international credit. The report revealed a shift in Bank lending practices from providing assistance for developmental concerns to tying aid to "comprehensive policy reform."[61]

The World Bank's premise for the shift was that the postcolonial development states were overbureaucratic and inefficient on the one hand, and unresponsive to their citizenry on the other. In the World Bank's major report of 1989 on sub-Saharan Africa, "shrinking" the state was now reinterpreted as a political reorganization of state administration to encourage populist initiatives. Of course, some of these observations are credible; there are many examples of authoritarian government, corruption, and "hollow" development financing—such as Zaire President Mobutu's lavish global-set lifestyle and Ivory Coast President Félix Houphouët-Boigny's construction in his home village of a larger-than-the-original replica of St. Peter's basilica in the Vatican. Nevertheless, the solutions proposed, and imposed, by the Bank substitute growing external control of these countries in the name of financial orthodoxy.[62]

In its 1989 report entitled, significantly, *Sub-Saharan Africa From Crisis to Sustainable Growth: A Long Term Perspective Study,* the Bank advanced the idea of "political conditionality." It proposed "policy dialogue" with recipient states leading to "consensus forming." This is a sophisticated way of constructing political coalitions within the recipient state that embrace economic reforms proposed by the multilateral agencies.[63] One observer noted: "It has become an explicit target of the institutions, and the World Bank in particular, to shift the balance of power within governments towards those who expect to gain from the policy reforms encouraged by the institutions and/or those who are in any case more sympathetic towards such changes."[64]

This strategy is actually a way of remaking states, through "institution building." It continues the practice discussed in Chapter 2, whereby the administration of Bank projects gives greatest weight to the input of technical experts in national planning. The new phase of Bank involvement deepens by organizing coalitions in the state that are committed to the redefinition of the government's economic priorities. The state sheds its accountability to its citizens, who lose input into their own government.

Jonathan Cahn, using information from confidential Bank documents, told of the conditions imposed on an unnamed debtor country. The Bank provided $9 million to an interministerial commission to manage the structural adjustment process, with a "technical committee" established to perform the commission's work.[65] In the Bank's words, this new administrative unit was "designed to assist . . . the Government in implementing its structural adjustment program successfully."[66]

One clear implication of this practice is an expanding trusteeship role for the multilateral agencies. This procedure not only compromises national sovereignty but also subordinates national policy to the demands of the global economy. It illustrates the growth of global regulatory mechanisms that may override national policy making. Under these conditions, the World Bank, which is now the principal multilateral agency involved in global development financing, plays a definite governing role. It "dictate[s] legal and institutional change through its lending process," and, since its 1989 report, it now asserts that evaluating governance in debtor countries is within its jurisdiction.[67]

Despite the new emphasis on human rights and democratization as conditions for reform and financial assistance, the World Bank remains unaccountable to the citizenry in developing countries. And when the IMF and the Bank stabilize and make long-term loans to a debtor, they assume "a governance role that may best be likened to that of a trustee in bankruptcy," except that trustees are accountable to the bankruptcy court. The IMF and the Bank remain accountable to no one other than their powerful underwriters.[68] Further, after a loan is approved, U.S. corporations and citizens are given access to economic—and political—intelligence reports prepared by the Bank. The political asymmetry is obvious, lending support to the idea that global rule without law is being institutionalized.[69]

In sum, the debt regime shifted economic managerial power from former Third World states to global agencies. Countries surrendered their economic sovereignty as First World governments and financiers, both private and public, concentrated managerial control of the global economy in their own hands. World Bank and IMF programs of adjustment were substituted for a true multilateral management of the debt crisis. These conditions imposed standard rather than locally tailored remedies on indebted states. Governments and business elites in the former Third World countries certainly collaborated in this enterprise, often for the same reasons they had promoted development financing in previous decades. They are usually well placed to benefit most from infusions of foreign capital, and the debt burden is borne disproportionately by the poor. The social and political consequences of restructuring are examined in Chapter 5.

Summary

The divergence of growth patterns in the former Third World intensified through the 1980s. According to the World Bank, the East Asian share of Third World real incomes rose from 22 percent to 33 percent while all other regions had lower shares, especially Latin America and sub-Saharan Africa, where income share fell by 6 and 5 percentage points, respectively.[70]

Two trends were emerging. One was the further polarization of wealth and growth rates within the Third World. The rising tide was lifting some regions and swamping others. The countries of the Third World, which had stood together as the Group of 77, were no longer able to identify and pursue common interests because some were experiencing a level of prosperity so much greater than that of others. The defeat of the New International Economic Order initiative was a turning point. The other trend was the consolidation of the organizational features of the global economy, with the lending institutions assuming a powerful trusteeship role in the debtor nations.

We began this chapter by looking at how global financial organization matched the global production system emerging through Third World export strategies. Offshore money markets redistributed private capital to states as loans, and transnational corporations invested capital in production for global markets. These two trends combined in a frenzy of developmentalist projects as Third World states sought to equal the success of the newly industrializing countries. Public investments complemented and underwrote private enterprise. When credit dried up in the 1980s, debt repayment schemes reversed both aid-for-development programs and investment by the transnationals. Debt rescheduling was conditioned on the privatization of state agencies and projects. And the rescheduling process concentrated financial power in the hands of the multilateral agencies. Developmentalist states were turned inside out as global managerialism emerged. It emerged institutionally as the multilateral agencies restructured policy priorities and administrations in these states, and it gathered ideological force in the growing faith in the authority of the market. In short, the debt crisis was a rehearsal for the globalization project, discussed in Chapter 5.

PART III

The Globalization Project
(1980s–)

5

The Rise of the Globalization Project

Global economic integration played a substantial role in the development project. Right from the beginning, when the Bretton Woods system was formed, the postwar world order rested on two pillars. One was the nation-state, the arena in which development was to be pursued. The other was the international institutional structure, including the Bretton Woods agencies, and the development establishment, such as the Ford and Rockefeller Foundations, the U.S. Agency for International Development (USAID), and the international agricultural institutions—the International Wheat and Maize Improvement Center (whose Spanish acronym is **CIMMYT**) and the **International Rice Research Institute (IRRI).** These institutions shared common assumptions and procedures regarding development.

The development project had offered a *universal* blueprint for national economic development. Technologies and infrastructural programs were universal hardware. Modernization was a universal ideal. The nation-state was to be the vehicle of these shared goals in the postwar era (see Chapter 1). It was the logical political unit in which to mobilize populations around the ideal of modernization—not only because national independence and material advancement were high on the agenda but also because states themselves were power centers that were able to coordinate such mobilization. And membership in a system of states, in which sovereignty concerns were paramount, oriented states toward multilateral and bilateral programs of assistance. In this way, national and international development initiatives were intertwined.

Now we begin our evaluation of the *post-developmentalist* era. It did not begin on any particular date, but it signifies a new stage of thinking about development, as represented in the time line at the beginning of this book. The debt crisis shifted the terms of development from a national to a global concern. States still pursue development goals, but these goals are less and less nationally managed. Certainly some specific assistance projects are cast in terms of national developmentalism (often at the subnational level), but the infrastructure of economic development at large has been shifted mainly to the level and goals of the globalization project. These goals involve development of a world market in which states expect to share the benefits. The development project has shed its national characteristics and is now undergoing reformulation as the globalization project. It is important to understand who is doing the reformulating; we explore that issue in this chapter.

The rise of global managerialism was examined in Chapter 4. Of course, its roots go back to the Bretton Woods and Cold War institutions, which coordinated a framework for managing national economies. But the global managers emerging on the scene in the 1980s made explicit claims about managing a global economy. These managers included the development establishment in the Bretton Woods institutions as well as governments reformed by monetarism and debt rescheduling. They also included transnational corporate and political elites across the world—arguably a global ruling class, whose shared interest in an expanding global economy was embedded in the multilateral and restructured national institutions. A consensus, with a good deal of financial coercion, formed around the redefinition of development to mean *participation in the world market.* The task of this chapter is to explore the elements of this consensus and how they contribute to the new globalization project.

Postdevelopmentalism

Postdevelopmentalism refers to the demise of the project in which states pursued nationally managed economic growth. In this project, development dovetailed with nation-building in the postcolonial world. It had a definite political arena: the national territory. This initiative is now disintegrating. Key indicators are the current fragmentation of some nation-states into ethnoregional segments and the universal dismantling of public supports for populations, especially the underprivileged sectors. These signs suggest that a new project is under way. It no longer simply addresses the postcolonial world. It is universal, and it concerns the attempt to build a global economy under global management. All states are involved, even those of the Second World, now that the Soviet bloc has unraveled and China, Vietnam, North Korea, and Cuba are entering the world market.

Under these circumstances, states are exploring new ways of governing. There are simultaneous processes of *decentralization* of central state authority (as an example, the U.S. federal government is divesting itself of certain social budgetary responsibilities, shifting these down to states and municipalities) and processes of *centralization* of power (such as the formation of macro-regional groupings in which member states agree to certain common economic rules about trade and investment). Everywhere, states are renegotiating their reach, often along bureaucratic lines beyond the control of their citizenry. Some of this has to do with global integrating trends. As one sociologist has observed: "In circumstances of accelerating globalization, the nation-state has become `too small for the big problems of life, and too big for the small problems of life.'"[1] Out of this uncertain foundation, the globalization project arises.

In the 1970s, the World Bank proclaimed the model postdevelopmentalist strategy for development to be successful participation in the world economy. The newly industrializing countries were held up as exemplars of the new strategy of export-led growth. By the 1980s, the definition of development was extended to include a policy of broad *liberalization*—in particular, privatization of public functions and the application of market principles to the administration of wages, prices, and trade. President Reagan reiterated this theme in his 1985 State of the Union address: "America's economic success . . . can be repeated a hundred times in a hundred nations. Many countries in East Asia and the Pacific have few resources other than the enterprise of their own people. But through free markets they've soared ahead of centralized economies."[2] These principles guided the structural adjustment measures imposed on debtor nations by the debt managers in the 1980s.

The successful newly industrializing nations (NICs) of East and Southeast Asia, however, did not actually follow these principles. South Korea is notorious for its "centrally managed capitalism." And the pretenders to NIC status—Malaysia, Thailand, and Indonesia—combined successful export-led growth with strong import-protectionism. Their strategy depended on growing Japanese offshore investment in the 1980s (compared with the dearth of foreign investment in Latin America).[3] In East and Southeast Asia, then, a managed flying-geese pattern of regional expansion, with Japan in the lead, scored enormous success without adhering to the free market ideal.

Two trends resulted from these developments. First, like the idealized Western model that inspired the development project, the NIC model has also been idealized. Neither model corresponded to historical reality; each merely represented an ideal version of that reality. That is, they served ideological purposes. In fact, the free market ideal has been turned *against* the protectionism of the Asian NICs as well as Japan, principally by U.S. bilateral trade pressures on these states since the mid-1980s to open up to foreign trade and investment. Second, the United States has led a parallel attempt to institutionalize this free market consensus globally. Thus, the long, drawn-out negotiations of the GATT Uruguay Round (1986–1994) led to the formation of a World Trade Organization (WTO) designed to anchor a new "free trade regime" on a global scale. These trends are central to the emerging globalization project.

The Globalization Project

Although the globalization project replaces the development project, "development" has not lost its currency. Its frame of reference has simply shifted, especially at the initiative of proliferating nongovernmental organizations (NGOs) that increasingly fill the vacuum as states withdraw, or lose, their capacity to assist subnational groups and causes. Thousands of community and regional development projects continue at the local level, attempting to improve conditions at these levels or stabilize communities affected one way or another by the restructuring of their states. And at the global level, the development establishment focuses on developing the global economy. At both levels, a new conception of **sustainable development** has gained currency. It is used by both grassroots movements and global managers (for example, the World Bank), but it does not always mean the same thing. The new frames of reference proliferate as the certainty of the development project's singular framework has disappeared. We address these frames in turn.

The Strategy of Liberalization

Most important, the globalization project emerges in the *wake* of the development project. Its centerpiece is the belief in market liberalization that took hold under the debt regime. Debtor governments that reduced their size and role were rewarded by the debt managers with credit released in tranches (staggered portions) to ensure their continuing compliance with loan conditions. Thus, national economies were opened up to global forces; they were increasingly globalized, or turned inside out. National governments, in varying degrees, embraced global rather than national criteria of economic growth. As suggested in the following case study of Chile, such pressure to gain international financial solvency has its costs and consequences—polarizing wealth, compromising the security of domestic populations, and threatening the sustainability of local resources.

Chile—the Model of Economic Liberalization

Chile is perhaps the model case of economic liberalization. Although not regarded as a newly industrializing country, Chile's significance lies in its political history. A military coup in 1973 eliminated the democratically elected socialist president Salvador Allende, coinciding with the beginnings of the postdevelopmentalist era. General Augusto Pinochet pursued a radical free market reform masterminded by economists trained at the University of Chicago, a center of neoclassical economics. Over the next two decades, 600 of the country's state enterprises were sold; foreign investment expanded into strategic sectors like steel, telecommunications, and airlines; trade protection dwindled; and the dependence of the Chilean GDP on trade grew from 35 percent in 1970 to 57.4 percent in 1990. In other words, Chile was structurally adjusted before structural adjustment became fashionable.

The Chilean experiment was hailed as a miracle. Between 1977 and 1981, private consumption, especially of consumer durables, increased by about 10 percent a year, with some trickle-down of consumption from middle to skilled working classes. Real wages went up by roughly a third for the employed, and improvement was made in other social indicators, such as infant mortality rates. At the same time, however, poverty rates remained high, at around 35 percent; unemployment rates among the poorer, unskilled segments of the population were at least 15 percent; and social amenities were maldistributed across classes and across the urban-rural divide. So the benefits of the Chilean miracle were in fact quite uneven.

Chile was always known as the most democratic of Latin American nations prior to the assault on its parliamentary and civil institutions by the Pinochet military junta and its economic reforms. In the 1980s, however, when Chile restructured its debt, social polarization increased. The share of national income of the richest 10 percent of the people rose from about 35 percent to 46.8 percent, while that of the poorest half of the population declined from 20.4 percent to 16.8 percent. Chilean social spending continued to fall, wages were frozen, and the *peso* was seriously devalued. Under these conditions, domestic production faltered as deindustrialization set in, unemployment levels rose to 20–30 percent, and real wages suffered a 20 percent reduction. Thus, when Pinochet resigned at the end of the decade, about 40 percent, or 5.2 million, of the 13 million Chilean people were defined as poor in a country once identified by its substantial middle class. In sum, the pursuit of "efficiency in the global marketplace" had weakened the domestic fabric of social securities and local production.

In conjunction with military rule, socioeconomic polarization also compromised democratic renewal. Cathy Schneider, a Latin American scholar, observed: "The transformation of the economic and political system has had a profound impact on the world view of the typical Chilean. . . . It has transformed Chile, both culturally and politically, from a country of active participatory grassroots communities, to a land of disconnected, apolitical individuals."

Sources: Bello, 1994, pp. 42, 44–45, 59; George, 1988, pp. 131–132; Schneider, quoted in Chomsky, 1994, p. 184.

Another dimension of liberalization concerns the commercial exploitation of national resources to service international debt. This exploitation is universal; for example, in Canada, which is home to 10 percent of the world's forests, about 1 million hectares of woodland disappear annually to logging. In the province of British Columbia, the Mitsubishi Corporation has the largest chopstick factory in the world, converting aspen stands into chopsticks at the rate of 7 to 8 million pairs a day.[4] Under the debt regime, natural resources were routinely mined beyond sustainable proportions. The close correlation between debt and high rates of deforestation worldwide is well known.[5]

In Chile, timber exports doubled in the 1980s, reaching beyond industrial plantations to the logging of natural forests. Illegal cutting spread among Chile's poor rural population, about half of whom (700,000) live on native forest land; this is a survival strategy that responds to Japan's insatiable demand for wood chips and depletes Chile's old-growth rain forest.[6] In addition, toxic runoff from unregulated mining and from pesticides used on fruits grown for export has combined with overfishing to jeopardize the annual sardine catch. Chile's export boom in the 1980s overexploited the country's natural resources beyond their ability to regenerate.[7]

In Africa, the World Bank's model of structural adjustment, Ghana, had a 3.8 percent growth rate in the 1980s, stimulated by extensive aid. Exports of mining, fishing, and timber products accelerated to close the widening gap between cocoa exports and severely declining world prices of cocoa. From 1983 to 1988, timber exports increased from $16 million to $99 million, reducing Ghana's tropical forest to 25 percent of its original size.[8] The organization Development GAP reported that deforestation

> threatens household and national food security now and in the future. Seventy-five per cent of Ghanaians depend on wild game to supplement their diet. Stripping the forest has led to sharp increases in malnutrition and disease. For women, the food, fuel, and medicines that they harvest from the forest provide critical resources, especially in the face of decreased food production, lower wages, and other economic shocks that threaten food security.[9]

Widespread export-led debt servicing involves two dynamics: (1) selling domestic resources to global firms that supply the global economy and delivering the revenues to multilateral lenders as debt repayment, and (2) eroding the country's natural resources (the "commons") that provide subsistence security to the poor. In the long run, removing domestic protections to meet short-run payment schedules threatens social and environmental sustainability.

Expanding exports to earn foreign currency with which to service debt appears to be a logical strategy for individual debtor nations to pursue. But when all debtor nations try to export their way out of debt, the fallacy of the structural adjustment blueprint becomes clear. When 70 countries submitted to the liberalization programs of the multilateral agencies, the resulting glut of exports produced the lowest commodity prices seen on the world market since the 1930s. For example, in West Africa, between 1986 and 1989, cocoa producers expanded their exports by 25 percent only to suffer a 33 percent price fall on the world market. The nongovernmental organization Oxfam named this syndrome the "export-led collapse."[10]

Biotechnical substitution compounds the problem of export reliance. Many prepared foods and drinks now substitute high-fructose corn syrup for sugar. Before 1985, sugar was the common sweetener; since that time, all U.S. soft drinks have been sweetened with sugar substitutes, and U.S. sugar imports have fallen by half. As a result, producers in Brazil, India, the Philippines, Thailand, and several poor African and Caribbean countries lost markets just at the time when their debt servicing demanded increased exports.[11]

It appears, then, that the push to liberalize national economies severely compromises the capacities of governments to deliver on the promise of the development project. The flow of credit to debt-stressed nations has been premised precisely on the renunciation of national development criteria. But the example of the export-led collapse reveals the risks associated with greater participation in an unequal world market. The terms of participation are not necessarily favorable. Thus, in place of national priorities, global priorities such as debt service, expanded trade, and renewal of foreign investment opportunities gain the upper hand. The next case study illustrates these effects in Eastern Europe and China.

CASE STUDY

Restructuring in Eastern Europe and China

The restructuring programs of the International Monetary Fund and the World Bank extended to more than half the former Second World. By 1986, Hungary, Romania, the former Yugoslavia, Poland, Vietnam, and China were subject to IMF supervision of their economies. Many of these states had started borrowing from Western financial institutions during the 1970s, often to pay for basic consumer items demanded by their increasingly restive civilian populations. In 1986, Mikhail Gorbachev was formulating plans for *perestroika* (restructuring) in exchange for membership in the Bretton Woods institutions. Earlier, in 1982, the IMF had tendered an austerity plan in Hungary on condition that centrally planned production be replaced by "market-responsive" and "financially-disciplined" enterprises, along with reductions in subsidies of food, transportation, heating fuel, and housing. These subsidies were the foundation of the well-established basic *economic* rights of the socialist systems. During the 1980s, most commodity prices were shifted to a supply/demand basis, small-scale state enterprises were privatized, and assembly line workers found that instead of a steady wage they were now earning piece rates determined not by the work performed (as with the union contract common in the United States) but by the profit rate of the enterprise. Social equality was being redefined as the equality of private opportunity that characterizes Western market ideology. Of course, former public officials had the lock on private opportunity, not only in Hungary but throughout the former Second World. They enriched themselves and their relatives at the moment of transition from state to private ownership of property. When Eastern European economies were opened to the world market through massive IMF loans of foreign currency, domestic prices moved up to world price levels while wages held constant. As Joyce Kolko remarks: "During the 1980s there was growing resentment in the general population at the rising prices, falling living standards, and the new rich."

Deregulations throughout these once centrally regulated social systems had consequences quite similar to those in the former Third World. By the early 1990s, Eastern European per capita income levels resembled those of the former Third World. The per capita incomes of Poland and Mexico were about the same, as were those of Hungary and Brazil. Because Eastern European populations have higher levels of education and stable population growth rates, they differ from former Third World societies. But the collapse of their formerly comprehensive system of state subsidies and social consumption put their populations in a short space of time at the mercy of the market. This is the reason some observers say Eastern Europe has experienced "Third Worldization."

Whereas Eastern Europe's level of urbanization resembled that of the Latin American countries, China demonstrates some of the common patterns associated with rural restructuring in the more agrarian societies of Southeast Asia and Africa. China has a strong tradition of private land ownership compared to Russia, and the IMF-style reforms in both regions have reinforced these traditions, as Mark Selden points out. The rural regions of China were once the site of tightly organized rural communes (a collection of several villages) that stabilized the population and delivered surpluses to the state for redistribution to poorer regions. Massive decollectivization has occurred in rural China since the 1970s, speeding up under IMF guidance in the 1980s. In 1978, about two-thirds of rural income came from the communes, but by 1985 more than three-quarters came from households. As land has been privatized, agricultural management has shifted from the commune to the household level. Agricultural productivity rose initially with privatization, generating a process of enrichment for former Party members. Social, and regional, inequalities rose. The expanding "special economic zones" (equivalent to the export processing zones introduced in Chapter 3) on the coast and especially in South China near Hong Kong acted as an industrial magnet for ex-commune members making the most of their new geographical and social mobility as well as for peasants displaced by private land concentration.

Sources: Kolko, 1988, pp. 278–296; Pepper, 1988; Selden, 1994; Kagarlitsky, 1995.

The globalization project, then, began with market liberalization. The debt regime fostered this liberalization by forcing governments to downsize. It was a regime precisely because it established new economic rules to which indebted states conformed in order to sustain their flow of credit. But, in doing so, they surrendered their powers to manage their national economic growth. Sale of public enterprises and reduction of social subsidies effectively remade Third World states and restructured societies, placing the burden on lower classes, especially women in these lower classes. Scaling back public capacity transformed nation-states into states that administer globally based flows of money and goods alongside increasingly tenuous local economies in which states lack public capacity to pursue nationally coordinated development initiatives. The transformation is reflected in governments' greater dedication to market rather than social (welfare) principles in their growth strategy.

The Comparative Advantage Axiom

The development strategy of the globalization project depends on the world market rather than the domestic market for its stimulus. It is premised on the neoclassical concept of **comparative advantage**: that national prosperity derives from specialization in those forms of economic activity in which a country does best. It obviously contradicts the development project's ideal of a series of integrated national economies. This is why the restructurings during the 1980s were strategic in shifting the terms of development. The case study of Singapore that follows is a contemporary example of successful economic restructuring, although it comes at the cost of considerable political authoritarianism.

Under the theorem of comparative advantage, international prosperity derives from the more efficient exchange among countries of their comparative advantage in goods and services. The theorem applies strictly to competitive situations in which countries that might replicate each other in industrial capacities nonetheless will find their level of specialization through the competitive processes of international trade. David Ricardo, an English political economist, used the example of Portuguese wine exchanging with English cloth to illustrate how comparative advantage applies to competitive situations where producers specialize through trade.[12] The colonial division of labor was established through force rather than competition, so comparative advantage does not strictly apply to the colonial era.

CASE STUDY

Restructuring in Singapore: A Successful Mini-Dragon

Singapore is an exceptional city-state that is highly dependent on foreign investment. It has experienced over three decades of paternal rule under the People's Action Party (PAP) since gaining independence in 1959 from Britain and its subsequent expulsion from the Malaysian federation in 1965. Along with Hong Kong, Taiwan, and South Korea, Singapore is one of the four newly industrializing countries (NICs) of Pacific Asia known as the "mini-dragons." Its status as a NIC depended on centralized planning that brought together state bureaucracies, public enterprise, and transnational companies. It also rested on a corporatist (developmentalist) political system that silenced political opposition, turned labor unions into tools of the state, and elaborated a social discipline based on Confucian ethics of loyalty.

In 1985, at the height of a local recession and the reorganizations underway in the global economy, a government economic committee recommended a new strategy to liberalize the economy. Beginning with Singapore Airlines, the government began a gradual process to privatize its substantial public sector and to foster local enterprise and high-tech foreign investment. The recent technological upgrading in financial services and manufacturing is part of a strategy to position Singapore as the source of specialized exports (including producer services such as computer technologies) to the fastest-growing region of the world economy, the Pacific Asian region. Restructuring also involves relocating lower-value and "dirty" pork production for the Singapore consumer to agro-export platforms in nearby Indonesia and Malaysia, and developing high-value and "clean" agro-technology parks within Singapore. Meanwhile, the PAP's strategy of using social investments—in nearly universal public housing, universal public health services and education, and vocational retraining—allows it to coordinate wage levels with economic strategies and, most important, to continue its tradition of low unemployment levels and social cohesion.

Sources: Deyo, 1991; Ufkes, 1995.

Ricardo formulated his theorem of comparative advantage over a century ago, and it has retained a certain currency among neoclassical economists. Until now, it represented a minority strand of economic thought, partly because it was out of step with social history. In particular, social movements such as organized labor demanded social entitlements and protections from the free market, especially after the Great Depression of the 1930s. Now, the globalization project has brought into the foreground of contemporary economic thought the notion that liberalization brings greater economic efficiency. The postwar consensus built around Keynesian ideas of state economic intervention and public investment has crumbled. The evidence is all around us in various guises—in welfare reform or reversal, in wage cutting, and in privatization schemes. It is a universal process, most dramatically played out in the former Second World countries, where public resources have been sold at rock-bottom prices to well-placed new capitalists (usually former state officials) and markets have been released from government regulation.

On reflection, you see that as states open up and pursue global efficiency—with wage cuts, for example—other states are compelled to follow or suffer offshoring of their capital to these cheaper zones. In these conditions, comparative advantage in cheap labor determines strategy. Individual states may offer specific packages to attract foreign investment, but the *global* labor force finds its wages trending downward. Inevitably, each state participates in a process that spirals downward and over which they have little control as long as they participate in the world market.

The globalization project includes an explicit vision of global order, which is quite distinct from that of the post–World War II modernization era. At that time, the slogan was "Learn from, and catch up with, the West." Now, under comparative advantage, the slogan is "Find your niche in the global marketplace." While the first held out *replication* as the key to national development, the second presents *specialization* as the path to economic prosperity. But specialization in different commodity chains does not alter the reality that the mechanisms of specialization—wage cutting, foreign investment concessions, privatization, and reduction of social entitlements—are repeated everywhere.

Whereas the development project emphasized the national market, the globalization project emphasizes development through global markets. But when global markets are so volatile and unevenly structured, there are no guarantees of success. As shown most clearly in the poorer regions of the world, finding a niche in the global marketplace through specialization often results in the "export trap," exacerbated by First World protectionism and leading, in the case of Africa, to a process of economic marginalization.

The Infrastructural Dimension

Shifts in World Bank lending patterns also illustrate the evolution of the globalization project. Traditionally, the Bank focused on *project* loans for public infrastructure in Third World states. Project loans have continued into the present, but in the 1980s the Bank shifted its emphasis from projects to *policy* loans. It linked loans to policies that pursued market-oriented economic growth strategies, especially the structural adjustment loan (SAL).

In 1983, the World Bank president, A. W. Clausen, remarked: "The fundamental philosophy of our institution is to help countries diversify their exports . . . and to have an export orientation." From 1983 to 1985, concessional loans from the International Development Association (IDA) for the poorest countries were reduced about 15 percent, while there was a 35 percent rise in loans to private firms through the **International Finance Commission (IFC)**, a Bank affiliate. Most important, the IDA redirected its lending from the poorest countries (those with a per capita income of $400 or less) to those "making the greatest efforts to restructure their economies," according to President Clausen.[13] By reducing its global welfare function, the Bank reversed its 1970s basic needs policy. The priority had shifted to the stabilization of global, rather than local, organization.

Global Governance

In addition to restructuring their economies and societies to serve global priorities, states face a new world order in which global institutions have assumed a different governing role. This role is by no means absolute, and it requires compliance from the states themselves. Pursuing efficiency in the world market is one such form of compliance.

The most immediate form of governance is the leverage gained through debt. Most people who own credit cards know of the discipline that debt can exert on their spending habits, especially in an era when credit ratings abound. This is true for states as well: all states are now subject to universal credit ratings. Debt became a powerful form of political leverage under the debt regime when the multilateral financial agencies strengthened their control over national policy making by assuming the lending role.

During the 1980s, the composition of loans to the former Third World changed dramatically. In 1981, 42 percent of net loans came from commercial banks and 37 percent from the multilateral financial agencies; by 1988, the banks supplied only 6 percent and the multilaterals 88 percent of net loans.[14] In effect, during that decade the multilaterals loaned public funds to help indebted states repay the debt they owed private banks. The result was that the recomposition of the debt of the former Third World centralized financial power in official hands. Because this financial power extracted major political concessions from those states, it amounted to an informal practice of global governance.

By the 1990s, global debt management was firmly institutionalized in the World Bank and the IMF. As these institutions were ultimately beholden to the so-called Group of 7 (G-7) "Northern" powers (the United States, Britain, France, Germany, Italy, Canada, and Japan), the newly formed South Commission made a provocative declaration in 1990:

> What is abundantly clear is that the North has used the plight of developing countries to strengthen its dominance and its influence over the development paths of the South. . . . While adjustment is pressed on them, countries in the North with massive payments imbalances are immune from any pressure to adjust, and free to follow policies that deepen the South's difficulties. The most powerful countries in the North have become a *de facto* board of management for the world economy, protecting their interests and imposing their will on the South. The governments of the South are then left to face the wrath, even the violence, of their own people, whose standards of living are being depressed for the sake of preserving the present patterns of operation of the world economy.[15]

This declaration continues the Third Worldist tradition of identifying the cause of underdevelopment in the North/South division. What it does not address in doing so is the decline of living standards in the so-called North. But the South Commission's declaration also draws attention to a new dimension in development discourse: the priority given to managing the world economy as a *singular entity*. Certainly there have been institutional forms of international management in the past. The Bretton Woods monetary regime, for example, maintained international financial stability during the long postwar boom (1950–1970). But the priority during that regime was on managing national economic growth within an ordered international economic system.

During the next two decades, however, as the debt regime took over, international financial stability depended on preventing default by Third World states and restructuring national economies. The outcome, as we have seen, was a general reorganization of the international system in such a way that national currencies and national economic policies became thoroughly interdependent.

In these circumstances, global financial management has become a practical necessity. For example, when the Mexican *peso* devalued by 30 percent in December 1994, Latin American stock and bond markets fell sharply. The international financial community hastily assembled a financial loan package of $18 billion to stabilize the *peso*. The United States committed $9 billion (and more), while the Bank for International Settlements in Switzerland, owned by the European Central Banks, provided $5 billion, Canada contributed $1 billion, and a dozen global banks, including Citibank, added a $3 billion line of credit. Finally, the International Monetary Fund was called in to lend both money *and* its stamp of approval to restore investor confidence in the Mexican economy.

The continuing lesson has been that the bailouts of Mexico (1982, 1995) were in fact necessary to restore confidence in the operation of the global economy. If Mexican financial instability was not resolved quickly, confidence in the functioning of the international financial system would decline. U.S. President Clinton remarked in 1995: "Mexico is sort of a bellwether for the rest of Latin America and developing countries throughout the world."[16]

Perhaps more important, confidence in the new North American Free Trade Agreement (NAFTA) was also at stake. If NAFTA were to unravel, a protectionist countermove by governments around the world would follow. Needless to say, the condition of Mexico's more recent bailout was reminiscent of the conditions under the debt regime, though less drastic. Mexican wages (already devalued) and prices were frozen, and public spending was slashed. The optimism surrounding NAFTA and Mexico's recent entry into the Organization for Economic Cooperation and Development evaporated as President Ernesto Zedillo Ponce de León proclaimed: "The development of Mexico demands that we recognize with all realism that we do not constitute a rich country but a nation of grave needs and wants."[17] In other words, Mexican adjustment was the condition for stabilization of the global economy.

Concern with management of the global economy arises from several sources but converges as the globalization project. This is a new threshold in world affairs, and it has two essential and related aspects: (1) international financial stability has a higher priority than national development planning; and (2) countries are so embedded (through debt as much as other mechanisms) in the global system that financial stability considerations actually drive economic policy making. In these circumstances, global governance is embedded in state policy.

GATT: The Making of a Free Trade Regime

The debt regime elevated the Bretton Woods institutions to positions of global governance by way of economic management, with the former Third World as the target. By contrast, the whole world became the target of the Uruguay Round, begun in 1986 in Punte del Este, Uruguay, under the auspices of the GATT organization. The Uruguay Round attempted to establish a systematic set of world trade rules, including rules concerning freedom of investment and protection of intellectual property rights. To administer this new "free trade" regime, it put into place a new global institution called the **World Trade Organization (WTO)** in 1995. The WTO is perhaps the first institution of truly global governance, even though its powers are far from absolute.

The General Agreement on Tariffs and Trade (GATT) was established in 1947 to reduce constraints on trade. From 1947 through 1980, GATT successfully reduced tariff rates on trade in manufactured goods by more than 75 percent.[18] In 1955, the United States insisted that agriculture be excluded from GATT considerations; it was concerned with protecting its farm supply policies, which used price supports and production controls to establish a floor for farm prices. But the U.S. government removed these agricultural supply constraints for several years during the mid-1970s and adopted a green power strategy of agro-export expansion (see Chapter 2). Then, at the end of the 1970s, a world economic recession produced a rising tide of trade protectionism. At this time, over 100 governments around the world signed on to a new "Uruguay Round" of GATT negotiations, which included reform of agricultural trade.

The United States initiated the Uruguay Round, because it wished to extend GATT liberalization measures to agriculture and other areas such as services (banking, insurance, telecommunications). First World countries recognized the advantages they had in these areas, but Third World countries were quite skeptical. In the early 1980s, many had been subjected to a range of "voluntary" export constraints (VERs) against their cheaper exports of steel products, footwear, electronic products, and agricultural products. India and Brazil, two of the largest Third World states, led the resistance to broadening GATT. But First World pressure and the promise of open markets, including agricultural markets, won the day.[19] A GATT ministerial meeting recognized an "urgent need to bring more discipline and predictability to world agricultural trade by preventing restrictions and distortions, including those related to structural surpluses, so as to reduce the uncertainty, imbalances and instability in world markets."[20]

The liberalization movement was supported by an activist lobby of "free trader" agro-exporting states, called the Cairns Group: Argentina, Australia, Brazil, Canada, Chile, Colombia, Fiji, Hungary, Indonesia, Malaysia, the Philippines, New Zealand, Thailand, and Uruguay. The widespread belief was that free trade would enhance the farm commodity exports of the members of the Cairns Group and of the United States. The United States took the initiative also to consolidate its green power strategy in the belief that European Community farm exports would decline under a new trade regime. It also wanted further liberalization of markets to facilitate the freedom of enterprise that it had promoted under the development project.

Not surprisingly, the transnational corporations supported GATT-style liberalization. In fact, 14,000 firms—including General Motors, IBM, and American Express—formed a multinational trade negotiations coalition to lobby GATT member nations. It was in the interest of agribusinesses such as Cargill, Ralston-Purina, General Mills, Continental Grain, RJR Nabisco, and ConAgra to use GATT to challenge agricultural regulation. This regulation included national trade controls on import quantities, farm subsidies that inflate domestic prices for agricultural commodities, and supply-management policies that restrict the demand for farm inputs like fertilizer and chemicals. Such regulations all compromise the flexibility of transnationals to use the lower-priced products of their global sourcing operations as a competitive market weapon against high-priced producers.[21]

Free trade versus the less-protected farmer. The goal of the Uruguay Round was to establish new trade rules to regulate the global economy. Such rule making necessarily generates tension between global rules and national policies, that is, between global firms and national manufacturing and agricultural sectors—and their firms, farmers, and workers. The tension in agriculture is particularly salient because farming is associated with territory, and the Uruguay Round focused on agriculture. Global firms favor liberalization because it opens up global sourcing possibilities, especially desirable to the spatially mobile transnationals. They stand to gain if they can sell farm products all over the world; they benefit from seasonal differences, from different and shared diets, and from the opportunity to seek the lowest-cost producers.

Alternatively, commercial farmers are spatially fixed. They traditionally have depended on national farm policy—input and price subsidies, farm credit, and import controls—for their economic viability. They invariably oppose farm sector deregulation, which exposes them directly to world prices. Because of the inequality of land productivity and cost variation, not to mention export subsidization by wealthier governments, most farmers need protection from price competition. These factors are in addition to the normal price instability that attends the variabilities associated with farming, such as unpredictable weather and crop blight.

The *absence* of trade rules during the closing years of the development project showed in the widespread use of *export subsidies*. The impact of subsidized exports was especially clear in the 1980s, as the United States and the European Community (EC) farm blocs competed for market share with their agricultural surpluses. While First World farmers reaped the benefits of having powerful states behind them, Third World farmers faced falling agricultural commodity prices, especially since their governments had become used to importing food, as discussed in Chapter 2.

Farm subsidies quadrupled in the United States and doubled in the European Community in the early 1980s, generating ever larger surpluses to be dumped on the world market. These American and European surpluses substantially depressed world agricultural prices—from a mean of 100 in 1975 down to 61 in 1989, a decline of 39 percent. The relatively wealthy agro-exporter Argentina experienced a 40 percent fall in earnings from cereals and vegetable oil seeds in the 1980s—and these products accounted for 50 percent of its export earnings in 1980.[22] Many Third World farm sectors were adversely affected by such commercial dumping, which deepened food import dependency, especially in sub-Saharan Africa. In Zimbabwe, for example, U.S. corn dumping forced that country's grain marketing board to cut domestic producer prices almost in half in 1986 and to reduce its purchase quota from these producers.[23]

GATT-style liberalization of agricultural trade claims to stabilize commodity markets, but it does not guarantee survival of Third World farmers. Global firms monopolize trade in agricultural commodities; they market 70 percent to 80 percent of all global trade in primary commodities.[24] This share means they are in a position to manipulate prices to secure markets. Church leaders of the European Ecumenical Organization for Development, implicitly referring to global managerialism, claimed: "With four grain corporations controlling over 80% of world cereals trade . . . market liberalization would simply transfer authority from governments to corporate leaders whose activity is guided by the profit motive. We reject this starting point on ethical grounds."[25]

In addition, wealthier farm sectors have all kinds of infrastructural advantages (transport systems, subsidized irrigation and other inputs), as well as related economies of scale (the larger the producer, the greater the cost spread). For example, the comparative advantage of U.S. corn producers over their considerably smaller counterparts in Mexico includes a productivity differential of 6.9 tons versus 1.7 tons per hectare. Under the NAFTA agreement, the Mexican government agreed to a phaseout of guaranteed prices for staples such as corn and beans.[26] The future of Mexican small producers is therefore in doubt. As Herman Daly, former World Bank senior economist, observed: "U.S. corn subsidized by depleting topsoil, aquifers, oil wells and the federal treasury can be freely imported [to Mexico, and] it is likely that NAFTA will ruin Mexican peasants."[27]

The Mexican agreement under NAFTA anticipates an ultimate goal of the free traders, which is to phase out special treatment for many of the farmers in the former Third World. In the rules established originally in GATT, Third World countries received special and differential treatment. That is, they were not required to match First World liberal trade reforms "inconsistent with their development, financial and trade needs." Although this position was reaffirmed at the opening of the GATT Uruguay Round (for the 47 least-developed countries), proposals have since been made to remove such special treatment except for the very poorest countries, mainly those in sub-Saharan Africa.[28]

Trade liberalization is understood as an efficiency move on the one hand and a leveling of the playing field on the other. But the playing field looks quite different depending on the vantage point from which you view it. The Jamaican government, for example, demanded that GATT distinguish between First World subsidies that may finance overproduction and dumping and Third World subsidies that may promote food self-reliance, rural employment, and sustainable agriculture.[29] The issue demonstrates the opposition between global and national goals, where global goals are largely those of the wealthier states and their firms.

Free trade versus food security. The opposition between global and national goals is particularly divisive around the question of *food security.* The goal of food security is to provide populations with sufficient and predictable food supplies. How to attain that goal varies, as food supplies are not always local—and how *local* is defined varies by regional ecology and economic organization. At its inception, GATT's Article XI included food security provisions that permitted member nations to implement "export prohibitions or restrictions temporarily applied to prevent or relieve critical shortages of foodstuffs or other products essential to the exporting contracting party."[30]

In the Uruguay Round, however, the United States challenged this provision on the grounds of the superior efficiency of free world markets in food:

> The U.S. has always maintained that self-sufficiency and food security are not one and the same. Food security—the ability to acquire the food you need when you need it—is best provided through a smooth-functioning world market. . . . In the food security context, we have also proposed that the permission to restrict or inhibit exports of agricultural food products to relieve critical food shortage be removed from Article XI.[31]

This global conception of food security stems from the superior position of U.S. farm exports in the world economy. But it is more than a market superiority; it is backed by the institutional legacies of the postwar international food regime and the green power strategy. The 1985 U.S. Farm Bill continued this goal of reorganizing the world food market by drastically cheapening prices of U.S. agro-exports. In 1986, Agricultural Secretary John Block remarked:

> The push by some developing countries to become more self-sufficient in food may be reminiscent of a bygone era. These countries could save money by importing food from the United States. . . . The U.S. has used the World Bank to back up this policy, going so far as making the dismantling of farmer support programs a condition for loans, as is the case for Morocco's support for their domestic cereal producers.[32]

This is a remarkably clear statement of the viewpoint, and practice, of global economic management. This view depends, of course, on the existence of breadbasket regions and/or the organization of global provisioning by transnational food companies. From a North/South perspective, global thinking such as this aims to subordinate Southern states to global/Northern institutions; indeed, some perceive globalism as a process of "recolonization."[33] However, globalism goes beyond the North/South divide in this respect. It also demands universal trade liberalization.

Since the mid-1980s, the universal reach of trade liberalization has driven the U.S. demands for trade freedom, especially with South Korea and Japan, but also including Taiwan, Singapore, Hong Kong, Thailand, Indonesia, India, and Brazil. Deploying the Super-301 clause of the 1988 trade act, which allows the United States to retaliate against states it deems to be practicing unfair trade, the United States put tremendous trade pressure on South Korea and Japan to open up their heavily protected rice sectors. Rice protection created a price differential of roughly 1 to 7 between world-market and domestic East Asian prices. To the free trader, this is economic inefficiency. But, as we saw above, price differentials ignore additional inputs, or externalities, not to mention domestic food security.

In both Japan and South Korea, rice has traditionally been a sacred cultural symbol, and in the postwar era it has also symbolized national food security. The dilemma for them is that they are both super-exporters of manufactured goods. They need to optimize their access to world markets for these goods, so it was only a matter of time before the logic of liberalizing rice markets would triumph. But this liberalization requires dislocating both a long-standing self-sufficiency in rice and a form of paddy farming that is environmentally constructive.[34]

Freedom of enterprise under a GATT regime. Under the terms of the Uruguay Round, trade liberalization means more than the freer movement of goods, especially since much of this movement is intra-firm transfer. Liberalization includes three other key issues: (1) ensuring freedom of investments by eliminating local regulation of foreign investment, such as specifications of how much local content and equity should be involved in such investments; (2) ensuring freedom of trade in services, a rapidly growing area of foreign investment where, for example, global banks purchase local banks; and (3) ensuring freedom of intellectual property rights—protection of technological licenses from imitation and protection of corporate patents across national borders.

All in all, the GATT regime codifies new spheres of *global economic activity*, with new regulations that would streamline the global economy largely for the benefit of global firms. For example, when global corporations extend patents over seeds, they potentially monopolize genetic resources developed by local communities of producers over centuries of cultural experimentation. It is not surprising that Indian farmers have strongly protested corporate intentions to use the GATT regime for seed patenting, which removes local control over genetic resources. In early 1993, the Karnataka Farmers Union in Bangalore protested against the patenting intentions of Cargill Seeds, demanding preservation of the law against patents on all life forms in the Indian Patent Act (1970). This action was followed by a demonstration in Delhi of 40,000 farmers, protesting against "gene theft" and the GATT proposals.[35]

These events are mirrored by African farmers' concern that if firms can patent traditional seed stock, farmers planting traditional crops that their families have cultivated for centuries may be liable for patent infringement.[36] Cause for this concern came as firms such as I.C. Industries and Pioneer Hi-bred sought licensing rights to use a gene from an African cowpea. When inserted into crops like corn and soybeans, this gene increases pest resistance. As the Rural Advancement Foundation International (RAFI) asked: "The question is, who are the inventors? [The scientists] who isolated the gene? Or West African farmers who identified the value of the plant holding the gene and then developed and protected it?"[37]

The World Trade Organization

A major outcome of the GATT Uruguay Round was the creation of the World Trade Organization (WTO) in 1995. This organization, with 117 voting members, assumes unprecedented power to enforce GATT provisions. The WTO has independent jurisdiction, like the United Nations, and oversees trade in manufactures, agriculture, services, investment, and intellectual property protection. The rules it administers reflect the power of the free market/transnational corporation lobby in the global economy. Whereas earlier any state could ignore a GATT ruling, the WTO's rules are binding on all members.[38] That is, it has global governing powers.

The WTO has an integrated dispute settlement mechanism. If a state is perceived to be violating free trade obligations in one area, such as curbing investments in timber cutting to protect a forest, it can be disciplined through the application of sanctions against another area of economic activity, such as some of its manufactured exports. Member states can lodge such complaints through the WTO, whose decision holds automatically unless every member of the WTO votes to reverse it.[39]

The WTO has the potential to overrule state and local powers in regulating environmental, product, and food safety. As an example of this potential of a WTO overruling, a GATT body ruled in 1991 that the U.S. Marine Mammal Protection Act of 1972, which prohibits imports of tuna caught in drift nets that kill large numbers of dolphins, was an "illegal trade barrier" and therefore should be reversed. Further, the international standards for food safety are set by Codex Alimentarius, a U.N. group with near majority representation from food, chemical, and agribusiness companies as well as representatives from consumer and health groups. One standard recommended by Codex was the use of chemicals long banned in the United States; in particular, it allows up to 50 times the residues of DDT permitted under U.S. laws in grains, meat, and dairy products.[40]

The WTO can require nations to alter such domestic laws to bring them in line with its provisions, overriding national regulatory powers. Furthermore, the WTO staff are unelected bureaucrats, who answer to no constituency other than an abstract set of free trade rules. Their proceedings are secret, denying citizen participation. In other words, citizens are excluded from making and evaluating policy. In its confidential bureaucratic guise, such global authority displays a clear preference for the universal rule of the market over the individual rule of states. This is a remarkable development: states, the historical site of democratic politics, potentially become the instruments of abstract rules.

In this sense, the WTO expresses the essence of the globalization project, even though its implementation is hardly complete. In this arrangement, global managers assume extraordinary powers to manage the web of global economic relations lying across the states, at the expense of those state organizations, including their democratic achievements. What is so remarkable is that the reach of real economic globalization itself is so limited in terms of the populations it *includes,* and yet its impact is so extensive. The impact is extensive precisely because states have been absorbed into the project. Just as nation-states were the ideal vehicle of the development project, so restructured states convey the globalization project to their populations. Such restructuring of political authority is multilayered, however, as it includes a macro-regional dimension between states and global managers.

Regional Free Trade Agreements

The macro-regional dimension of the globalization project lies in the recent spread of free trade agreements (FTAs). These are agreements among neighboring countries to reform trade and investment rules governing their economic intercourse. Free trade agreements range from the North American FTA (known as NAFTA and including originally Canada, the United States, and Mexico) to the Southern Cone of Latin America, where Brazil, Uruguay, Argentina, and Paraguay participate in the Mercosur Treaty. There is the South African Development Community, including Angola, Botswana, Lesotho, Malawi, Mozambique, Namibia, South Africa, Swaziland, Zambia, and Zimbabwe, and the so-called northern growth triangle linking southern Thailand with four Malaysian provinces and northern Sumatra in Indonesia. Then there is the South China region, linking Taiwan, Hong Kong, and the Chinese province of Guandong. The emerging mega-regions are NAFTA, centered on the United States; the European Community (EC), centered on Germany; and the Asian Pacific Economic Community (APEC), centered on Japan. They are considered mega-regions because they currently produce about 62 percent of world manufacturing output and 77 percent of world exports.[41]

Regionalist groupings encourage liberal economic reform at an intermediate level within the nation-state system. They subscribe to the global principles of free trade but implement them among neighboring states as a logical, intermediate step. For example, NAFTA was logical for Canada and Mexico, which conduct 70 percent of their trade with the United States.[42] Such a grouping is considered an intermediate step for two reasons: first, because it anticipates globalism through the signing of regional FTAs; and second, because it is a competitive weapon against other regional groupings. In addition, trade blocs represent an alternative to a GATT-type global regime, should it ever really materialize.

As regional integration occurs, states elsewhere may respond with local regional groupings, anticipating the possible exclusion of their exports from other trading blocs. In this sense, regionalism is a defensive, or preemptive, strategy. Much has been written, for example, about the threat to Japanese and U.S. producers of the European Community's attempts to establish a European-wide common market, termed "Fortress Europe," and the resulting movement toward integration in the Asia-Pacific region and the Americas. The United States and Japan conduct 74 percent and 64 percent of their trade, respectively, *outside* their regions. Compare this with a figure of only 30 percent for the EC members and their European Free Trade Association.[43] It was therefore strategic in the early 1990s for the United States and Japan to embrace regional integration as a fallback, should the global free trade movement fracture into regional blocs. However, with Japan running a persistent trade surplus with the United States and the EC, by the mid-1990s the possibility of forming an Atlantic free trade zone, linking North America with Europe, was under investigation.[44]

Regionalism embodies the tensions between global and national authority that exist in the globalization project. It just occurs at a more intermediate, and perhaps a more immediate, level. The European Community has revealed these tensions in its movement toward a common governance in the 1980s, symbolized in the rejection by Danish voters of the Treaty of Maastricht in 1992. When the secrecy of the technocratic decision making behind the formation of the European Union (EU) was challenged in the European Court of Justice in Luxembourg, lawyers for the European Council of Ministers responded by stating that "there is no principle of community law which gives citizens the right to EU documents." As one observer argues: "The Treaty of Maastricht seeks to create a supranational, centralized, bureaucratic state—a homogenized union. It would destroy the pillars on which Europe was built—its nations. . . . The strength of the European Parliament and the [European] Commission is in inverse proportion to that of the national democratic institutions."[45] This question of national sovereignty is explored in the following case study.

CASE STUDY

NAFTA and the Question of Sovereignty

The North American Free Trade Association (NAFTA), founded in 1994, has generated a continuing debate about the implications of regional rules for local sovereignty. NAFTA is an unelected and confidential bureaucratic entity, which regulates flows of goods, services, and capital between the three member nations (Canada, the United States, and Mexico) according to abstract market rules rather than national and subnational decisions. In effect, like GATT, national and local regulations regarding health, labor, and environmental standards are subjected to the rules of freedom of trade. For example, NAFTA rules proposed that the United States could not limit imports of a product based on its production method (child or unprotected labor, or environmentally damaging practices such as drift netting for tuna).

NAFTA formalized a decade-long process of turning the Mexican political economy inside out. The real erosion of national sovereignty occurred as the Mexican state restructured prior to gaining acceptance into the free trade agreement. The structural adjustment programs of the debt regime laid the groundwork by liberalizing markets and privatizing enterprise.

In Mexico, in a World Bank/IMF-proclaimed model privatization, more than 80 percent of the 1,555 companies run by the government were sold or dissolved during the 1980s to pay the country's debt and appease Bank managers by demonstrating a commitment to liberalization. Although many of these were inefficient, their sale enriched the fabled 13 wealthy families of Mexico and eliminated employment and services for tens of thousands of other Mexicans. As Mexican export composition shifted from oil to manufactured goods, 85 percent of which crossed the northern border, the Mexican government secured this export relation by depressing wages further—a decline of 60 percent since 1976—and signing a series of agreements to preempt U.S. protectionism. Average Mexican tariffs fell from 27 percent to 8 percent between 1982 and 1992, agricultural subsidies were reduced, infrastructural investments in rural areas were cut by 65 percent between 1981 and 1989, and regulations were relaxed on foreign ownership of land.

Preparation for NAFTA, then, was a decade-long process of establishing Mexico's liberal credentials at the expense of its national economic coherence and its poorer majority. In the debates leading up to the signing of NAFTA, the opposition presidential candidate, Cuauhtémoc Cárdenas, argued that "exploitation of cheap labor, energy, and raw materials, technological dependency, and lax environmental protection should not be the premises upon which Mexico establishes links with the United States, Canada and the world economy."

On the other side, a GATT director endorsed Mexican progress since joining GATT in 1986: "Mexico is one of the new trading powers of the world that has helped to maintain the pace for bringing about an ambitious reform of the world trading system." In other words, Mexico has been a model state, anchoring the implementation of a global free trade regime. The globalization project is deeply rooted in the Mexican reforms, and vice versa.

NAFTA did not decree thoroughgoing opening of the Mexican economy. For example, Mexico agreed to allow foreign banks to enter the country gradually, permitting them to obtain up to a 15 percent share by 1999; it also reserved exemptions for several state enterprises, including railroads and satellite operations. But the 1994 debt crisis in Mexico, stemming from the preparations for NAFTA over the past decade, compelled the Mexican government in 1995 to try to raise funds by allowing 100 percent ownership of Mexican financial institutions and selling off its railroads and its satellite operations. In this sense, regional agreements are intertwined with the same processes that make up the globalization project.

Sources: DePalma, 1993; Barkin, 1991, p. 35; Schwedel, 1991, p. 25; Schwedel & Haley, 1992, pp. 54–55; Fenley, 1991, p. 41; Resource Center Bulletin, 1993, p. 2; Fidler & Bransten, 1995.

The Globalization Project as a Utopia

The development project was an ideal that some say was a confidence trick or an illusion because the world economy has always rested on an exploited base, or periphery;[46] others say it was a success because it was never intended to be absolute.

> Some critics make the mistake of proclaiming that development has failed. It hasn't. Development as historically conceived and officially practised has been a huge success. It sought to integrate the upper echelons, say ten to

forty per cent, of a given third world population into the international, westernized, consuming classes and the global market economy. This it has accomplished brilliantly.[47]

Whatever the case, it is clear that the development project was a process wherein states *attempted* to manage national economic integration, but the integration was often incomplete. This was because the process of development often spread benefits unequally. It was also because segments of the domestic economy were either absorbed into, or marginalized by, the growing global reach of new commodity chains. In either case, states often exploited weaker communities in their hinterlands (such as forest dwellers or peasant villages displaced by dams), justifying this action in the name of national development. Global financiers and firms funded this activity, as we have seen. In short, large social segments of the Third World remained on the margins or experienced dislocation as the development project took hold.

The globalization project is essentially similar. Indeed, as our case studies have suggested, if there was a national integrating trend under the development project, there appears to be a disintegrating trend at the national level under the globalization project because of an integrating trend at the global level. This is not necessarily a homogeneous integration. Although it is certainly true that more people across the world now consume standardized products, it is also true that the people who produce these products do so under quite diverse labor conditions. Any integrating trends in the composition of labor under twentieth-century forms of national capitalism are reversing as economic globalization deepens.

We know that the recent history of formation of Western welfare states rested on a common organizing drive by the working classes of those nations, demanding adequate wages, job and employment protections, the right to organize into unions, and a voice in national politics.[48] This trend has subsided recently as industrial restructuring, offshore investment, public works downsizing, labor demobilization, and rising unemployment have swept across the First World. The other side of this process has involved, as we have seen, the incorporation of new labor forces across the world into commodity chains of global production. Peasant contractors, *maquila* workers, child labor, casual female and male labor, sweatshop work, plantation labor, homework, and even slave labor constitute a quite heterogeneous tapestry of labor in the global economy. And with transnational corporations using global sourcing employment and countries cutting back the national work force, employment insecurity rises across the world. In short, the world market standardizes consumption but differentiates production and disorganizes producing communities.

If this is in fact the dominant scenario under the globalization project, likely to become more tenuous with further social and national disintegration, then the globalization project looks more and more like a utopia itself. The point of thinking about it this way is to emphasize that the globalization project, like the development project, is likely an unrealizable ideal on two counts. First, as suggested, the expectations do not square with the reality in which either project is pursued. Neither nation-states nor world community is singularly composed of market-oriented individuals: there are class, gender, and ethnic relations that divide people to begin with. There is a historical context in which some regions are more equal than others. And there are powerful institutional forces that actually organize and reorganize markets, with profits rather than social welfare in mind. Second, as we see in Chapter 7, there are social movements in the world, of various ideological hues, and state organizations that actively resist and/or qualify the globalization project. Many of these movements reject belief in the self-regulating global market as the most logical principle of social organization. Some movements aim to protect their communities by reregulating the market; others see withdrawing from the market as the most satisfactory form of resistance. Whatever the alternatives, the globalization project is only one way, albeit the most powerful we have seen, of reorganizing the world.

The globalization project is the most powerful force so far, in part because it has not had to confront its contradictory effects in any fundamental way. Some of these effects are spelled out in the following chapter. But one effect is already causing alarm in the inner circles of global management: the fragility of the world monetary system. The United States is the most indebted state in the world, but to date it has avoided having to tighten its financial belt under the kinds of conditions laid down by the International Monetary Fund during the debt regime. The United States is arguably the most powerful member of the multilateral financial community, and the dollar standard still holds, even though Japan holds the majority of the world's financial reserves. In 1994, a group called the Bretton Woods Commission, headed by former Federal Reserve Board chairman Paul Volcker, suggested that the world monetary system required overhauling and that this implied bringing all countries (including the United States) under IMF discipline.

The Bretton Woods Commission reported that, since "the early 1970s, long-term growth in the major industrialized countries has been cut in half, from about 5% a year to about 2.5% a year."[49] The reason for this was the instability of exchange rates. (Recall that President Nixon removed the dollar from gold parity in 1971, leading to fluctuating exchange rates.)

Where exchange rates fluctuate, currency speculation flourishes. This change results in resource misallocation, such as endless financial mergers, which cultivate an uncertain business climate. Such "financialization," rather than productive investment, explains the mixed record of economic growth over the last quarter of a century.[50]

Although the G-7 countries have attempted to stabilize the system, the Commission continued: "There has been no reliable long-term global approach to coordinating policy, stabilizing market expectations, and preventing extreme volatility and misalignments among the key currencies."[51] Confirmation of this volatility came the following year, 1995, when the American dollar went into a free-fall against the Japanese yen. The trade war between the United States and Japan intensified, and the members of the G-7 experienced great discomfort as President Clinton's government allowed the dollar considerable space to fall.

In the same year, the perception of a growing possibility that an international discipline might be imposed on the United States provoked a deadly bomb attack on a U.S. federal government office building in Oklahoma City, allegedly by a citizen militia group anxious to stem such a challenge to U.S. sovereignty. The point of this story is that the globalization project contains some powerful tensions. State, or national, sovereignty may have a hard shell in the United States, home of the ideal of national self-determination.

Whereas the United States may be in the driver's seat in the globalization project in general, as it was in the development project, its seating arrangement is only as good as the willingness of the world to use the dollar, or its own willingness to assert its military superiority globally. We can only speculate on how the globalization project, as a new organizing principle for the world, will play out. In the meantime, in June 1995 the G-7 powers created a worldwide emergency fund to bail out states on the verge of national bankruptcy. The United States, along with its European allies, pursued this initiative to stabilize the world monetary system. It had three essential aspects. The first was to shift the burden of such bailouts from the United States, which bore the brunt of the Mexican bailout of 1994. The second was an expectation that the prosperous Asian countries would underwrite the fund with their financial surpluses—in effect a way of redistributing the world's financial wealth so that money would continue to make the world go around. Finally, the third involved a plan to establish an "improved early warning system" based on comprehensive public disclosure by member states of financial information (such as foreign exchange reserves) hitherto confidential—using IMF leverage to deepen financial surveillance of the system at large.[52]

Summary

This chapter has recounted how the development project incubated a new direction in the world capitalist order, which hatched during the 1980s debt crisis. This new direction is the globalization project, an alternative way of organizing economic growth that corresponds to the growing scale and power of the transnational banks and corporations. The increasing volume of economic exchanges and the greater mobility of money and firms require forms of regulation beyond the reach of the nation-state.

All markets have institutional supports. That is, they require certain kinds of political and social regulation to work. When monetary exchanges began to govern European productive activity in the nineteenth century and industrial labor markets emerged, central banks and state bureaucracies stepped in to regulate and protect the value and rights of these flows of money and labor, respectively. Markets in money and labor could not work automatically. Similarly, when global money markets became dominant in the 1970s and then the flows of credit needed to be protected in the 1980s, the International Monetary Fund stepped in to regulate the value of international currency.

The new global regulatory system subordinated states' labor protections to financial credit protection. This new balance of power marked the transition from the development project to the globalization project. Indebted states remained viable regulators of market exchanges, but only through agreeing to restructure their institutions and their priorities. They were turned inside out; that is, they downgraded their social functions of subsidizing education, health, food prices, producer credit, and other social services and beefed up their financial and commercial export ministries. Overall, with variation according to capacity and indebtedness, states became surrogate managers of the global economy. These tendencies are also replicated in regional free trade agreements, which express goals similar to those of the globalization project.

The imposition of austerity measures by indebted governments deepened inequalities within their societies. Their surrender of public capacity yielded power to global institutions. Economic liberalization and currency devaluation heightened competition among states for credit and investment, consolidating Third World disunity. Structural adjustment programs required the reduction of social infrastructure, privatization of public enterprise, and deregulation of protective laws regarding foreign investment, national banking, and trade policy. And so were laid the foundations for the new globalization project, the components of which are summarized in the following insert.

What Are the Elements of the Globalization Project?

The globalization project combines several strands: (1) an emerging consensus among policy makers favoring market-based rather than state-managed development strategies; (2) centralized management of global market rules by the G-7 states; (3) implementation of these rules by the multilateral agencies: the World Bank, the IMF, and the WTO; (4) concentration of market power in the hands of transnational corporations and financial power in the hands of transnational banks; (5) subordination of former Second and Third World states to these global institutional forces; and (6) subordination of First World states to these global institutional forces—a subordination as yet by no means as severe as in the former two Worlds, in part because First World societies have more institutional and political coherence, so a smaller proportion of their population is marginalized.

The standardized prescriptions for liberalization reorganize regions and locales: from the removal of Mexican *campesinos* from long-held public lands, through the rapid dismantling of public ownership of the economies of Eastern Europe, to the proliferation of export processing zones and agro-export platforms. Many of these mushrooming export sites suffer the instability of flexible strategies of "footloose" firms, as they pick and choose their way among global sourcing sites. Social protections decline as communities lose their resource bases (as forests dwindle) or their employment bases (as firms downsize or move offshore).

Under these conditions, globalization is everything but universalist in its consequences. It assigns communities, regions, and nation-states new niches or specialized roles (including marginalization) in the global economy. The development project proposed social integration through national economic growth under individual state supervision. Alternatively, the globalization project offers new forms of authority and discipline according to the laws of the market. Whether these forms of authority and discipline are based in global institutions like the World Trade Organization or in national institutions managing the global marketplace within their territories, they perform the governance functions of the globalization project.

6

The Globalization Project in Action

There are two sides to the globalization project: (1) the goal of global economic growth, managed by advocates of the free market ideal, and (2) the untidy social reality generated in the wake of the development project and the emerging globalization project. The process of global integration is not unproblematic. It transforms social structures and introduces new, undemocratic forms of governance, where whole populations lose any formal representation in decisions about their material future. Development may be thought of as an economic process, but it is also profoundly political.

In this chapter we consider some of the social effects of global integration that have the most substantial impact on our future. These are (1) a growing global labor surplus, including global migrations of labor; (2) intensified informalization of economic activity; and (3) the crisis of governmental legitimacy at the national level. Although these three effects could be considered the *underside* of globalization, they have important long-term implications. Some of these provide the stimulus to the oppositional social movements examined in Chapter 7. Here we document the structural trends that accompany the globalization project, beginning with the labor surplus.

A Global Labor Surplus

In the shadow of globalization lurks a rising dilemma: the redundancy of labor. For example, in France the GNP grew by 80 percent between 1973 and 1993, but unemployment grew from 420,000 to 5.1 million.[1] Two major trends seem to contribute to labor redundancy, one secular and the other cyclical. The *secular* or linear trend is the ongoing process of "depeasantization." The process that expelled peasants from the land and forced them to migrate to urban centers has, of course, been occurring for centuries. But it has accelerated outside the First World since the post–World War II era, as more and more areas of land and forest are absorbed into the global marketplace. The resulting pools of labor create the low-cost zones sought out by firms in their global sourcing operations. Secular growth in labor productivity, without a matching reduction of the working day/week/year, also expels some workers from production.

The *cyclical* trend is the instability of employment under competitive capitalist production systems and competitive labor markets. As firms re-tool or go out of business, they shed labor. Private enterprise systems do not guarantee alternative employment, although during the era of welfare capitalism governments established various safety nets. As the world moves (backward) to competitive capitalism, these safety nets are fraying.

Globalization combines these trends. As peasant farmers lose markets to cheaper imported foods or surrender their land to larger commercial agro-export operations, they flood the towns and cities looking for work. When barriers to trade and investment fall, the cheaper labor these peasants can provide attracts foreign investment as firms scour the world, or the region, to reduce production costs. The following case study of Mexican *campesinos* illustrates this trend.

CASE STUDY

The Mexican *Campesino* Shapes the Global Labor Force

Of the more than 500,000 workers in the Mexican *maquiladoras*, roughly 70 percent moved there from the countryside during the 1980s. The border region is a low-wage enclave; wages there were lower in 1993 than were Mexican industrial wages in 1981, even though productivity rose 41 percent during the same period. The implication is that the mere presence of such a labor pool depresses wages, and we know that the Mexican government enforced low wages in its preparation to join NAFTA. A further implication is that a low-wage enclave can have an eroding effect on a higher-wage system once firms are free to relocate. Harley Shaiken observed that "Mexican plants achieving U.S. productivity levels at one-seventh the wages offer a powerful incentive for many U.S. firms to relocate production or lower their labor costs by threatening to move or both."

The border region of Mexico, according to Shaiken, has become "almost a 51st state in terms of production" as the automation of *maquiladoras* has proceeded. In the state of Chihuahua in 1993, the Ford engine plant paid assemblers $1.55 an hour (compared with $17.38 in the United States) and skilled workers $2.87

an hour (compared with $20.21 across the border). The trend of substituting semi-automated assembly in Chihuahua for fully automated assembly in the American Midwest is illustrated by Ford's moving the manufacturing of dashboard gauges from a factory in Saline, Michigan, to a *maquiladora* in Chihuahua, which Ford named Altec. This *maquiladora* has a labor force of 3,000 producing radios and other car parts, with 700 people producing dashboard gauges, replacing 400 Michigan workers.

One consequence of this process is a stratification of Mexican industrial workers, as wages for some auto work on the border drift up with rising skill levels—on the order of a 40 percent increase between 1990 and 1994, even though the pay differential across the border is still more than 6 to 1. While the border region acts as a magnet for jobs in the United States, the automation process south of the border has its own local job-displacing effect. The mayor of the city of Chihuahua claimed in 1993: "I would say that the unemployment rate in the city has risen to 8 percent or more, double what it was three years ago. This does not include housewives who worked and now don't. We don't count them as unemployed."

Sources: Shaiken, 1993; Uchitelle, 1993b; Harper, 1994.

In a global marketplace, where products must meet global standards, producers all across the world must conform. In the former Third World, this may mean leapfrogging a phase of industrialization to remain competitive. The manager of an African textile mill explained why the mill was so automated:

[It is] because African labor, unused to industrial work, would make mistakes, whereas automated machinery does not make mistakes. The quality standards demanded today are such that my product must be perfect to be able to find a market. . . . Surely my task is to eliminate the human factor.[2]

The Role of Free Trade Agreements in the Race to the Bottom

The free trade agreement (FTA) tends to merge national labor forces into a global labor force. Labor costs vary within and across national arenas, depending on local historical conditions. In the U.S./Mexican comparison, there is variation between an industrial or service-based post-industrial society and a semi-industrial society. Their unification into a single market includes mature labor forces and first-generation wage laborers from rural communities. The wage differential is enormous. On the other hand, between Canada and the United States, which signed an FTA in 1988, the differential is the social wage—the Canadian system having a more comprehensive social security system than the United States. In the United States, for example, approximately two-thirds of the more than 8 million unemployed in 1986 received no compensation.[3]

In both cases, United States/Mexico and Canada/United States, free trade has a harmonizing effect on policies regarding levels of wages and social services. "Harmonization" means reducing the differential in the direction of the minimal standard, given the competitive advantage of the lower-cost regions. This process is known as downward leveling, or "the race to the bottom."[4] It was clearly articulated by the former president of the Canadian Manufacturer's Association, J. Laurent Thibault:

> As we remove trade restrictions and move more and more towards an open flow of goods, it is obvious that we reduce the degree of political independence in Canada. There is nothing sinister in that. It is simply a fact that, as we ask our industries to compete toe to toe with American industry under a full free product flow basis, we in Canada are obviously forced to create the same conditions in Canada that exist in the US, whether it is the unemployment insurance scheme, Workmen's Compensation, the cost of government, the level of taxation, or whatever . . . and that means that we would have less freedom to create in Canada an environment that is very much different from that which exists in the United States.[5]

From the U.S. side, the harmonization process is also at work. Industries that shift to Mexico are those in which women are disproportionately employed, such as apparel, consumer electronics, and food processing. Many of these women entered the work force in the late 1970s and 1980s because families could no longer get by on a single wage. Once their already low-wage jobs move south, the possibility lessens for these women to find equivalent work. The pressure on family livelihood increases. The general downward pressure on the U.S. wage heightens as Mexico's cheaper labor comes on line.

Consequences within the United States are further declines in real wages (a clear trend since 1972), rising poverty rates, increased family stress and social disorder, rising public health costs, and so on. The foundations of social cohesion crack. A study issued in 1995, entitled *Families in Focus,* found that family decay is worldwide; this situation is attributed largely to the trend of women assuming a greater role as income earners. These jobs are usually inferior, requiring longer hours of work than men's work and leading to new stresses in households.[6]

Proposed retraining schemes to help American workers adjust to a shifting employment scene are often ineffectual. Indeed, the United States Labor Department issued a report in November 1993 evaluating a long-standing $200 million annual program for retraining manufacturing workers who lost their jobs to foreign trade. It concluded

> that only 19 percent of the "retrained" workers found jobs that demanded their new skills and paid at least 80 percent of their former wages; 20 percent remained jobless; most of the rest sank into low-wage slots that they occupied for just eight months. In Buffalo [New York], once a manufacturing power-house, formerly unionized steel and auto workers now compete for openings in the top employment categories of retail salesperson, office clerk, waiter, janitor or maid, secretary and food-counter worker. More people have jobs than ever before in that region's history, but deskilling, not reskilling, is the trend, as 86 percent of all new jobs there are in services paying an average of $5.60 an hour.[7]

Retraining is likely to be ineffectual when governments surrender the prerogative to regulate investment and labor markets to global market forces. In the global marketplace, product cycles are unstable, as consumer fashions and sourcing sites change relentlessly. The loss of jobs is not simply an economic transfer from one nation to another; more fundamentally, it represents the "hollowing out" of a nation's economic base and the erosion of social institutions that stabilize the conditions of employment and habitat associated with those jobs. A century of institution-building in labor markets, in corporate/union relations, and in communities can disappear overnight when the winds of the market are allowed to blow across uneven national boundaries. Those who have work find they are often working longer hours to make ends meet, despite remarkable technological advances.

Structural Unemployment in the Global Economy

Structural unemployment, where redundant workers cease rotating into new labor markets, has grown dramatically in the centers of the global economy since the 1960s. One cause is automation, a tactic of competitive advantage pursued by firms in the global marketplace. In the United States between 1980 and 1985, about 2.3 million manufacturing jobs disappeared as robotization spread. The other cause of structural unemployment is the competition from offshore export zones. This competition for unskilled labor began in the late 1960s in the textile, apparel, furniture, rubber, and plastic industries and then moved to the more skilled industries such as shipbuilding, steel, machinery, and services by the 1980s.[8]

Around 65,300 U.S. footwear jobs disappeared between 1982 and 1989. Part of the reason was that during this time Nike stopped making athletic shoes in the United States, relocating most of its production to South Korea and Indonesia. In the early 1990s, a worker, usually female, in the footwear industry in Indonesia earned $1.03 per day compared to an average wage in the U.S. footwear industry of $6.94 per *hour*.[9]

Under competition from cheap labor overseas, core industries in the United States and the United Kingdom had lost the power to set wages and stimulate local supplier industries by the late 1970s. By the mid-1980s, the same decline was occurring in Japan.[10] This loss of core function was part of the industrial hollowing-out phenomenon. Some Japanese manufacturing had shifted offshore to Southeast Asia, as Japan increasingly supplied components and production machinery, such as robots, to other countries for use in final product assembly. Japan, too, is becoming a high-tech economy specializing in services and information-based industries. These trends are indicators of postindustrialism, explained in the following insert.

What Is Postindustrialism?

Postindustrialism describes a society that has moved beyond its industrial phase of economic growth and social development. Services now predominate as the major economic activity. These include public and private work, referred to as "people-processing" work by C. Wright Mills in his classic sociological work, *White Collar*, which addresses the decline of blue-collar work in the United States in the 1950s. Services include clerical work, retailing, health care, restaurant work, finance, and education. The assumption is that the society is sufficiently technologically advanced that only a small proportion of the labor force is employed in agriculture and industry. Three puzzles are associated with the idea of postindustrialism: (1) Have industrial jobs moved offshore? (2) Because some postindustrial jobs, such as data processing and insurance processing, have also moved offshore, where does this leave us? (3) Why are many of the new postindustrial jobs, often referred to as "pink-collar" work, so low paying and impermanent?

Whether postindustrial services (retailing, health care, restaurants, finance, security) are the basis of future economic expansion is hotly debated. Some see many service jobs as inferior to manufacturing jobs, whereas others argue that service jobs such as design and sales are generated by manufacturing systems as they become more sophisticated.[11] Service employment is not, however, immune to relocation. Many new jobs in the Caribbean, for example, are data processing jobs that large U.S. insurance, health industry, magazine subscription renewal, consumer credit, and retailing firms have shifted offshore at a lower cost. Swissair recently transferred all its revenue accounting to Bombay, and many U.S. software firms subcontract labor-intensive programming to Bangalore.[12]

Since 1970, manufacturing employment has fallen 50 percent in Britain, 8 percent in the United States, 18 percent in France, and 17 percent in Germany, although most of these jobs were in "low-tech" industries, such as footwear, textiles, and metals.[13] This hollowing-out of First World industrial bases intensified under the debt regime. Deflationary conditions to the south slowed economic growth rates and middle-income consumption, thereby reducing imports from the First World. Overall, the growth rate of world exports to the former Third World fell from 7.9 percent to –0.2 percent between 1969–1981 and 1981–1988.[14]

One solution would be to pursue a form of global Keynesianism, wherein public monies are redistributed across the world to stimulate public employment that would counterbalance falling productive investments and stimulate new purchasing power. This idea informed the failed New International Economic Order (NIEO) initiative in the 1970s. But the idea is presently preempted by the pervasive belief that minimizing public investment and allowing the market to work its magic is the proper course. Britain offers such an example. After a decade of conservative government restructuring of the British labor force (weakening union rights, eliminating minimum wages, reducing jobless benefits), Britain in the 1990s became a new site for offshore investment from Europe—mostly in part-time jobs (electronic assembly, apparel, clerical tasks) undertaken by women at considerably lower wages than would be paid in Europe.[15] Typically, "Third World" working conditions are just as likely to appear in the global centers under the policy of economic liberalism. Garment sweatshops are a recurring phenomenon, for example, in New York City, and a range of "Third World" jobs has spread in First World cities over the past two decades.[16] This process is further advanced in the United States, which, unlike European states, has allowed companies to hire part-time employees without traditional full benefits, thus creating millions of new jobs.[17]

Meanwhile, in the former Third World, over half the labor force was unemployed or underemployed in the 1980s.[18] In the early 1990s, the count approached approximately 1 billion, according to estimates by the International Labor Organization. In the Organization for Economic Cooperation and Development (OECD) countries, approximately 35 million people were officially unemployed in 1993. In the ex-Communist countries of Eastern Europe, the proportion of unemployed was more than double that in the OECD countries. In the United States, where 60 percent of new jobs were part time, President Clinton acknowledged a "global crisis of unemployment." He added: "All the advanced nations are having difficulty creating new jobs, even when their economies are growing. . . . We have to figure out how to unlock the doors for people who are left behind in this new global economy."[19]

Arguably, the problem is that the new global economy habitually leaves people behind, as jobs are automated, shed, or relocated under the competitive pressure of the global marketplace. Competition compels firms not only to go global, but to keep their sourcing flexible and, therefore, their suppliers—and their workers—guessing. The women's wear retailer Liz Claiborne, which divides its sources mainly among the United States, Hong Kong, South Korea, Taiwan, the Philippines, China, and Brazil, claims: "The Company does not own any manufacturing facilities: all of its products are manufactured through arrangements with independent suppliers. . . . The Company does not have any long-term, formal arrangements with any of the suppliers which manufacture its products."[20]

Legacies of First World Labor Importing

Labor redundancy on such a grand scale contributes to social disorder across the world, as restructuring and relocation of firms destabilize organized labor markets, industrial districts, and human habitats. The quickened movement of the global economy stratifies populations across, rather than simply within, national borders. With provocative imagery, Jacques Attali, former president of the European Bank for Reconstruction and Development, distinguishes *rich nomads* ("consumer-citizens of the world's privileged regions") from *poor nomads* ("boat people on a planetary scale"). In a gloomy projection in the wake of the "lost decade," Attali suggests:

> In restless despair, the hopeless masses of the periphery will witness the spectacle of another hemisphere's growth. Particularly in those regions of the South that are geographically contiguous and culturally linked to the North— places such as Mexico, Central America, or North Africa—millions of people will be tempted and enraged by the constant stimulation of wants that can't be satisfied. . . . With no future of their own in an age of air travel and telecommunications, the terminally impoverished will look for one in the North. . . . The movement of peoples has already begun; only the scale will grow: Turks in Berlin, Moroccans in Madrid, Indians in London, Mexicans in Los Angeles, Puerto Ricans and Haitians in New York, Vietnamese in Hong Kong.[21]

Such latent fears, founded in stereotypes, underlie the concern of the global managers and the First World "consumer citizens" to stem the tide of global labor migration. During the NAFTA debate, one study claimed that failure to implement NAFTA would devastate the Mexican economy to the degree that "at least 500,000 extra migrants would sneak north each year throughout the next decade."[22] A year later, following sharp devaluation of the peso, the Clinton Administration argued that if the United States did not increase the Mexican bailout fund from $9 billion to $40 billion, an additional 430,000 Mexicans would cross the border into Texas and California.[23]

A cursory glance at the First World newspapers of the 1990s confirms the broad anxiety about the ethnic composition of the global labor force, often manifested in outbreaks of racist violence toward "guest workers." This attitude has been particularly manifest in Europe, where 20 million immigrants from other world zones live. It is well to remember that in the postwar development decades states actively promoted the guest worker phenomenon—when European firms needed a cheap labor force while its basic industries were expanding, and when Southwestern U.S. industrial and agribusiness firms needed cheap Mexican labor under the *bracero* program, an official labor immigration policy. Continuing immigration is in the interests of firms needing cheap labor and of privileged people needing servants, even though it has become the focus of cultural backlash and political fear campaigns. The scope of labor migration is the focus of the following case study.

CASE STUDY

The Global Labor Force in Circulation

At the beginning of the 1990s, as many as 80 million people were estimated to be living as expatriate laborers around the world. One Geneva-based journalist observed: "A woman gynecologist from Romania sells bananas in a downtown supermarket here. Polish engineers pick grapes in Swiss alpine vineyards, earning in five weeks what it would take them five months to make at home. Thai bar girls in Tokyo ride the Japanese economic boom together with 700,000 workers from Korea. Expatriates from more than 100 countries work in graying Italy, where Roman matrons connive with Borgian resolve for the services of cleaning women. Among the 2.8 million foreign workers . . . in the Middle East last year were 17,000 Vietnamese. Hundreds of thousands of Indonesians harvest rubber and copra in Malaysia for the same pocketbook reasons that Mexicans pump gasoline in Los Angeles. In Germany, there are more than 1,000 mosques for resident Turkish workers."

Source: Montalbano, 1991, p. F1.

Labor: The New Export

Just as money circulates the globe seeking investment opportunities, so labor increasingly circulates seeking employment opportunities. Migration is of course not new to the late twentieth century. The making of the modern world in particular has involved the unrelenting separation of people from the land. Colonialism propelled migrations of free and unfree people across the world. Between 1810 and 1921, 34 million people, mainly Europeans, emigrated to the United States alone.[24] The difference today is largely one of scale.

During the 1980s, spurred by debt regime restructurings, there was an internal migration in the former Third World of between 300 and 400 million people.[25] This pool of labor, then, contributes to current levels of global migration from overburdened cities to metropolitan regions as it seeks to earn money for families back home. Estimates suggest that roughly 100 million kinfolk depend on remittances of the global labor force. Also spurred by debt, labor export has become a significant foreign currency earner: Filipino overseas earnings are estimated to amount to $3–$5 billion, for example. About 2 million Filipinos work overseas as contract laborers (seamen, carpenters, masons, mechanics, or maids).[26]

The government of the Philippines has a *de facto* labor export policy, which has become an important component of an export-led development strategy.[27] In addition to products, labor is exported, mainly to the oil-rich Middle East, where contractors organize the ebb and flow of foreign labor. One contractor, Northwest Placement, a privately run recruiting agency, receives 5,000 pesos ($181)—the maximum allowed by the Labor Department—from Filipino applicants on assurance of a job; this covers the costs of a medical check, visas, and government clearance fees. Not surprisingly, there are plenty of unlicensed agencies operating also.[28]

The conditions of foreign labor, or guest workers, are often devoid of human rights. Workers in the Gulf states, for example, are indentured, with no civic rights, no choice of alternative jobs, and no recourse against poor employment conditions and low wages—which are determined by the income levels of the country of origin. Migrant workers must surrender their passports on arrival; they reportedly work 12 to 16 hours a day, seven days a week. Governments in the migrant workers' home countries in Asia, dependent on foreign currency earnings, are reportedly resigned to the exploitation of their nationals. International labor union organizations have been ineffectual, especially as Middle Eastern states have united to suppress discussion in international forums of working conditions inside their countries.[29]

The Politics of Global Labor Circulation

In the United States, labor comes from all over the world, principally Mexico (around 60 percent in 1990), Asia (22.1 percent), Europe (7.3 percent), South America (5.6 percent), and Africa (2.3 percent). About 33 percent of the population of Los Angeles County is foreign-born, a number that has tripled since 1970. "Latinos, now 28 percent of California's population, will likely be the majority by 2040."[30] The scale is large enough that immigrants retain their cultural and linguistic traditions rather than assimilate, as they did earlier in the formation of U.S. society. Robert Reich has commented that "the old American 'melting pot' is now cooking a variegated stew, each of whose ingredients maintains a singular taste."[31]

The juxtaposing of distinct cultures in countries to which labor migrates creates this *multicultural* effect. The United States took a turn in this direction in 1965, when the Immigration and Nationality Act Amendments abolished the previous policy of organizing immigration according to the already established patterns of cultural origin. "During the 1950s there were nine times as many European immigrants as there were Asians. Following the passage of the new Immigration Act, the proportions were sharply reversed."[32] However, in the context of economic restructuring in the United States, a heightened "nativism" is appearing—a local backlash in response to the economic, social, and cultural uncertainties associated with this trend. Since 1965, the polled percentage of Americans objecting to immigration has almost doubled—from 33 percent to 60 percent.[33] The following case study examines the effects of one particular immigrant group in France.

Increasingly, given the scale of labor migration, minority cultures are forming identifiable communities in their new labor sites, maintaining a certain distance from the local culture. The inhabitants of these "transnational communities" have regular contact with their sending countries and other migrant communities through modern electronic communication (e-mail, fax), transportation, and media developments; they establish their own cultural beachhead within the host society. Such communities may engage in what Benedict Anderson has referred to as "long-distance nationalism"; they are activists residing in an immigrant community but involved politically in their country of origin.[34] Such offshore activities distort politics in the countries of origin.

The circulation of cultures of labor binds the world through multiculturalism. However, the conditions in which labor circulation has intensified have made multiculturalism a fragile ideal. Labor export arrangements deny rights and representation to the migrant work force. Deteriorating economies and communities in the centers of the global

CASE STUDY

Dilemmas of Multiculturalism in France

In France, the question of multiculturalism has been tested recently with the growing presence, and fundamentalism, of the 3.5 million Muslims living in that country. Muslims comprise a quarter of the total immigrant population (mostly from European countries). Their presence stems from French policy to import large numbers of North African men for factory and construction work from the 1960s through 1974, after which families were allowed to join the men. Arab and African immigrants and their French-born children form an increasingly distinct suburban underclass in French society. The children are referred to in French slang as "beurs," a reversal of the syllables of the French word for Arab. A principal of a Parisian school with a considerable immigrant population remarked in 1993: "In the 1970s and 1980s, we promoted multiculturalism. We had a day of couscous, a day of paella, it was 'vive la différence' much of the time. Now the pendulum is going the other way."

The pendulum change registers the growing number of Muslim immigrants in France, the charge made by the right-wing National Front party that the official number of immigrants is about the same as the number of unemployed workers, and a 1991 poll showing that 77 percent of the French agreed that the million or so "illegal" aliens, mostly African, should be expelled.

Source: Riding, 1993.

---

economy spark exclusionist politics that scapegoat cultural minorities. In the days of the development project, a more inclusive attitude prevailed, rooted in broad-based class movements and political coalitions committed to cultural integration and the redistribution of resources. In the present context, inclusion is threatened by separatist politics. The race to the bottom has profound destabilizing tendencies.

Informal Activity

The globalization project is accompanied by another social process arising from the limits of the development project—a growing culture of informal, or marginal, activity. This culture involves people working on the fringes of the market, performing casual and unregulated labor, working in cooperative arrangements, street vending, or pursuing what are deemed illegal economic activities. This culture did not just appear, however. With the rise of market societies, the boundaries of the formal economy were identified and regulated by the state for tax purposes; but they have always been incomplete and fluid, often by design and certainly by custom. An army of servants and housecleaners, for example, routinely works "off the books." Casual labor has always accompanied small-scale enterprise and even large-scale harvesting operations where labor use is cyclical. Also, a substantial portion of labor performed across the world every day is unpaid labor—such as housework and family farm labor.

It is somewhat artificial, then, to distinguish between a formal economy with its legal/moral connotations and an informal sector with its illegal/immoral connotations. They are often intimately connected and mutually conditioning. The distinction is made by economists concerned with models of economic activity that can be measured. And the measurement is done by governments who are concerned with their records and their tax base. We continue to make the distinction here because it helps to illuminate the limits of official, formal development strategy on the one hand and to identify alternative, informal livelihood strategies on the other.

Our point is that those who are bypassed or marginalized by development often form a culture parallel to the market culture. There is, of course, a question as to whether this informal culture is a real alternative or simply an impoverished margin of the formal culture. This may be an issue of scale, or it may depend on the context. For example, withdrawal from the formal economy in the countryside may revive subsistence farming that represents an improvement in living standards over working as a rural laborer or existing on the urban fringe, as long as land is available. The scale of marginalized populations grows with de-peasantization and the labor redundancy discussed in the previous section. That is, these trends are often connected, so that informalization is a direct outgrowth of expanded formal economic activity or the concentration of resources in fewer corporate hands.

One source of the quite dramatic expansion of the informal sector has been the hyper-urbanization in former Third World countries. Agricultural modernization routinely expelled peasants and rural labor from secure rural livelihoods; they migrated to the urban centers where, as they had heard on the radio and through the migrant labor networks, jobs and amenities were available. One vivid account of this trend is given by Hernando De Soto, a libertarian critic of developmentalism:

Quite simply, Peru's legal institutions had been developed over the years to meet the needs and bolster the privileges of certain dominant groups in the cities and to isolate the peasants geographically in rural areas. As long as this system worked, the implicit legal discrimination was not apparent. Once the peasants settled in the cities, however, the law began to lose social relevance. The migrants discovered that their numbers were considerable, that the system was not prepared to accept them, that more and more barriers were being erected against them, that they had to fight to extract every right from an unwilling establishment, that they were excluded from the facilities and benefits offered by the law. . . . In short, they discovered that they must compete not only against people but also against the system. Thus it was, that in order to survive, the migrants became informals.[35]

In effect, then, development engendered a growing marginal population. Of course, these *peri-urban* communities, as they are known, have been expanding throughout the twentieth century: the urban South has grown from 90 million in 1900 to nearly 1 billion in 1985, with an increase of over 40 million a year. Its share of world urban population increased from 39 percent to 63 percent between 1950 and 1990. The United Nations estimates that in the former Third World there will be 2 billion city dwellers by the year 2000 with increases of 109 percent in Africa, 50 percent in Latin America, and 65 percent in Asia.[36]

With globalization, the lines are drawn even more clearly, on a larger scale, and possibly more rapidly. There are professional and managerial classes who participate within global circuits (involved with products, money, electronic communications, high-speed transport) linking enclaves of producers/consumers across state borders. Many of these people increasingly live and work within corporate domains. For the United States, Robert Reich termed this the "secession of the successful," meaning the top fifth of income earners in America, who "now inhabit a different economy from other Americans. The new elite is linked by jet, modem, fax, satellite and fiber-optic cable to the great commercial and recreational centers of the world, but it is not particularly connected to the rest of the nation."[37] And there are those whom these circuits bypass, or indeed displace. These are the redundant labor forces, the structurally unemployed, the marginals, who live in shantytowns and urban ghettos across the world. Some join the global labor force as migrants and/or refugees, and others enter the informal, or underground, economy.

Informalization is not new, but under economic globalization it has some different facets. One facet is the industrial decay or downsizing that occurs as the global labor market comes into play. The labor expelled in this process is quite distinct from first-generation peasants forced to leave the land. Middle-class people are now entering the ranks of the structurally unemployed daily in the United States.

Projections abound concerning the impact of a GATT regime. Only time will tell how accurate they are. The former chair of the Group of 77, Luis Fernando Jaramillo, predicted in January 1994 that "the industrialized countries, which make up only 20% of the membership of GATT, will appropriate 70% of the additional income to be generated by the implementation of the Uruguay Round."[38] According to a GATT report released nine months later, the big winners would be the United States and the European Union. It stands to reason that the "level playing field" under a GATT regime would privilege the strongest markets, but it is by no means clear that there will be a rising tide of global economic activity. The Organization for Economic Cooperation and Development predicts that after a decade of a GATT regime Africa will lose an additional $3 billion of trade income annually; wheat and corn prices will rise, while cocoa and coffee prices will continue to fall.[39] Finally, in 1994, European Member of Parliament James Goldsmith reported in a U.S. Senate inquiry that 4 billion people are joining the world economy as the Cold War, which held them separate in the Second World, has ended:

> The application of GATT will also cause a great tragedy in the third world. Modern economists believe that an efficient agriculture is one that produces the maximum amount of food for the minimum cost, using the least number of people. . . . It is estimated that there are still 3.1 billion people in the world who live from the land. If GATT manages to impose worldwide the sort of productivity achieved by the intensive agriculture of nations such as Australia, then it is easy to calculate that about 2 billion of these people will become redundant. Some of these GATT refugees will move to urban slums. But a large number of them will be forced into mass migration. . . . We will have profoundly and tragically destabilized the world's population.[40]

Informalization

Refugees such as those described by Goldsmith are likely to enlarge the social weight of informal activities across the world. That is, with an enlarging mass of people existing on the fringes of the formal economy, informalization may rise. Informalization (as a term describing a *social movement*) reputedly first defined the consolidation of informal activity in Africa in the 1970s, a trend that grew out of successive development failures.[41] Serge LaTouche argues that informal activity actually constitutes a society rather than an atypical and invisible economic reality—if not a legal society, certainly an alternative to legal society. It proceeds first from a negative description in which marginal types—for example, women and their work—are perceived by planners as nonformal, unwaged, unorganized, outside the realm of official statistics, and so forth. Such negative description parallels common First World perceptions of Third World people. According to Arturo Escobar, non-European people often tend to be perceived by what they lack—capital, entrepreneurship, organization and political conscience, education, political participation, infrastructure, rationality.[42] This perception underlay the assumptions of the development project.

The positive description of the informal economy transcends the negative definition. Fantu Cheru calls it the "silent revolution," referring to the defensive response of African peasants to the failure of trickle-down policies: they dropped out. Exiting was the choice for producers and workers consistently bypassed by state policies. Self-defense "has required the resuscitation of rural co-operatives, traditional caravan trade across borders, catering services and other activities that had once fallen into disuse, depriving the state of the revenue that traditionally financed its antipeople and anti-peasant development policies."[43] LaTouche views the informal as

> comprehensive strategies of response to the challenges that life poses for displaced and uprooted populations in peri-urban areas. These are people torn between lost tradition and impossible modernity. The sphere of the informal has, incontestably, a major economic significance. It is characterised by a neo-artisanal activity that generates a lot of employment and produces incomes comparable to those of the modern sector. . . . Resolving practical problems of living spaces and daily life has all sorts of economic ramifications, so much so that the practical importance of the "informal economy" is no longer a matter of debate. Some 50–80% of the population in the urban areas of these countries live in and from the informal, one way or another. Moreover, the "informal economy" and more generally the "informal society" do not constitute a closed world. There are all sorts of bridges and ties into "formal" national and international structures.[44]

In many ways, informalization has become more and more prominent because more and more people are disenchanted with the economic models associated with the development and globalization projects. So the discovery of survival strategies among the poor and dispossessed has become an academic industry. Activists are finding these communities to be sources of hope rather than despair. Ivan Illich, for example, notes that "up to now, economic development has always meant that people, instead of doing something, are instead enabled to buy it."[45] In this parable he finds that the "development castaways" constitute a proliferating culture of alternatives.

The "lost decade" intensified pressures to consolidate new livelihood strategies in already overburdened cities. In Latin America, whereas formal employment rose by 3.2 percent annually in the 1980s, informal jobs rose at more than twice that rate. Presently about a third of urban jobs in Asia and Latin America and more than half in Africa are estimated to be informal.[46] Among the poor in urban Mexico, collective pooling of resources to acquire land, shelter, and basic public services (water, electricity) was one widespread strategy for establishing networks among friends and neighbors to build their own cheap housing.[47]

Many different strategies contribute to the *culture of the new commons*, a social inventiveness arising on the fringes of industrial society and drawing on traditional collective interaction to allow people to make ends meet. Mexican intellectual Gustavo Esteva observes:

> Peasants and grassroots groups in the cities are now sharing with people forced to leave the economic centre the ten thousand tricks they have learned to limit the economy, to mock the economic creed, or to refunctionalize and reformulate modern technology. The "crisis" of the 1980s removed from the payroll people already educated in dependency on incomes and the market people lacking the social setting enabling them to survive by themselves. Now the margins are coping with the difficult task of relocating these people. The process poses great challenges and tensions for everyone, but it also offers a creative opportunity for regeneration.[48]

Growth and Marginalization

Arguably, the culture of the new commons may spread, as more and more regions across the world decay from neglect. The neglect has two sources. First is the incapacity of debt-stressed state organizations to support regions that do not contribute to the global project. For example, in the poorer states, with borrowed funds earmarked to promote export production to service debt, little remains to subsidize sectors and communities on the margins. In sub-Saharan Africa, total debt servicing amounts to $10 billion annually, four times the amount spent on health and education.[49] The First World is not immune to this fiscal stress—the United States continues to confront its rising debt burden by slashing social services.

Second, the hallmark of a market regime is inequality—the reinforcing of growth poles and the neglect of the remainder. We already can see this in practice:

1. During the 1980s, the North/South gap widened such that the average-living-standards differential was 10 to 1.[50]

2. According to U.N. calculations, within the three super-regions— the United States, Europe, and Japan (the "Triad")—cross-border

investment tripled between 1980 and 1988, accounting for one-third of such investment worldwide. "In terms of trade, interactions within the Triad have outpaced both interactions in the rest of the world, and interactions between the Triad and the rest of the world, indicating a faster rate of integration within the Triad than between the Triad and the rest of the world."[51]

3. Between 1990 and 1993, foreign direct investment in the former Third World nearly tripled, but 60 percent of it was concentrated in Asia (China, Singapore, Malaysia, Thailand, Hong Kong, Taiwan, and Indonesia).[52]

4. The African share of world exports is now about 1.3 percent, whereas Latin America's is around 4.3 percent.[53]

5. Bleak images of "Europe's periphery, Africa, [as] a lost continent" abound: "Since 1970, Africa's share of the world markets has been reduced by half; its debt has been multiplied by twenty and now equals its total gross product; and income per capita in sub-Saharan Africa has fallen by one-quarter since 1987."[54]

The globalization project is likely to be considerably more selective in its reach. Just because its progenitors speak of globalization does not mean there is universal and homogeneous development. Weaker regions of the world have no real channels of representation. They can attract attention from investors only by making themselves weaker through further structural adjustment. The selectivity of the globalization project distinguishes it from the direct interventions in the non-European world under colonialism and from the aid and geopolitics of the development project. The globalization project appears to be a recipe for marginalization.

As noted in the development literature, conditions in sub-Saharan Africa are expected to deteriorate further, and some fear that the reconstruction of Eastern Europe will draw assistance monies away from the African continent. According to Brown and Tiffen, "Africa is being marginalised as never before, as the single European market, the American continental trade bloc and the Japanese Pacific Rim—the 'triad'—become the foci for capital investment and the target markets for the products of that investment."[55] Over and above the neglect, there are the maturing industrial and biotechnological substitutes for tropical exports (such as sugar, rubber, oils, fish protein, and cocoa). Robert Schaeffer terms this scenario indifferent **imperialism,** where the wealthy countries "have so greatly increased their technological advantages that they do not *need* to exploit the whole world, just some of it."[56]

Informalization is one consequence of marginalization. Another is the loss of governmental legitimacy. In the kind of transition through which

we are living, the erosion of national capacities expresses itself in the erosion of representative politics. No one votes for global management systems. Yet, as governments undertake such managerial functions for the
global economy, they shed their own representative role, and their citizens
lose faith—as we see in the final section of this chapter.

Legitimacy Crisis

The third social impact of economic globalization is a growing **legitimacy
crisis** of government. This means that citizens lose faith in their government or that government policies exacerbate social divisions within the
population between classes and regions. We have already seen that global
managerialism generates new forms of governance—either as regulation
by global institutions or as surrogate global management by individual
states themselves. Both of these new forms of governance pose problems
for national governments in relation to their citizens, because both erode
national sovereignty. Erosion takes many forms—from foreign ownership
of essential national resources (banking and energy infrastructures),
through the undoing of political coalitions formed around national development projects, to the dismantling of social services provided by governments to their needier populations. All these trends erode government
capacity or social responsibility. With the disappearance of social protections, described in the following insert, the government's legitimacy becomes more fragile.

Also eroding the legitimacy of nation-states is their loss of coherence or
definition, resulting from the growing integration of economic regions,
currency exchanges, and cultures across the world. This integration is
sometimes termed "coca-colonization"—in metaphorical reference to the
process by which the ubiquitous soft drink replaces local drinks and rede-
fines thirst. Former United Nations University President Soedjakmoto
commented:

> In the process of interdependence, we have all become vulnerable. Our soci-
> eties are permeable to decisions taken elsewhere in the world. The dynamics
> of inter-dependence might be better understood if we think of the globe not
> in terms of a map of nations but as a meteorological map, where weather
> systems swirl independently of any national boundaries and low and high
> fronts create new climatic conditions far ahead of them.[57]

It is important to remember that these interdependencies have not
come just with the globalization project, nor has globalization created the
legitimacy problems of governments of the former Third World. These

---

What Are Social Protections?

When capitalist economies came into being, they undid the tight-knit, sometimes oppressive, community relationships of the premarket society. Peasants, expelled from the land to work as wage laborers in the cities, found that they were in a fiercely competitive labor market and at the mercy of their employers. Over time, the new working classes banded together and fought for their right to organize in unions, and then they demanded the right to vote. Once able to exercise some power through the electoral systems, they were in a position to demand social rights— that is, entitlements to unemployment protection, health and welfare benefits, work safety laws, and other safeguards. They had the power to get their way in the early twentieth century as governments needed their loyalty for military and taxing purposes. Also, as industry grew, labor held increasing power with its threat of a strike. The politics of social protection is of course more complex than this, but it does involve these various kinds of economic, political, and social relationships. By the mid-twentieth century, the welfare state was quite well established, at least for a time.

---

states always had legitimacy problems of one kind or another, in part because of the colonial legacy. For instance, African states did not necessarily coincide with nations, and colonialism's disorganizing impact compromised their economic resources and social coherence. But anticolonial movements and the new governments saw the *centralized state* as the key to overcoming the colonial legacy. They mobilized different class and ethnic groupings behind the pursuit of material improvements associated with the development project. The developmentalist state was the primary actor.

Development Project Legacies

Two elements of the development project, however, typically compromised Third World states in their pursuit of modernity: the network of military alliances in the Cold War and the urban bias of economic growth strategies. *Urban bias* channeled wealth away from the rural sector in Africa, inflating public works in the cities at the expense of small farming. The deterioration of sub-Saharan African economies through the development decades undercut states' capacities and their ability to deliver on their citizens' heightened expectations from the anticolonial struggle. Citizens disengaged from the formal economy, pursuing activities such as hoarding, currency exchanging, smuggling, and bartering. Ghana's head of state, Jerry Rawlings, referred to the "culture of silence,"[58] and in the 1980s Fantu Cheru documented the African states' weakened capacity to regulate social and economic relations under the pressures of the debt regime in his book *The Silent Revolution in Africa* (1989).

Militarization, through aid packages from the Cold War superpowers and through choices made by military or authoritarian regimes, diverted scarce funds from developmental programs. Between 1960 and 1987, military spending in the Third World rose almost three times as fast as in the First World, as the Third World more than doubled its share of global military spending—from 7 percent to 15 percent. Meanwhile, the Third World's share of global income stayed below 5 percent. In 1992, 18 former Third World countries devoted more to military spending than to their education and health budgets, and eight of these were among the world's poorest nations.[59]

These spending decisions, however, reflect far more than simply the diversion of resources. The militarization of governments and societies carries vast consequences. Basic human rights and potential civil rights suffer in states whose regimes hold power through terror and intimidation of their subject populations. Legitimacy is always compromised in states that rule through coercion rather than consent. It is true that certain states like South Korea managed to establish some legitimacy by providing material benefits to the population while suppressing their political rights. Having North Korea as a neighbor, of course, helped, and this proximity explains why the Cold War was so critical to the implementation of the development project. If governments were balancing their developmental needs with security needs in a hostile world, then coercion (and military aid) was more readily justified.

Development and Democracy?

Even in circumstances where militarization compromised or slowed political development, the expectation was that economic growth would eventually lead to political democratization. This was the model held out to the Third World. But it was controversial, because many newly industrializing countries and middle-income states grew economically while their governments remained bureaucratic, authoritarian, and militaristic. The term **bureaucratic-authoritarian industrializing regimes**

(BAIRs) was coined to describe this type of government.[60] The former prime minister of Singapore, Lee Kuan Yew, justified authoritarianism in his characteristic paternalist way: "I do not believe that democracy necessarily leads to development. I believe that what a country needs to develop is discipline more than democracy. The exuberance of democracy leads to indiscipline and disorderly conduct which are inimical to development."[61] Lee Kuan Yew may have meant that when different classes put conflicting demands on the state—industrial-capitalists seeking propitious business conditions, workers asking for higher wages, farmers requesting subsidies—the bureaucratic elites have less flexibility. In addition, a docile labor force is a strong incentive for foreign investment. But economic change and the restructuring of economic opportunity do alter a country's social structure, which in turn changes the balance of social and political forces.

South Korea is a case in point. It appeared to confirm the dictum that development does bring about democracy. During the 1980s, as it modernized on an expanding base of heavy industry, a sequence of political challenges was directed at the regime. The national economy was experiencing stress, as rising labor costs were affecting the competitiveness of Korean export manufacturing. Powerful industrialists, a burgeoning middle class, and a mobilized working class all put pressure on the state to adjust the economic system to improve their respective conditions. Hagen Koo observed at the time: "The capitalist class has grown too strong to be easily dominated by the state, and workers are not as docile and quiescent as they once were. At the same time the presence of a relatively large, well-educated middle class exerts pressure on the state for political democratization."[62] In 1987, a political explosion occurred, as labor unrest and broad demonstrations directly challenged the paternalism of the South Korean regime, starting a movement for greater democracy in the electoral system.[63]

The relationship between development and democracy is always complex, depending at a minimum on the mix of local conditions and the global position of states and economic actors. The development project was always infused with the expectation that development would lead to democracy. But as the globalization project takes shape, declining state legitimacy *also* encourages movements for democracy. The shrinking of the state can open space for political activism as patronage systems lose their funds. It can also stimulate political upheaval when urban communities lose resources as their states restructure. These complex relationships are illustrated in the following case study of Brazil.

CASE STUDY

Development, Class, and Democracy in Brazil

The relationship between development and democracy is generally mediated by class politics. How central class politics becomes depends on the particular case. Middle-income states (such as the newly industrializing countries) typically have substantial domestic economies and therefore quite mature industrial structures in which class politics features centrally. These circumstances came together in Brazil.

The Brazilian economic "miracle" followed the 1964 military coup, which had dismantled the previous government's developmentalist alliance. Although it encouraged foreign investment in the auto and auto-parts, electrical goods, and capital goods sectors, the military junta squeezed wages, demobilized labor unions, and repressed political rights. The new working class that emerged in this private industrial sector erupted in the late 1970s, demanding improved wages and working conditions and forming a Workers Party; soon after, a new national trade union organization was established. These workers were a different breed from the public-sector workers the junta had demobilized in the 1960s. The earlier work force had been incorporated politically into the state's developmentalist alliance; the new labor force had direct class concerns—for economic rights (improved working conditions) and political rights (to organize independently of the state). Also, these workers came from communities denied social resources, as the developmentalist alliance had been dismantled. Labor activism included demands for community resources, known as social-movement unionism. These demands spread to other classes, and in the 1980s the military government was brought down by a broad new coalition of social forces demanding a democratized political system.

Gay Seidman has shown in a comparative study of Brazil and South Africa that in such industrializing middle-income countries democratization requires specific conditions—primarily, a show of real power by the new industrial working class at a moment when there is conflict between industrialists and the state. In the Brazilian situation, relatively skilled labor forces had to deploy factory-based organizations to disrupt production before the state or large employers would consider extending them political rights or economic benefits. The opportune moment came when Brazilian industrialists found that the international business climate had moved against them, pushing them into a confrontation with industrial policy makers in the state. At that moment, in the 1970s and 1980s, labor had its way and established a new democratic beachhead.

Sources: Hewitt, 1992, pp. 86–89; Seidman, 1994, pp. 260–263.

The democratic impulse spread throughout the Second and Third Worlds in the 1980s, albeit unevenly. It was often based in relatively new industrial working classes. But they tended to focus on their falling living standards; that is, they were not following a sequence of democratization on a wave of development. This was particularly true in Eastern Europe. Mass resistance built on growing dissatisfaction throughout the Soviet bloc. The focus was the inability of the centrally planned regimes to raise living standards as they had promised and the continued repression of political rights. The Polish Solidarity movement began the challenge to the communist political system in the early 1980s. Indebted states submitted to the conditions of loans from the International Monetary Fund, but rather than saving these regimes, the conditions sank them. Privatization posed new problems because "the state could no longer compensate itself for its expenses out of the profits of enterprises" as it had done under the central planning system, and so it went deeper into debt, bringing ever-declining living conditions. These regimes had crumbled from within by the end of the decade.[64]

As citizenship demands have mushroomed in Eastern Europe, the instant markets promoted by the global managers encouraged Mafia-like activity, the formation of private militias, and self-enrichment for the former members of the party-states, as well as a general social disintegration. The tidy link between democracy and development no longer appears to hold in this region of the global economy. It seems that under a restructuring global system the politics of economic change no longer follow a clear formula.

The collapse of the Second World coincided with the collapse of the Third World. This was a major threshold, marking the end of the development project and the simultaneous incorporation of all regions into the liberalizing thrust of the globalization project. This thrust came in the form of loan conditions laid down by the debt managers. It occurred in a period of heightened tensions. Across the former Second and Third Worlds, so-called *IMF riots*, described in the following case study, marked the end of the development era. These large-scale, sometimes coordinated urban uprisings protested the austerity measures of their governments, with the rioters often breaking into food banks to help themselves. Between 1976 and 1992, some 146 riots occurred in 39 of the approximately 80 debtor countries (including Romania, Yugoslavia, Poland, and Hungary).[65]

CASE STUDY

The IMF Food Riots

Food riots, associated with the historic transition to market society, reemerged on a broad, global scale around the mid-1970s, coinciding with the erosion of the development project. The target of these uprisings was the continuing austerity measures meted out in Latin America, Eastern Europe, and Africa. Walton and Seddon define these austerity protests as "large-scale collective actions including political demonstrations, general strikes, and riots, which are animated by grievances over state policies of economic liberalization implemented in response to the debt crisis and market reforms urged by international agencies." The authors documented 146 incidents of protest between 1976 and 1992, noting that protests within each country were characteristically well-organized movements that spread simultaneously across several urban centers.

These austerity protests addressed the unequal distribution of the means of livelihood, targeting policies that eroded urban dwellers' social supports. The collapsing social supports included a range of subsidized items or services necessary to members of hyper-urbanized environments, including food, health care, education, transportation, housing, and others. The supports were the elements of the social pact made between the developmentalist state and its urban population during the period of industrialization by way of import-substitution; the services were to be delivered in return for the people's political loyalty.

The *classical* food riot, which signaled the destabilization of traditional food markets during the transition from customary to market society, occurred during the era of European state-building in the eighteenth and nineteenth centuries. By contrast, the *contemporary* food riot signals a new transition, occurring across a world experiencing the hollowing-out of the national economic project. The conception of the public household—a state-underwritten program of public welfare—arose in the First World as states replaced communities. This conception also shaped Second and Third World state policies as these governments supervised national economic development. It is now undergoing a dramatic reversal as structural adjustment policies universally enforce austerity. The consequences are more drastic outside the First World where social security nets are thinner. Austerity protests seek to restore lost social rights within the national project. At the same time, they bear witness to and in some cases identify globalization as the driving force behind the shrinking of the public household.

Source: Walton & Seddon, 1994.

The IMF riots symbolized the link made by protestors between IMF conditions and the loss of capacity and legitimacy of governments, especially as "developers." One scholar has observed that the logic of the structural adjustment program "is to further weaken the motivation of the state to respond to the popular demands that have been built into the process of postcolonial state formation."[66] The protests were not simply indicators of a linear decline in states' power. They also were a recognition of the restructuring of states according to reformist criteria imposed and adopted by the global managers. This restructuring exacerbated the sense of a declining government legitimacy.

Political Reforms

Pressures for political reform under the conditions of adjustment have not always been successful. The African state most successful in meeting World Bank economic criteria has been Ghana, where the military rule of Jerry Rawlings persists. Another model of adjustment has been Uganda under the authoritarian rule of President Yoweri Museveni, who took power at the end of decades of bloody civil war in 1986. According to one commentator, Museveni "has for many years succeeded in defying international pressure that makes aid contingent on democratization efforts."[67] He is reported to reject multiparty systems, arguing that they are products of Western industrial societies with fluid class divisions, while African societies are divided vertically, along fixed tribal lines. A multiparty system may, therefore, divide along tribal lines, leading to additional ethnic conflict. Museveni's solution is to use "national resistance councils," organized at the local level, to bring local concerns into the national arena. Critics charge that this is a one-party state by another name.[68]

Elsewhere, African one-party states have unraveled with democratizing trends, drawing inspiration and example from the collapse of the Eastern European one-party states and responding to governance pressures from the global managers. With the demise of one-party rule and in the context of declining economic opportunity, protective ethnic lines have been drawn. These lines often become the basis for civil wars and struggles for control over national resources. In the normal course of events, such conflicts then present themselves as ethnic clashes, as if the disintegration of national cohesion were essentially based in tribal divisions.

An example occurred in West Africa, where a movement for democracy in the oil-producing Congo followed hard on the heels of the collapse of the Cold War. The one-party rule by a Marxist government ended and democratic elections were held in 1992. Newly elected President Lissouba replaced the transitional, multi-ethnic cabinet with people of his ethnic origin, the Nibolek. He also formed an ethnically homogeneous presidential guard, distinct from the regular military force. Political opponents then organized along ethnic lines, based in the Pool Lari and the Mbochi groups. These divisions subsequently shaped clashes in Brazzaville between government and oppositional militia. A Congolese economist was quoted in the *New York Times* as remarking: "Democratic elections were the worst thing that ever happened in this country. It's unleashed a Pandora's box of tribal hatreds that may take generations to heal."[69] The problem is that ethnic conflict is usually only the tip of the social iceberg, and in order to avoid jumping to simple conclusions about African disunities, we need to understand the context in which states formed through the decolonization process and were then reformed, or deformed, by the process of restructuring in the 1980s.

In 1994, the world was shocked by massacres of tens of thousands of people in Rwanda. These occurred during a military conflict between the majority ruling ethnic group—the Hutu—and the Rwandan Patriotic Front, composed largely of minority Tutsi, the traditional ruling group, who were challenging their removal from power. The ethnic hierarchy derived from precolonial times, was reinforced under colonialism, and was left in place in the new postcolonial state—until the reform period of the last decade, when Tutsis were forced into exile. The Angolan Ambassador to Zimbabwe, Alberto Bento Ribeiro, commented: "The outside powers,

Belgium, France, the U.S., they all exerted a lot of pressure on Rwanda. They wanted to get the Hutu into the power structure, to move them up in the army. All that upset the established order, which had Tutsi at the top."[70]

Ethnically defined tensions coincide with the economic depression that has stretched across the continent of sub-Saharan Africa over the last two decades. The shadow of colonialism also lies across this region. For example, former French colonies (Senegal, the Comoros, Burkina Faso, Equatorial Guinea, Ivory Coast, Chad, Benin, the Central African Republic, Congo, Gabon, Niger, Togo, Cameroon, and Mali) suffered a destabilizing currency devaluation in 1994 when France cut the local French-backed currency, the C.F.A. franc, by 50 percent, causing extensive price increases for food and pharmaceutical products as well as creating wage freezes.[71]

These instances suggest that sub-Saharan Africa struggles with enormous dilemmas, in which economic adjustment often fans social divisions over dwindling resources. The divisions often express themselves in ethnic conflict as economies stagnate and political reforms promote multiparty systems. Spreading civil war signals the inability of some states to maintain any internal authority, especially in a world where global forces are now considerably more selective. The characteristic export dependency of many African states handicaps their ability to maneuver in a technologically changing world economy. The legitimacy crises of these states have deep roots.

One dramatic manifestation of the loss of political cohesion of some African states is an exploding refugee population. The United Nations makes a distinction between "international refugees" and "internally displaced persons." The latter category, generated through ethnopolitical conflict (such as that in Somalia, Rwanda, Sudan, and Liberia), soared in sub-Saharan Africa in the late 1980s and early 1990s, affecting about 16 million, or 60 percent of the world total of displaced persons. In addition, there are over 6 million international refugees out of a total regional population of 600 million. Africa now leads the world in both categories.[72]

Loss of cohesion is not confined to Africa, however. On a world scale, the number of international refugees mushroomed from 10.5 million in 1984 to close to 23 million in 1994, in addition to the 26 million internally displaced persons—from places as far apart as Bosnia and Burma, Iraq and Sri Lanka.[73] Although economic and political authority has been centralizing in the hands of transnational institutions, military power has remained at the state level—whether held as a monopoly of the state itself or subdivided between warring factions within the state.

With these destabilizing movements, further global governance mechanisms have come into play. The United Nations is assuming an expanding role in policing the world. In 1994, for example, that organization was involved in preventive diplomacy or peacemaking in 28 conflicts (compared with 11 in 1988) and deployed 17 peacekeeping operations (compared with 5 in 1988) involving 73,393 military personnel (compared with 9,570 in 1988).[74]

Policing the world has an air of recolonization about it. In 1993, U.S. marines landed in Somalia. In the absence of a functioning government, they were uninvited, but the U.N. Security Council approved the action on humanitarian grounds, in order to stem the destruction of civil war. This reappearance of "trusteeship," historically associated with colonialism, generated a provocative observation by Paul Johnson, a U.S. historian:

> We are witnessing today a revival of colonialism, albeit in a new form. It is a trend that should be encouraged, it seems to me, on practical as well as moral grounds. There simply is no alternative in nations where governments have crumbled and the most basic conditions for civilized life have disappeared, as is now the case in a great many third-world countries. . . . The appeals for help come not so much from Africa's political elites, who are anxious to cling to the trappings of power, as from ordinary, desperate citizens, who carry the burden of misrule.[75]

One year later, African scholar Ali Mazrui was quoted in a Kenyan newspaper as asking: "As the whole state machinery collapses in one African country after another, is Africa in need of recolonization?" This conception, however, was of self-colonization—where African states might administer malfunctioning neighboring states under a mandate from the international community.[76] Alternatively, one journalist has suggested that "new overlords" in Africa are already in place in the form of the International Monetary Fund and the World Bank.[77]

Summary

The globalization project has many social and political consequences and implications for the future of the world. We have examined just three phenomena: the global labor surplus, informalization, and the legitimacy crisis of state organizations. None of these is unique to the global project. They have all appeared in previous eras, but possibly not on the scale found today. The three are linked; indeed, they are mutually conditioning processes, being three dimensions of a single process of global restructuring affecting all states, although with variations.

As the world market becomes more consequential, competition among firms heats up. It takes the form of technical upgrading, movement to cheaper labor zones, and constant product innovation. All three competitive strategies, taken together, undermine the stability of labor markets. Labor redundancy rises. And this, in combination with the growing international migration of labor forces, generates political intolerance where ethnic hierarchies (constructed historically) are used to fuel tensions between the culturally different labor forces. In this way, labor is even more divided and distracted from addressing the root cause of its insecurity: economic globalization. Labor organization on a world scale is still very much in its infancy, partly because of the divisive role of ethnic politics.

The technological shedding of labor and the downsizing and stagnation produced by structural adjustment programs extend informalization. Indeed, the institution of wage labor is undergoing substantial change across the world. Not only is wage employment contracting, but wage labor is also displaying a *casualizing* trend, where jobs become part-time and impermanent. The strategies of flexibility embraced by firms contribute to this informalization as much as does the growing surplus of workers. Some observers see in informalization a countermovement to the official economy and to state regulation—the new commons. Whether informalization is the source of future alternatives to the formal market economy, there is no doubt that it is the site of a diverse array of livelihood strategies, some of which are embedded in community or personal relations.

Finally, the legitimacy crisis is substantial under the globalization project because of the relative indifference or incapacity of states in a market regime to resolve the breakdown of social institutions. The breakdown marks the crossing of a threshold from the national-development era to a new era in which international competition and global efficiency increasingly govern nations' policy and growth strategies. But in such breakdown there are signs of a renewal, as people across the world push for democratic participation. Movements for democracy have emerged in the moment at which already overextended states, sometimes riddled with unproductive cronyism (pork-barrel politics), are under pressure to end the pretense of development and repay the debts built up over two decades of development financing. The emperor really doesn't have on any clothes, and disillusioned citizens, repressed workers, and neglected rural communities have demanded the opening of their political systems. This demand coincides with the reorganization of states as surrogate global managers. The globalization project amplifies the contradictory features of developmentalism on the national and the global scale. This is the subject of Chapter 7.

PART IV

Rethinking Development

Social Responses to Globalization

The globalization project is a relatively coherent perspective and has a powerful set of agencies working on its behalf. Nevertheless, it is by no means the only game in town. Like the development project, the globalization project is an attempt to fashion the world around a central principle through powerful political and financial institutions. Because the principle is framed in the liberal discourse of rights and freedom, its power ultimately depends on consent.

Most governments feel the pressure to play by the new and emerging global rules, but their citizens do not always share their outlook. And where globalization weakens nation-states (by eroding their public welfare function, increasing social and regional polarization, and reducing state patronage systems) citizens have fresh opportunities to renew the political process. This chapter surveys some of the social responses of these citizen groups, exploring their origins and goals and highlighting the range of opposition. Examining each movement offers a particular angle on the dilemmas associated with both the development project and the emerging globalization project. Although the various opposition movements have emerged in different ways and places and at different overlapping times, there is a sense in which they converge. As you encounter each broad movement, you will see how each expresses a common condition across the world. This condition may be represented as an escalating tension between global (or universal) and local (or particular) understandings of how humanity should proceed as the globalization project subsumes the development project. We consider the following social movements and assess their impact in the development debate: fundamentalism, environmentalism, **feminism,** and **cosmopolitan localism.**

Fundamentalism

Fundamentalism usually expresses a desire to return to the simplicity and security of traditional codes of behavior. But it is never quite so simple. First, who decides what is traditional? There may be sacred texts, but they are open to interpretation. And fundamentalist movements are usually split by factional differences and power struggles. Second, what are the conditions in which fundamentalism comes to the fore? These conditions are likely to shape the leadership and the interpretation of tradition. In the United States at present, the broad-based fundamentalism espousing family values, among other things, can be understood only in the context of a significant decline in the proportion of the population that is actually a part of the traditional nuclear family structure. Even then, the nuclear family is not exactly traditional; the extended family is the more traditional structure. What may be traditional is the unquestioned power of the family patriarch.

In uncertain times, fundamentalism often moves to the front burner. People gravitate to fundamentalism for protection and security. We have seen a variant of this in the rising use of ethnic politics as competition for jobs grows while the economy shrinks. Nothing is absolute or definite about the content of fundamentalism or about the elevation of ethnic identity as a way of drawing boundaries between people. The interpretation of ethnicity is quite plastic and depends very much on the historical and social context in which people reconstruct ethnic divisions.[1] Nevertheless, in an increasingly confused and uncertain world, the presumed essentialism of ethnic identity either comforts people or allows them to identify scapegoats. The current challenge to affirmative action in the United States represents one such reaction. In whatever form, fundamentalist politics has become a powerful weapon for mobilizing people as the political and class coalitions of the development era crumble. The illustration that follows is one of the early landmark fundamentalist responses to the development project that has since fueled growing opposition across the world to the globalization project.

In the early 1970s, with oil prices rising sharply, the Shah of Iran boasted that Iran would now catch up rapidly to the West. His country, he predicted, would be the world's fifth greatest military power by 1980, would equal West Germany's per capita income by 1986, and would eradicate class divisions on the way.[2] Iranian oil revenues financed more than $10 billion worth of military hardware purchased from the United States, identifying Iran (along with Israel) as the guardian of the Middle Eastern status quo. Meanwhile, the Shah plunged Iran into a modernization program designed to reduce its dependence on oil. But land reforms were ineffectual because their recipients had no technological assistance, and agricultural modernization relied on capital-intensive agribusiness investments from abroad. Between 10 percent and 20 percent of oil revenues financed food imports. The focus on militarization choked industrial growth. In the end, conspicuous consumption by the beneficiaries of rising oil revenues intensified inequality and cultural divisions. Mohammed Reza Shah Pahlavi's regime was ultimately overthrown in 1979 by a conservative Islamic-led counterrevolution against Iranian westernization.[3]

The limits of the development project in this case were not set simply by a reliance on oil-financed militarization. The resulting uneven social impact empowered a growing opposition to modernity and its symbols. Leadership of the opposition was claimed by the Ayatollah Khomeini and the urban network of fundamentalist *mullahs*, Islamic leaders who sought power through a reassertion of Islamic rule. But the revolution was multi-class in its composition, including students, intellectuals, middle-class professionals, the traders of the bazaar, and workers, particularly those in the oil fields. A good part of the social base of the counterrevolution was the mass of displaced peasants driven into the cities at the rate of 8 percent a year in the 1970s.[4] The catch-up game, driven by a fixation on military power, generated its own political limits—in the form of an unruly surplus of rural labor generated by rapid modernization.

Fundamentalist opposition to westernization was a powerful symbolic movement that served the interests of the Islamic establishment in Iran. The fundamentalists attacked various secular interests in Iran, including nontraditional women, leftist organizations, and liberal or centrist political groups—in fact, anyone who espoused democratic-secular rather than Islamic rule. In Nigeria, in the same year the Shah of Iran was deposed, a Muslim fundamentalist movement was suppressed. Members of this group had been aroused by the social impact of the country's new oil wealth, but their protest was held down forcibly by the newfound military power of the Nigerian state, ruled by a Muslim president. Like the Iranian fundamentalists, the Nigerian fundamentalists' targets were Western-style consumerism and the venality of the social and political elites. As suggested above, the content and appeal of fundamentalism depend largely on its context. In Nigeria and Iran a shared context of westernization drove the resurgence of Islamic politics, but quite different outcomes resulted from the different capacities and roles of the fundamentalist movement in each state. The Nigerian case involved a more radical Islamic group. As such, it had no broad-based political program with which to attract social groups beyond its base in the informal urban sector.[5]

Indeed, Islam is known for having two faces. It has been used conservatively (in Iran, Turkey, Pakistan, and Indonesia) to secure the status quo and radically (in Algeria, South Yemen, Libya, and within the Palestine Liberation Organization) to promote egalitarianism.[6] Either way, it has also been a general movement of opposition to Western forms of capitalist democracy.

The Iranian case illustrates religious fundamentalism presented as a cultural alternative to developmentalism. It also shows how developmentalism, whether based in oil wealth or not, fuels fundamentalist opposition in overcrowded cities. In Turkey, for example, Istanbul's population has doubled every 15 years. When the modern Turkish Republic was created in 1923, only 15 percent of its population of 13 million was urban. Now two-thirds of Turkey's 60 million people live in urban areas. These city dwellers offer fertile ground for an Islamic revival challenging Kemalism, the secular politics associated with the founder of the early-twentieth-century Turkish republic, Kemal Ataturk.[7] The anti-westernism challenges both developmentalism and globalism and will be a major fracture line in the future.

In Egypt, growing discontent with economic failure and political corruption in the government has emboldened Islamic fundamentalism. Its ranks have expanded among the urban poor, partly because Islam offers community and basic services in the midst of the disorder of huge, sprawling cities such as Cairo. Fundamentalists have mounted a cultural offensive against Egyptian secular institutions (education, media, courts, and the arts). In 1994, a fundamentalist member of the Egyptian parliament, Galal Gharib, accused the minister of culture, Fariq Husni, of promoting Western pornography to "demolish Islamic religious and moral values." He condemned specifically a Gustav Klimt painting of Adam and Eve, an Egyptian adaptation of a Bertolt Brecht play, and government sponsorship of ballet schools, movie festivals, and translations of foreign literature. In southern Egypt's public schools, fundamentalist teachers have reimposed the veil on girls as young as six and have revised schoolbooks to emphasize Islamic teachings. They argue that secularization has suppressed Egypt's deep Islamic and Arab roots in the pursuit of a communion with Western culture.[8]

Opposition to the cultural implications of the development project extends easily to the new globalization project. India, a leader of the Non-Aligned Movement, was perhaps the last significant holdout among former Third World states against IMF-style economic liberalization. In 1991, the Indian Finance Ministry acceded to the borrowing conditions set out by the International Monetary Fund, and India joined the "structural adjustment" club. Right-wing Hindu groups, once advocates of economic liberalism, then organized a "Buy Indian" campaign against imports and the efforts to globalize the Indian economy on the part of Prime Minister P. V. Narasimha Rao. The Swadeshi Jagran Manch (SJM), an organization promoted by a Hindu revivalist group (Rashtriya Swayamsewak Sangh), urges Indians to boycott foreign-made goods such as toothpaste, shaving cream, soaps, detergents, cosmetics, soft drinks, paint, canned food, and even crayons. The convenor of the SJM, S. Gurmurthy, wears homespun cotton clothes to invoke the economic nationalism of India's beloved anti-colonial leader Mahatma Gandhi. Gurmurthy declared:

> We want to create a nationalist feeling that every nation has to evolve a mind of its own in economics. The integration of India with the rest of the world will be restricted to just one percent of our population. . . . A nation should largely live within its means and produce for its own market with trans-country commerce restricted to its needs.[9]

In sum, the fundamentalist movements springing up around the world have two main features. First, they articulate the uncertainties and distress brought about by the social decay that populations experience as a result of the limits of developmentalism and the increasing selectivity of globalization. Second, they often take the form of a nationalist resurgence against perceived threats to their culture. The combination frequently involves contesting the universalist assumptions of global development, presenting alternative ways of organizing social life on a national or local level.

Environmentalism

Environmentalism as a social movement involves questioning modern assumptions that nature and its bounty are infinite. It has two main strands. One derives from growing environmental awareness in the West, initially inspired by the publication of Rachel Carson's *Silent Spring* in 1962. This path-breaking book documented the disruption in the earth's ecosystems that was being caused by modern economic practices such as the use of agricultural chemicals. Its title refers to the absence of bird songs in the spring. Carson's metaphor dramatized the dependence of life on sustainable ecological systems. It also emphasized the shortcomings of Western rationalism insofar as it perceives nature as "external" to society. This perception encourages the belief that nature is an infinitely exploitable domain.[10]

A range of "green" movements has mushroomed throughout the First World as the simple truths revealed by Carson's study have gained an audience. First World "greens" typically challenge the assumptions and practices of unbridled economic growth, arguing for scaling back to a renewable economic system of resource use. One of their focuses is agricultural sustainability—that is, reversing the environmental stress associated with capital- and chemical-intensive agriculture. A key goal is maintaining a natural aesthetic to complement the consumer lifestyle, the emphasis being on preserving human health on the one hand and enhancing leisure activities on the other.

The second strand of environmentalism appears in active movements to protect particular ecological regions from environmentally damaging practices. In the former Third World, human communities depend greatly on the viability of regional ecologies for their livelihood. Such movements are therefore often distinguished by their attempts to protect existing cultural practices. In contrast to First World environmentalism, which attempts to regulate the environmental implications of the market economy, so-called Southern environmentalism questions the benefits of unregulated market forces. This is especially true where states and firms seek to "monetize" and harvest natural resources on which human communities depend.

Local communities have always challenged environmentally damaging practices where natural conservation is integral to local culture. Opposition has run from the protests of eighteenth-century English peasants at the enclosure of the commons, through the resistance of nineteenth-century Native Americans to the takeover of their lands and the elimination of the buffalo, to Indian struggles against British colonial forestry practices.

Recently, in the late twentieth century, forest dwellers across the tropics have been the focus of attention. Indigenous communities such as these are involved in a common attempt to preserve tropical rain forests from the extensive timber cutting associated with commercial logging. Timbering and the pasturing of beef cattle in degraded forest areas intensified with the agro-export boom of the 1980s, spawning Southern environmentalism. First World forms of environmental regulation also began to be demanded in order to address environmental stresses from overuse of natural resources resulting in desertification, excessive water salinity, and chemical contamination associated with the green revolution.

The common denominator of most environmental movements is the belief that natural resources are not infinitely renewable. The finiteness of nature has been a global preoccupation, from the neo-Malthusian specter of population growth overwhelming available supplies of land and the food grown on it to anxiety about the dwindling supplies of raw materials, such as fossil fuels and timber, that are essential to modern economies.

Lately, however, this rather linear perspective has yielded to a more dynamic one that sees a serious threat to essential natural elements such as the atmosphere, climates, and biodiversity. Trees may be renewable through replanting schemes, but the atmospheric conditions that nurture them may not be so easily replenished. As Paul Harrison implies, the world has moved to a new threshold of risk to its sustainability:

> It used to be feared that we would run out of non-renewable resources—things like oil, or gold. Yet these, it seems, are the ones we need worry least about. It is the renewables—the ones we thought would last forever—that are being destroyed at an accelerating rate. They are all living things, or dynamic parts of living ecosystems.[11]

Furthermore, the very survival of the human species is increasingly at risk as pollution and environmental degradation lead to public health epidemics. These include lead poisoning, new strains of cancer, cataracts from ozone destruction, immune suppression by ultraviolet radiation, and loss of genetic and biological resources for producing food and medicines.[12]

There has been a change in thinking in several quarters. First is the rise of what are termed "new social movements" (discussed briefly in the following insert). These include modern-day feminism, environmentalism, and cooperatives. Their appearance on the historical stage reflects the demise of developmentalism and the search for new directions of social and political action.[13]

What Are the New Social Movements?

The new social movements, such as the greens, feminism, and grassroots or *basismo* politics, share criticism of the development project. Where the development project advocated state economic management, the new movements tend to reject centralism and stress community empowerment instead. Where the development project emphasized industrialism and material abundance, the new movements tend to seek post- or preindustrial values of decentralization, flexibility, and simplicity; and where the development project championed state and market institutions, the new social movements seek grassroots autonomy and the reassertion of cultural values over those of the market. In short, the new social movements are distinguished by their *expressive politics* and their challenge to the economism and instrumental politics of the "developed society" model. They have grown as the institutions of the welfare state (including labor organizations) have receded, and they have contributed to the declining legitimacy of the development project. (*Sources*: Buttel, 1992; Lehmann, 1990)

The second indication of a change in thinking is a growing awareness of the limits of "spaceship earth." From the late 1960s, space photographs of planet earth dramatized the biophysical finiteness of our world. The dangerous synergies arising from global economic intercourse and ecology were driven home by the Brundtland Commission's declaration in 1987: "The Earth is one but the world is not. We all depend on one biosphere for sustaining our lives."[14]

Third, there have been various grassroots movements focusing attention on the growing conflict on the margins between local cultures and the global market. For example, the Kayapo Indians of the Amazon strengthened their demands by appealing to the global community for defense of their forest habitat from logging, cattle pasturing, and extraction of genetic resources. One response by the Brazilian government to this kind of demand was the creation of *extractive reserves* for native tribes and rubber tappers to protect them from encroaching ranchers and colonists. These reserves are relatively large areas of forest land set aside, with government protection, for extractive activities by forest dwellers.[15]

Finally, from the 1970s on, the pressure on natural resources from the rural poor has intensified. This pressure stems from the long-term impoverishment of rural populations forced to overwork their land and fuel sources to eke out a subsistence. As land and forest were increasingly devoted to export production in the 1980s, millions of rural poor were pushed into occupying marginal tropical forest ecosystems. Environmental degradation, including deforestation, resulted. Environmental movements have proposed both local and global solutions under the mantle of "sustainable development." The following case study illustrates opposition to a massive development project in India.

Sustainable Development

The concept of **sustainable development** gained currency as a result of the 1987 Brundtland report, entitled *Our Common Future*. The report defined sustainable development as "meet[ing] the needs of the present without compromising the ability of future generations to meet their own needs."[16] How to achieve this remains a puzzle. The Brundtland Commission suggested steps such as conserving and enhancing natural resources, encouraging grassroots involvement in development, and adopting appropriate technologies (smaller scale, energy conserving). While acknowledging that "an additional person in an industrial country consumes far more and places far greater pressure on natural resources than an additional person in the Third World," the Commission nevertheless recom-

CASE STUDY

Resistance to the Narmada Dam Project in India

Since the 1980s, the Indian government has been implementing a huge dam project in the Narmada River valley, with financial assistance from the World Bank. This massive development project involves 30 large and over 3,000 medium and small dams on the Narmada River, expected eventually to displace over 2 million people and their culture. In 1992, at the time of the Earth Summit, there was an embarrassing simultaneous release of an independent review (the first ever) of the Bank's Sardar Sarovar dam project in India. Commissioned by the Bank president, the review claimed "gross delinquency" on the part of the Bank and the Indian government in both the engineering and the forcible resettlement of displaced peasants. These revelations, and the growing resistance movement, the *Narmada Bachao Andolan* (Movement to Save the Narmada), had considerable success in forcing the Bank to withdraw its support for this project. Members of the grassroots opposition to the dam argue that the resistance "articulates . . . the critical legacy of Mahatma Gandhi . . . of the struggles all over the country that continue to challenge both the growing centralization and authoritarianism of the state and the extractive character of the dominant economic process—a process which not only erodes and destroys the subsistence economies of these areas, but also the diversity of their systems. . . . The movement is therefore representative of growing assertions of marginal populations for greater economic and political control over their lives."

Source: Kothari & Parajuli, 1993, p. 233.

mended continued emphasis on economic growth to reduce the pressure of the poor on the environment.[17]

The report did not resolve the interpretive debate over the root cause of environmental deterioration. This is the debate over whether the threat to our common future stems from poverty or from affluence. Those who argue the poverty cause consider the gravest stress on the environment to be impoverished masses pressing on resources. Population control and economic growth are the suggested solutions. Those who identify affluence as the problem believe the gravest stress on the environment comes

from global inequality and the consumption of resources to support affluent lifestyles. Measures of this effect abound, one of the more provocative
being the claim that each U.S. citizen contributes 60 times more to global
warming than each Mexican and that a Canadian's contribution equals
that of 190 Indonesians.[18] This perspective has generated the "impossibil-
ity theorem" of former World Bank economist Herman E. Daly that "a
U.S.-style high-resource consumption standard for a world of 4 billion
people is impossible."[19]

The Earth Summit

The terms of this debate infused the 1992 **United Nations Conference on
Environment and Development** (UNCED). Popularized as the Rio de
Janeiro "Earth Summit," it was the largest diplomatic gathering ever held.
The United Nations Environment Program (UNEP) organized the conference to review progress on the Brundtland report. Conference preparations resulted in a document, known as Agenda 21, that details a global
program for the twenty-first century and implicitly addresses all sides of
the debate.

The South, for instance, recognized that the First World had an interest in reducing carbon dioxide emissions and preserving biodiversity and
the tropical rain forests for planetary survival. It agreed to participate in
the global program in return for financial assistance, arguing that "poverty
is the greatest polluter," a phrase once used by the now deceased Indian
president Indira Gandhi. Accordingly, it called for massive investment by
the First World in sustainable development measures in the South, including health, sanitation, education, technical assistance, and conservation.[20]

In the end, UNCED detoured from the question of global inequities,
stressing that environmental protection should be a development priority,
but "without distorting international trade and investment."[21] The outcome was a shift in emphasis from the Brundtland report in two senses:
(1) privileging global management of the environment over local/national
concerns and (2) maintaining the viability of the "global economy" rather
than addressing deteriorating economic conditions in the South. The globalization project was alive and well.

Managing the Global Commons

Environmental management is as old as the need for human communities
to ensure material and cultural survival. *Global* environmental management preserves the viability and market culture of the global economy.

The difference is of scale and control of that economy. The global economy's limits are now planetary, of course. To the Southern greens, First World decision makers seem to focus on managing the global environment for the benefit of those who profit most from the global economy. This includes regulating the use of planetary resources and global waste sinks such as forests, wetlands, and bodies of water. Instead of linking environmental concerns to issues of social justice and resource distribution, the new "global ecology" has converged on four priorities: reducing greenhouse gas emissions, primarily from automobiles and burning forests; protecting biodiversity, mainly in tropical forests; reducing pollution in international waters; and curbing ozone-layer depletion.

The institutional fallout from UNCED strengthened global economic management. A **Global Environmental Facility (GEF)** was installed, geared to funding global ecology initiatives. The World Bank initiated the establishment of the GEF to channel monies into global environmental projects, especially in the four areas identified above; 50 percent of the projects approved in the GEF's first tranche were for biodiversity protection. Additionally, UNCED, via the **Food and Agricultural Organization (FAO)**, has plans to zone Southern land for cash cropping with the assistance of national governments. Under this facility, subsistence farming would be allowed only where "natural resource limitations" or "environmental or socioeconomic constraints" prevent intensification. And where governments deem marginal land to be overpopulated, the inhabitants are likely to be forced into transmigration or resettlement programs. The logic of this scenario is one of managing the "global commons."[22] That is to say, management of the world's natural environment, on which human life itself depends, would pass to a technical and bureaucratic elite accountable to no one. Given its past and current practices, which are both unrepresentative and favor global over local actors in managing the world's natural resource base, the global elite's conception of sustainable development has all the makings of an oxymoron (a contradiction in terms).

This unfolding global ecology movement, geared to environmental management on a large scale, has priorities for sustainability quite different from those of the remaining local environmental managers. It is estimated that there are 200–300 million forest dwellers in South and Southeast Asia, distinct from lowland communities dependent on irrigated agriculture. Some of these people have been given official group names assigning them a special—and usually second-class—status in their national society: India's "scheduled tribes" (*adivasis*), Thailand's "hill tribes," China's "minority nationalities," the Philippines' "cultural minorities," Indonesia's "isolated and alien peoples," Taiwan's "aboriginal tribes," and

Malaysia's "aborigines." Challenging their national status and elevating their internationally common bonds, these groups have recently redefined themselves as "indigenous."[23]

Indigenous and tribal people around the world have had their rights to land and self-determination enshrined in the International Labor Organization Convention. Nevertheless, they are routinely viewed from afar as marginal. The World Bank, in adopting the term *indigenous* in its documents, stated in 1990: "The term indigenous covers indigenous, tribal, low caste and ethnic minority groups. Despite their historical and cultural differences, they often have a limited capacity to participate in the national development process because of cultural barriers or low social and political status."[24]

Viewed through the development lens, this is a predictable perspective, and it carries a significant implication. On the one hand, it perpetuates the often unexamined assumption that these cultural minorities need guidance. On the other, it often subordinates minorities to national development initiatives, such as commercial logging or governmental social forestry projects involving tree plantations. More often than not, such indigenous peoples find themselves on the receiving end of large-scale resettlement programs justified by the belief that forest destruction is a consequence of their poverty. This has been the case recently on the Indonesian island of Kalimantan, where the state has been actively encouraging commercial logging at the expense of a sophisticated and centuries-old rattan culture practiced by the Dayak Indians. They have begun to form their own resistance, documenting their ownership of cultivars in the forest.[25]

The focus on poverty as the destroyer of forests guided the establishment of the Tropical Forest Action Plan (TFAP) in the 1980s by a global management group consisting of the Bank, the Food and Agricultural Organization, the **United Nations Development Program**, and the World Resources Institute. TFAP was designed to pool funds to provide alternative fuel-wood sources, strengthen forestry and environmental institutions, conserve protected areas and watersheds, and promote social forestry. It became the "most ambitious environmental aid program ever conceived" and, as such, attracted requests for aid from 62 Southern states looking for new, seemingly "green," sources of funds for extraction of forest products for export. TFAP projects were completed in Peru, Guyana, Cameroon, Ghana, Tanzania, Papua New Guinea, Nepal, Colombia, and the Philippines. Seeing their effects, however, and charging that the TFAP projects furthered deforestation through intervention and zoning, a worldwide rain forest movement mobilized sufficient criticism (including that of

Britain's Prince Charles) that the TFAP initiative ended. Forestry loans, however, continued through the World Bank.[26]

One such forestry loan was for "agro-ecological zoning" in the Brazilian Polonoroeste area of Rondônia and Mato Grosso to set aside land for farmers, extractive reserves for the rubber tappers, and protected Indian reserves in addition to national parks, forest reserves, and other protected forest areas. Typically, the minorities affected were not consulted, even though Chico Mendes wrote to the Bank president on behalf of the rubber tappers in 1988, voicing their concerns. He feared a repetition of the mistakes made when Rondônia was occupied in the 1980s by impoverished settlers who burned the Amazonian jungle in vain hopes of farming:

> We think that the extractive reserves included in Polonoroeste II only serve to lend the Government's project proposal to the World Bank an ecological tone—which has been very fashionable lately—in order to secure this huge loan. . . . What will be created will not be extractive reserves, but colonization settlements with the same mistakes that have led to the present disaster of Polonoroeste. In other words, a lot of money will be spent on infrastructures which do not mean anything to the peoples of the forest and the maintenance of which will not be sustainable.[27]

Mendes was later murdered for his part in championing the rubber tappers.

Despite protests from local nongovernment organizations, the Rondônian Natural Resources Management Project loan was approved in 1992, at the same moment the Brazilian land agency, INCRA, "was proceeding with plans to settle some 50,000 new colonists a year in areas that were supposed to be set aside as protected forests and extractive reserves for rubber tappers under the Bank project."[28]

On the other side of the world, a similar resettlement project was under way in Indonesia. In this transmigration project, millions of poor peasants were moved from densely populated inner islands of Indonesia, notably Java, to the outer islands of Kalimantan, Irian Jaya, and Sumatra to settle and cultivate cash crops for export, such as cacao, coffee, and palm oil. The outer islands were inhabited by non-Javanese indigenous tribes and contained 10 percent of the world's remaining rain forests. Critics saw this project as both a money-spinner for the Indonesian government and a security project against non-Javanese people who desired autonomy from the military government.

Building on the Indonesian government's initial resettlement of more than half a million people since 1950, the World Bank assisted a further resettlement of 3.5 million people between 1974 and 1990, with that many again moving to the outer islands as private colonizers. The project, by the Bank's own accounting, simply redistributed poverty spatially, from the inner to the outer islands; additionally, it caused roughly 4 percent of the Indonesian forests to disappear.[29]

Environmental Resistance Movements

In all these cases, there is a discernible pattern of collaboration between the multilateral financiers and governments concerned with securing territory and foreign exchange. Indigenous cultures, on the other hand, are typically marginalized. Indonesia's Forestry Department controls 74 percent of the national territory, and the minister for forestry claimed in 1989, "In Indonesia, the forest belongs to the state and not to the people. . . . [T]hey have no right of compensation" when their habitats fall to logging concessions.[30]

Under these conditions, grassroots environmental movements proliferate. They take two forms: active resistance, which seeks to curb invasion of habitats by states and markets; and adaptation to environmental depredation, which exemplifies the centuries-old practice of renewing habitats in the face of environmental deterioration. In the latter practice we may find some of the answers to current problems.

Perhaps the most dramatic form of resistance was undertaken by the Chipko movement in the Central Himalaya region of India. Renewing an ancient tradition of peasant resistance in 1973, the Chipko adopted a Gandhian strategy of nonviolence, symbolized in tree-hugging protests led primarily by women against commercial logging. Similar protests spread across northern India in a move to protect forest habitats for tribal peoples. Emulating the Chipko practice of tree planting to restore forests and soils, the movement developed a "pluck and plant" tactic. Its members uprooted eucalyptus seedlings—the tree of choice in official social forestry, even though it does not provide shade and does ravish aquifers—and replaced them with indigenous species of trees that yield products useful to the locals. Success of these movements has been measured primarily in two ways: by withdrawal of Bank involvement and the redefinition of forestry management by the Indian government; and by the flowering of new political associations, sometimes called "user groups," that are democratic and dedicated to reclaiming lands and redefining grassroots development.[31]

Environmental activism like this is paralleled across the South. In Thailand, where the state has promoted eucalyptus plantations that threaten massive displacement of forest dwellers, there has been an explosion of rural activism. . . . Small farmers are standing up to assassination threats; weathering the contempt of bureaucrats; petitioning cabinet officials; arranging strategy meetings with other villagers; calling on reserves of political experience going back decades; marching; rallying; blocking roads; ripping out seedlings; chopping down eucalyptus trees; burning nurseries; planting fruit, rubber and forest trees in order to demonstrate their own conservationist awareness. . . . Their message is simple. They want individual land rights. They want community rights to local forests which they will conserve themselves. They want a reconsideration of all existing eucalyptus projects. And they want the right to veto any commercial plantation scheme in their locality.[32]

In the Philippines, a successful reforestation program undertaken by the Ikalahan of the eastern Cordillera followed the decentralization of resource control from the Department of Energy and Natural Resources to management by the local community in the 1980s. The state in effect transferred ancestral land back to the community. On the island of Mindanao, indigenous communities have reclaimed state and pastoral lands for subsistence farming, organizing themselves democratically along Chipko lines.[33]

As grassroots environmentalism mushrooms across the South, community control gains credibility by example. At the same time, the institutional aspects of technology transfer associated with the development project come under question. An ex-director of forestry at the Food and Agricultural Organization, Jack Westoby, commented in 1987:

Only very much later did it dawn on the development establishment that the very act of establishing new institutions often meant the weakening, even the destruction of existing indigenous institutions which ought to have served as the basis for sane and durable development: the family, the clans, the tribe, the village, sundry mutual aid organizations, peasant associations, rural trade unions, marketing and distribution systems and so on.[34]

Of course, the point is that forest dwellers have always managed their environment. From the perspective of colonial rule and the developers, these communities did not appear to be involved in management because their practices were alien to the rational, specialized pursuit of commercial wealth characterizing Western ways beginning under colonialism. Local practices were therefore either suppressed or ignored.

Now, where colonial forestry practices erased local knowledge and eroded natural resources, recent grassroots mobilization, such as the Green Belt Movement in Kenya organized by women, has reestablished inter-cropping to replenish soils and tree planting to sustain forests. Where development agencies and planners have attempted to impose irrigated cash cropping, such as in eastern Senegal, movements like the Senegalese Federation of Sarakolle Villages have collectively resisted in the interests of sustainable peasant farming (sustainable in the social as well as the ecological sense).[35]

Hundreds of local communities have evolved new resource management practices as livelihood strategies, often with the aid of **nongovernmental organizations** (NGOs). For example, local environmental management in the Manya Krobo area of southeastern Ghana has revived in the wake of environmental deterioration visited on the forest land by cash cropping. Nineteenth-century colonialism promoted the production of palm oil, followed by cocoa cultivation, for export. The displacement of forest cover by monocultural cocoa crops led to severe degradation of the soils. With cocoa prices falling in the second half of the twentieth century, local farmers shifted to growing cassava and corn for local food markets; they also cultivated oil palms and activated a local crafts industry (distilling) used for subsistence rather than for export. Forest restoration technologies, combined with food crops, have emerged as a viable adaptation. These restoration methods are based on the preservation of pioneer forest species rather than the fast-growing exotics promoted by development agencies as fuel-wood supplies and short-term forest cover. The lesson is that the community of cultivators is "an originator of technology, rather than a consumer of technology packages."[36]

The challenge for grassroots environmental movements in the former Third World is therefore twofold: (1) to create alternatives to the capital- and energy-intensive forms of specialized agriculture and agro-forestry that are appropriate to the goal of restoring and sustaining local ecologies; and (2) to build alternative models to the bureaucratic, top-down development plans that have typically subordinated natural resource use to commercial rather than social ends. Perhaps the fundamental challenge to Southern environmental movements is the perspective stated in the Bank's *World Development Report, 1992*: "Promoting development is the best way to protect the environment."[37] Whether development, understood from the Bank's perspective, is a source of sustainability is the question. Thus, methods of environmental management and development, as ideas and practices, underlie the growing conflict between local and global forces.

Feminism

Where Southern grassroots movements entail protection of local resources and community, women typically play a defining role. This has always been so, but one consequence of colonialism is that this activity has become almost exclusively a women's preserve. As private property in land emerged, women's work tended to specialize in use of the commons for livestock grazing, firewood collection, game hunting, and seed gathering for medicinal purposes. These activities allowed women to supplement the incomes earned by men in the commercial sector. Women assumed a role as environmental managers, often forced to adapt to deteriorating conditions as commercial extractions increased over time.

The establishment of individual rights to property under colonialism typically privileged men. The result was the fragmentation of social systems built on the complementarity of male and female work. Men's work became specialized; in national economic statistics, it is routinely counted as contributing to the commercial sector. Conversely, the specialization of women's labor as "nonincome earning" work remains outside the commercial sector. Oppositions such as waged and non-waged work or productive and nonproductive work emerged. In modern national accounting systems, only productive work is counted or valued, leaving much of women's work invisible. The domain of invisible work in many cases involves the work of maintaining the commons.

When we trace the development of feminism, we find that it has circled back toward recovery of this sense of the commons. The journey has been both practical and theoretical—moving from bringing women into development to an alternative conception of the relationship of women to development. It began with the movement to integrate women into development in the early 1970s. The first U.N. world conference on women was held in Mexico City in 1975 and concentrated on extending existing development programs to include women. This movement was known as *Women in Development* (WID). Since then, the movement has changed gears, shifting from what Rounaq Jahan terms an "integrationist" to an "agenda-setting" approach, which challenges the existing development system of thought with a feminist perspective.[38] The goal includes involving women as decision makers concerned with empowering all women in their various life situations.

Feminist Formulations

The shift from integration to transformation of the development model has involved a redefinition of feminism from WID to *women, environment, and alternative development* (WED). The redefinition symbolizes a movement from remedies to alternatives.[39] There are two aspects to this shift. First, the WID position originally addressed the absence of gender issues from development theory and practice. The arguments are familiar: women's contributions were made invisible by economic statistics that measured only the contributions to development of income-earning units (waged labor and commercial enterprises). WID feminists have identified problems and formulated remedies in the following ways.

Women have always been *de facto* producers, but because of their invisibility, their technological and vocational supports have been minimal. Planners should therefore recognize women's contributions, especially as food producers for rural households and even urban markets, where males labor or migrate to the agro-export or cash-crop sector. Women also bear children, and a more robust understanding of development would include education, health care, family planning, and nutrition as social supports. Finally, because of patriarchal expectations that women perform unpaid household/farm labor in addition to any paid labor, development planners should pursue ameliorative measures. Findings reveal that where women can be incorporated into income-earning activities, a net benefit accrues to community welfare since male income is often dissipated in consumer/urban markets.

By contrast, the WED position is that economic development theory is Eurocentric (it understands non-European reality in Western terms), hierarchical, and male-biased in its assumptions about development strategy. Conventional economics excludes the contributions of women and nature from its models. Insofar as economic theory informs development practices, they have revealed a predatory relationship to each, in which women are exploited and socially and economically marginalized and nature is plundered. The human future is therefore depleted.

The second order of difference concerns our understanding of the world and how we replenish it. The WED position on developmentalism is that "the task is not simply to add women into the known equation but to establish a new development paradigm."[40] WED feminists argue that economic theory is incapable of reform because it is a rationalized form of knowledge, or paradigm, that is abstracted from practice and history and presumes to have universal application. An alternative form of knowledge is practical and rooted in cultural traditions.

WED feminists argue that Western traditions of rational science have devalued and displaced practical knowledge through colonialism and the development project.[41] That is, local cultures in both the European and the non-European worlds have yielded to the rationality of the marketplace. For example, craft traditions have been mechanized; multiple cropping and animal husbandry combinations have been separated, specialized, and infused with chemical inputs; and traditional health practices have been overriden by Western medical science. Similarly, "the work of caring for the environment, and women's role as nurturers, are also undervalued in the logic of development."[42] The difference between WID and WED feminism is further explored in the following insert.

What Is the Difference Between WID and WED Feminism?

The difference in the two perspectives is not just one of emphasis. It involves how we look at the world, including what we take account of. WID feminism tends to accept the developmentalist framework and look for ways within development programs to improve the position of women. For example, pushing for new jobs for women in the paid work force is because women's unpaid work was implicitly devalued and removed from consideration as activity contributing to livelihoods. The movement from WID to WED follows a conceptual shift from a universalist (rational) toward a diverse (expressive) understanding of the world. It is also a move from a linear (for example, *a* causes *b*, where independent forces act on one another) to a holistic understanding of development processes, where all forces are interrelated. In consequence, WED feminists question the separation in Western thought between nature and culture, where nature is viewed as separate from and acted on by culture rather than each shaping the other. In the WED view, stewardship of nature is understood as integral to the renewal of culture rather than being constructed as a program per se.

The WED position argues that, within the WID approach, women were presumed to be universally subordinate to men. Further, development was redefined as a mechanism of emancipation of women. But this perspective was seriously flawed; it resembled the colonial mission toward women, which was to rescue non-European women from the wretchedness of their own cultures (for example, Hindu widow cremation in India). The WID mission tended to judge Third World women's position against the ideal of the emancipated (economically independent) woman of the First World.[43]

In making this comparison, WED feminism stresses that development is a relative, not a universal, process and we should be aware of how our ideals shape our assumptions about other societies. Concerns for the empowerment of women in Third World settings should refer to those circumstances, not to abstract ideals of individual emancipation. In other words, women's role in sustaining cultural and ecological relations is complex, place specific, and incapable of being reduced to universal formulas. Reflecting this perspective was a women's tribunal held in Miami in 1991 to document women's environmental struggles. The outcome was the *Women's Action Agenda 21*, which combined women's voices across the divides of North/South, race, and class in a common vision of an alternative development practice to the Western model.[44]

Women and the Environment

At the practical level, women engage in multifaceted activity. Across the world, women's organizations have mobilized to manage local resources, to empower poor women and communities, and to pressure governments and international agencies on behalf of women's rights. Countless activities of resource management undertaken by women form the basis of these practices. Perhaps most basic is the preservation of biodiversity in market and kitchen gardens. In Peru, the Aguarunu Jivaro women nurture over 100 varieties of manioc, the local staple root crop. Women have devised ingenious ways of household provisioning beside and within the cash-cropping systems managed by men. Hedgerows and wastelands become sites of local food crops.[45] Forest products (game, medicinal plants, condiments) are cultivated and harvested routinely by women. In rural Laos, over 100 different forest products are collected chiefly by women for home use or sale. Women in Ghana process, distribute, and market game. Indian women anchor household income—with an array of nontimber forest products amounting to 40 percent of total Forest Department revenues—as do Brazilian women in Acre, working by the side of the male rubber tappers.[46] A particular success from Kenya is reported in the following case study.

Women, Poverty, and Fertility

Women's resource management is often ingenious, but often poverty subverts their ingenuity. For example, where women have no secure rights to land, they are less able to engage in sustainable resource extraction. Environmental deterioration may follow. When we see women stripping forests and overworking fragile land, we are often seeing just the tip of the iceberg. Many of these women have been displaced from lands converted for export cropping, or they have lost common land on which to subsist.

Environmental damage stemming from poverty has fueled the debate surrounding population growth in the former Third World. Population control has typically been directed at women—ranging from female infan-

CASE STUDY

The Kikuyu Cooperative in Kenya

In Kenya, the Kikuyu women in Laikipia have formed 354
women's groups to help them coordinate community decisions
about access to and use of resources. Groups vary in size from 20
to 100 neighbors, both squatters and peasants; members contribute cash, products, and/or labor to the group, which in turn dis-
tributes resources equally among them. The groups have been
able to pool funds to purchase land and establish small enterprises for the members. One such group, the Mwenda-Niire,
formed in 1963 among landless squatters on the margins of a
large commercial estate. Twenty years later, through saving funds,
by growing maize and potatoes among the owner's crops, and
through political negotiation, the group purchased the 567-hectare
farm, allowing 130 landless families to become farmers. Group
dynamics continue through labor-sharing schemes, collective
infrastructure projects, and collective marketing. Collective movements such as this go beyond remedying development failures.
They restore women's access to resources removed from them
under colonial and postcolonial developments.

Source: Wacker, 1994, pp. 135–139.

ticide through forced sterilization (as in India) to family planning interventions by development agencies. Feminists have entered this debate to
protect women from such manipulation of their social and biological contributions.

Feminists demand the enabling of women to take control of their fertility without targeting women as the source of the population problem.
On a global scale, the current world population of 5.7 billion is expected
to double by 2050, according to U.N. projections, unless more aggressive
intervention occurs. Studies suggest that female education and health services reduce birthrates. The 1992 World Bank report pointed out that
women without secondary education on average have seven children; if
almost half these women receive secondary education, the average declines to three children per woman.[47]

In addition, recent evidence based on the results of contraceptive use
in Bangladesh has been cited as superseding conventional theories of

"demographic transition." Demographic theory extrapolates from the Western experience a pattern of demographic transition whereby birthrates decline significantly as economic growth proceeds. The threshold is the shift from preindustrial to industrial society, in which education and health technologies spread. This is expected to cause families to view children increasingly as an economic liability rather than as necessary hands in the household economy or as a response to high childhood mortality rates.

Evidence from Bangladesh, one of the 20 poorest countries of the world, shows a 21 percent decline in fertility rates during the decade and a half (1975–1991) in which a national family planning program was in effect. The study's authors claimed these findings "dispute the notion that 'development is the best contraceptive,'" adding that "contraceptives are the best contraceptive."[48]

Feminist groups argue that family planning and contraception need to be rooted in the broader context of women's rights. Presently, almost twice as many women as men are illiterate, and that difference is growing. Poor women with no education often do not understand their rights or contraceptive choices. The International Women's Health Coalition identified the Bangladesh Women's Health Coalition, serving 110,000 women at 10 clinics around the country, as a model for future United Nations planning. This group began in 1980, offering abortions. With suggestions from the women it served, the Coalition has expanded into family planning, basic health care services, child immunizations, legal aid, and training in literacy and employment skills.[49] Similar success stories are presented in the following case study.

With supportive social conditions, fertility decisions by women can have both individual and social benefits. Fertility decisions by individual women usually occur within patriarchal settings—households or societies—as well as within definite livelihood situations. It is these conditions that the feminist movements and women's groups have identified as necessary to the calculus in fertility decisions. Over the past decade, the population issue has incorporated elements of the feminist perspective, which emphasizes women's reproductive rights and health, in the context of their need for secure livelihoods and political participation.[50] This view was embedded in the 1994 U.N. Conference on Population and Development document. Although contested by the Vatican and some Muslim nations (particularly Iran), the document states that women have the right to reproductive and sexual health, defined as "a state of complete physical, mental and social well-being" in all matters relating to reproduction.[51]

CASE STUDY

Women's Rights and Fertility

The correlation between women's rights and low fertility rates has ample confirmation. In Tunisia, the 1956 Code of Individual Rights guaranteed women political equality, backed with family planning and other social programs that included free, legal abortions. Tunisia is a leader in Africa, with a population growth rate of only 1.9 percent. The director general of Tunisia's National Office of Family and Population, Nebiha Gueddana, claims that successful family planning can occur in a Muslim society: "We have thirty years of experience with the equality of women and . . . none of it has come at the expense of family values."

In Kerala, where the literacy rate for women is two and a half times the average for India, and where the status of women has been high throughout this century relative to the rest of the country, land reforms and comprehensive social welfare programs were instrumental in achieving a 40 percent reduction in the fertility rate between 1960 and 1985, reducing the population growth rate to 1.8 percent in the 1980s.

Sources: Crossette, 1994b, p. A8; Bello, 1992–1993, p. 5.

Feminism has clearly made an impact on the development agenda since the days of WID's inception. However, the improvement of women's material condition and social status across the world has not followed in step, even if the statistical reporting of women's work in subsistence production has improved.[52] In 1989, at the end of a decade of structural adjustment, the United Nations made the following report in its *World Survey on the Role of Women in Development*:

> The bottom line shows that, despite economic progress measured in growth rates, at least for the majority of developing countries, economic progress for women has virtually stopped, social progress has slowed, and social well-being in many cases has deteriorated, and because of the importance of women's social and economic roles, the aspirations for them in current development strategies will not be met.[53]

Five years later, the United Nation's *Human Development Report 1994* found that "despite advances in labor-force participation, education and health, women still constitute about two-thirds of the world's illiterates, hold fewer than half of the jobs on the market and are paid half as much as men for work of equal value."[54] Even so, feminism has put its stamp on the reformulations of development, as the U.N. 1994 report declared in response to the crisis in the former Third World:

> It requires a long, quiet process of sustainable human development . . . [a] development that not only generates economic growth but distributes its benefits equitably, that regenerates the environment rather than destroying it; that empowers people rather than marginalizing them. It is development that gives priority to the poor, enlarging their choices and opportunities and providing for their participation in decisions that affect their lives. It is development that is pro-people, pro-nature, pro-jobs and pro-women.[55]

Cosmopolitan Localism

Perhaps the litmus test of the globalization project is that as global integration intensifies, the currents of multiculturalism swirl faster. Fractious mobilizations of communities—urban, rural, class/ethnic—across the world threaten national and regional orders. The politics of identity substitutes for the politics of nation-building. Regions and communities see self-determination as more than a political goal. It now includes the idea of cultural renewal, which includes recovering local knowledge. Wolfgang Sachs remarks:

> Today, more than ever, universalism is under siege. To be sure, the victorious march of science, state and market has not come to a stop, but the enthusiasm of the onlookers is flagging. . . . The globe is not any longer imagined as a homogeneous space where contrasts ought to be levelled out, but as a discontinuous space where differences flourish in a multiplicity of places.[56]

The new forms of imagination embody what Sachs terms **cosmopolitan localism,** that is, the assertion of diverse localism as a universal right. Cosmopolitan localism questions the assumption of uniformity in the global project. This is a protective response, insofar as communities seek to avoid the marginalization or disruption associated with unpredictable global markets. Such questioning also asserts the need to respect alternative cultural traditions as a matter of global survival. Finally, it is a question of preserving or asserting human and democratic rights within broader settings, whether a world community or individual national arenas.

The most potent example of cosmopolitan localism was the peasant revolt in Mexico's southern state of Chiapas, a region in which small peasant farms are surrounded by huge cattle ranches and coffee plantations.

About a third of the unresolved land reforms in the Mexican agrarian reform department, going back more than half a century, are in Chiapas. The government's solution over the years has been to allow landless *campesinos* to colonize the Lacandon jungle and produce subsistence crops, coffee, and cattle. During the 1980s, coffee, cattle, and corn prices all fell, and *campesinos* were prohibited from logging—even though timber companies continued the practice.[57] The revolt had these deepening classical class inequities as its foundation. But the source of the inequities transcended the region.

On New Year's Day, 1994, hundreds of impoverished peasants rose up against what they perceived to be the Mexican state's continued violation of local rights. Not coincidentally, the revolt fell on the day the North American Free Trade Agreement (NAFTA) was implemented. To the Chiapas rebels, NAFTA symbolized the undermining of the revolutionary heritage in the Mexican Constitution of 1917, by which communal lands were protected from alienation. In 1992, under the pretext of structural adjustment policies and the promise of NAFTA, the Mexican government opened these lands for sale to Mexican and foreign agribusinesses. In addition, NAFTA included a provision to deregulate commodity markets— especially the market for corn, the staple peasant food.

The Chiapas revolt illustrates cosmopolitan localism well because it linked the struggle for local rights to a political and historical context. That is, the *Zapatistas* (as the rebels call themselves, after Mexican revolutionary Emilio Zapata) perceive the Mexican state as the chief agent of exploitation of the region's cultural and natural wealth. In one of many communiqués aimed at the global community, Subcomandante Marcos, the *Zapatista* spokesperson, characterized the Chiapas condition:

> Oil, electric energy, cattle, money, coffee, bananas, honey, corn, cocoa, tobacco, sugar, soy, melons, sorghum, mamey, mangos, tamarind, avocados, and Chiapan blood flow out through a thousand and one fangs sunk into the neck of Southeastern Mexico. Billions of tons of natural resources go through Mexican ports, railway stations, airports, and road systems to various destinations: the United States, Canada, Holland, Germany, Italy, Japan—but all with the same destiny: to feed the empire. . . . The jungle is opened with machetes, wielded by the same campesinos whose land has been taken away by the insatiable beast. . . . Poor people can not cut down trees, but the oil company, more and more in the hands of foreigners, can. . . . Why does the federal government take the question of national politics off the proposed agenda of the dialogue for peace? Are the indigenous Chiapan people only Mexican enough to be exploited, but not Mexican enough to be allowed an opinion on national politics? . . . What kind of citizens are the indigenous people of Chiapas? "Citizens in formation?"[58]

In these communiqués the *Ejército Zapatista de Liberación Nacional* (EZLN) movement addresses processes of both decline and renewal in Mexican civil society. The process of decline refers to the dismantling of the communal tradition of the Mexican national state symbolized in the infamous reform of Article 27 of the Constitution. The Article now privileges private (foreign) investment in land over the traditional rights of *campesinos* to petition for land redistribution within the *ejido* (Indian community land held in common) framework. The *Zapatistas* argue that this reform, in conjunction with the new liberalization under NAFTA, will undermine the Mexican smallholder and the basic grains sector. They understand that the U.S. "comparative advantage" in corn production (6.9 U.S. tons versus 1.7 Mexican tons per hectare, including infrastructural disparities) seriously threatens Mexican corn producers, especially because under NAFTA the Mexican government has agreed to phase out guaranteed prices for staples such as corn and beans.[59]

The renewal side involves the renewal of "citizenship" demands by the Chiapas movement. This directly addresses the need for free and fair elections in Chiapas (and elsewhere in Mexico), adequate political representation of *campesino* interests (as against those of Chiapas planters and ranchers), and the elimination of violence and authoritarianism in local government. The EZLN's demands included a formal challenge to a centuries-old pattern of *caciquismo* (local strongman tradition) in which federal government initiatives have been routinely thwarted by local political and economic interests. A case in point has been in the patronage system, whereby the governor of Chiapas state has channeled federal government welfare funds (*Solidaridad* loans) to local political allies.[60]

The renewal side also includes the demonstration effect of the Chiapas revolt, because communities throughout Mexico have since mobilized around similar demands—especially because local communities face common pressures, such as market reforms. In challenging local patronage politics, the *Zapatistas* elevated demands nationally for inclusion of *campesino* organizations in political decisions regarding rural reforms, including equity demands for small farmers as well as farm workers. They also advanced the cause of local and/or indigenous development projects that sustain local ecologies and cultures.[61] Chiapas is a region with considerable inter-ethnic mixing (*mestizo*), although Tzoltal is the local language along with Spanish. The rebellion has a pan-Mayan identity rather than a specific ethnic character with ethnic demands, other than the demand for indigenous co-governors.

Arguably, the Chiapas rebellion is a model for the postnational developmental era. This model has several elements, many of which have been associated with the so-called new social movements that have sprung up across the world. These movements mark the demise of classical liberal politics—the framing ideology of modern national political-economic institutions.[62] Classical liberalism addressed issues of political representation, not to be confused with contemporary neoliberalism, which espouses private market initiatives. It nurtured the rise in the West of the labor movement, citizenship politics, and the notion of social entitlement; its demise now coincides with the dismantling of the welfare state. As we discussed earlier in this chapter, the new social movements tend to reject the interest-group politics of liberalism and espouse a more associative politics, connecting various social causes.

What is distinctive about the Chiapas rebellion is the *texture* of its political action. Timed to coincide with the implementation of NAFTA, it wove together a powerful and symbolic critique of the politics of globalization. This critique had two goals. First, it opposed the involvement of national elites and governments in implementing neoliberal economic reforms on a global or regional scale, reforms that undo the institutionalized social entitlements associated with political liberalism. Second, it asserted a new agenda of renewal involving a politics of rights that goes beyond individual or property rights to human, and therefore community, rights. The push for regional autonomy challenged local class inequalities and demanded the empowerment of *campesino* communities. It also asserted the associative political style of the EZLN, composed of a coalition of *campesino* and women's organizations. And this form of politics addressed conditions elsewhere in Mexico and the world.

The Mexican government responded to the rebellion by creating the "National Commission for Integral Development and Social Justice for Indigenous People" and promised more monies by way of the government's national solidarity program. The *Zapatistas* rejected these proposals, however, as "just another step in their cultural assimilation and economic annihilation."[63] The EZLN program rejects integration into outside development projects, outlining a plan for land restoration, abolition of peasant debts, and reparations to be paid to the Indians of Chiapas by those who have exploited their human and natural resources. Self-determination involves the development of new organizational forms of cooperation among different groups in the region. These have evolved over time into a "fabric of cooperation" woven among the various threads of local groupings. They substitute fluid organizational patterns for the bureaucratic organizational forms associated with modernist politics—such as political parties, trade unions, and hierarchical state structures.[64] In these senses, whether the *Zapatistas* survive or not, the movement they have quickened will intensify the unresolved tension between globalism and localism and between global managerialism and political representation.

Summary

We have toured some of the world's hot spots in this chapter, noting the particular forms in which social movements respond to the failures of developmentalism and the further disorganizing impact of globalism. Responses range from withdrawal into alternative projects (for example, Islamic fundamentalism, feminist cooperatives, recovery of noncapitalist agro-ecological practices) to attempts to reframe development as a question of rights and fundamental social protections (such as the feminist movement as opposed to developmentalism, social-environmentalism, micro-regional rebellions like the one in Chiapas, and even Western right-wing fundamentalism). All these responses express the uncertainties of social arrangements under globalizing tendencies. Many express a fundamental desire to break out of the homogenizing and disempowering dynamics of globalization and to establish a sustainable form of social life based on new forms of associative politics.

The opportunity for political renewal lies, paradoxically, in the weakening of the nation-state by globalization. The opportunity is that as states shed their public largesse, patronage politics loses its financial foundation. The developmentalist state loses its salience, resulting in austerity policies that force public scrutiny by the economically disenfranchised.[65] As we have seen, globalization involves states surrendering leverage to more powerful global private and public authorities over domestic policy and institutions. One of the consequences is the decline in the labor unions caused by the restructuring of work and corporate downsizing, as firms and states have pursued efficiency in the global economy.[66] Labor's response will be to forge new forms of organization, especially along the lines of the new labor internationalism that has emerged to present a solid front to footloose firms that would divide national labor forces and to states that enter free trade agreements that would undermine labor benefits.

The new labor internationalism was a key part of the political debate surrounding NAFTA. American organized labor took a big step in distancing itself from U.S. national policy, arguing that NAFTA was not in the interests of American labor. Led by the rank and file, organized labor joined a substantial national political coalition of consumers, environmentalists, and others in opposing the implementation of NAFTA.[67] Although the U.S. government pushed NAFTA through, it nevertheless argued that the absence of labor rights in the Mexican *maquiladoras* was a case of unfair competition in global labor markets. Similarly, the issue of labor rights was a substantial point of conflict in the debates of the GATT Uruguay Round negotiations as well as in the formulation of a social charter for the European Union.[68] We can conclude, therefore, that globalization is stimulating new forms of labor organization to protect hard-won rights and is encouraging renewed debate about human rights on a world scale. Both arenas are important for the preservation of social and political rights.

In sum, the road to the political future has several forks. Across the world, cosmopolitan localism is expressed in the organization of regional cereal banks in Zimbabwe, ecological campaigns by women's groups in West Bengal, campesino credit unions in Mexico, the emergence of solidarity networks among labor forces, and the defense of forest dwellers throughout the tropics. How effectively these movements will interconnect politically—at the national, regional, and global levels—is an open question. Another question is how these movements will negotiate with existing states over the terms of local and/or cultural sustenance. Potentially, the new movements breathe new life into politics. They transcend the centralizing thrust of the developmentalist states of the postwar era and present models for the recovery of local forms of social organization. Overriding questions include how new political movements will articulate with states and whether they will replenish nation-states. Many of the people and communities left behind by the development and globalization projects look to nongovernmental organizations (NGOs), rather than to states or international agencies, to represent them and to meet their needs. Indeed, we are currently in a phase of "NGOization," in that national governments and international institutions have lost much of their legitimacy, and NGOs take considerable initiative in guiding grassroots development activities. In the following, and concluding, chapter we examine how our future and the future of development are shaping up.

8

Whither Development?

We have come a long way since I asked you to reflect on the global dimensions of your lifestyle. We made that basic connection, then explored how it came about, its consequences for the world we live in, and the ways we might think about the future of this world. The nineteenth-century social thinkers, who gave us our theories of development, saw social development evolving along industrial-technological lines. Eventually the European colonies were expected to make the same journey. In many ways, development was the key concept of the social sciences. It spoke to the human condition, with universal expectation. This expectation was formalized in the development project, but it was an unrealizable ideal. It has been replaced with another unrealizable ideal—the globalization project, which speaks a similar language about the centrality of economic growth, but with different means. It is old wine in a new bottle. In this chapter, we review the implications of this reformulation of development.

Legacies of the Development Project

Three observations can be made about the development project and its underlying message. First, it represented a fork in the historical road, favoring the Western model over alternative models in the non-Western world. Second, this fork included a strong dose of economistic thinking, which now threatens to overpower all other conceptions of social organization. Third, because of the combined impact of these two forces, the world faces an uncertain future, and development itself is under serious question.

Historical Choices

Historical choices were made in the 1940s, but they grew out of previous historical relationships. Development is a long-standing European idea, woven from two related strands of thought. One is the Promethean self-conception of European civilization, underlying the Judeo-Christian belief in the progressive human domestication of nature. This progressivism evolved as the core ideal parallel to Europe's emergence as a world power and was expressed in the capitalist ethos of the endless accumulation of wealth as a rational economic activity. The second strand took root in this global endeavor. The inevitable comparison Europeans made between their civilization and the culture of their colonial subjects produced a conception of modernity as the destiny of humankind. It was this conception that governed the choice to institutionalize development on a world scale.

Two pillars of the development enterprise were *technological transfer* and *education*. Third World countries found that the promise of First World technologies was ambiguous. If green revolution technologies raised agricultural productivity, they also deepened social inequalities in many rural regions. There was also the problem of applying standard technologies to a variety of distinct local agro-ecologies. This problem was endemic to the schemes of technical assistance, which often had ambiguous results. Certainly, supplementary technical assistance such as water delivery and irrigation systems has improved many village and rural facilities. But wholesale introduction of some technical packages to modernize local economic systems has had decidedly mixed effects. The Tanzanian peanut scheme in the 1960s, for example, saw foreign experts overriding local aspirations and local conditions. The plan was to apply new technology to cultivate 3 million acres of peanuts, despite the misgivings of local farmers. The project was abandoned 10 years later because of rainfall miscalculations, soil abrasiveness that ruined metal plows, and persisting plant disease.

"Education for nation-building" was tied to the goal of the United Nations Educational, Scientific, and Cultural Organization (UNESCO): promoting scientific humanism as the basis for a development society. This goal energized planners and political elites alike. Education became a vehicle for introducing politics and bringing the advantages of political patronage down to the village level. As Hobsbawm remarked: "In a literal sense, knowledge meant power, most obviously in countries where the state appeared to its subjects to be a machine that extracted their resources and then distributed these resources to state employees."[1] Again, while some benefits were recorded, though fewer for women than for men, education has been routinely framed within the expectations of the development project. But critics have argued that formal schooling has encouraged economic rationalism and a consumer mentality at the expense of deepening pupils' understanding and appreciation of their own cultures and local ecologies.[2]

In short, the development project took the fork that led toward a common future, defined by the standards of the Western experience and bundled up in the idea of national economic growth. It rejected the other fork, the one of empowering local cultures—or at least allowing them to be replenished after the ravages of colonialism. Truly multilateral institutions would have been required to rebuild a world order that emphasized empowerment of local social needs rather than what were presumed to be common economic needs.

Notice that there is no suggestion here of how these social needs would be politically implemented, because there may have been alternatives to the national form of political organization. Certainly advocates of the pan-African movement in the 1950s understood that the national form was not appropriate to African needs at that time. It also appears that the nation-state may not have been appropriate to Central Europe 40 years earlier, and recently we have seen the violent implosion of Yugoslavia, Somalia, and Rwanda.[3] At the same time, macro-regions superimposed on neighboring nation-states are forming tentatively. In other words, the national form of political and economic organization may become only a moment in the longer sweep of history. Whether its democratic legacy will infuse future social organization, and how, is an open question.

Economism

Our second observation about the development project is that its fundamental economism has borne fruit, but not necessarily of a kind expected by some at its inception. Certainly, the capitalist form of economy has prospered, but its wealth and promise of technological abundance are quite unequally distributed. The development project brought all nations into line with the idea of national economic growth, even across the Cold War divide. But the pursuit of economic growth within the terms of the development project led to these terms being undercut by global economic relations, and the management of economic globalization erodes national sovereignty.

In the context of globalization, *neoclassical economic thought* has attained prominence. Proponents of neoclassical economics perceive national management and public expenditure as interfering with market efficiencies. They believe nationally managed economic growth is anachronistic in an era of global communications, corporate organization, and global freedom for goods and money—but not labor. It is these ideas that underlay the debt management program in the 1980s and still inform global management notions today. More significantly, these ideas guide national political elites on both the right and the left as nations scramble to survive in the global economy, triggering what some refer to as the race to the bottom. This scramble, of course, puts increasing distance between where the world is now and the tidy national framework of the development project.

The scramble reveals itself most dramatically in the *global reorganization of labor*. We examined this in Chapter 6, pointing out that as barriers to investment and trade fall, labor forces across the world become cost competitors with one another. Employment security has declined as firms have either downsized to remain competitive in a global market or relocated production to lower rungs on the global wage ladder. These changes have been in part responsible for the declining living standards in the North. In the United States, for example, while manufacturing jobs shrank by 15.6 percent between 1979 and 1992 and service jobs expanded by 40.8 percent during the same period, the average weekly wage in 1991 for service workers was only 73 percent of that of manufacturing workers. Half the 12 million new jobs created in the 1980s paid an annual wage lower than the official poverty level, and 80 percent of Americans have experienced a stagnation or decline in incomes since 1973. In addition, employment benefits such as health care and pensions have been on a downward slope since 1979, and more and more of the labor force finds itself in part-time, low-skill, and low-paying jobs. Furthermore, one-third of U.S. jobs are estimated to be at risk to the growing productivity of low-wage labor in China, India, Mexico, and Latin America.[4]

There are three important consequences of these changes. One is that the organization of Northern societies around stable employment patterns associated with the expectations of the development project is in serious flux. Another is that, no matter how much automation and post-industrialism may be celebrated as further economic progress, there is still the problem of stable employment—and this dilemma will occupy political elites and labor organizations for decades to come. A third consequence is that, as social entitlements for labor dwindle, antagonism toward immigrant labor groups intensifies. Current management of labor markets invokes racist divisions among segments of national populations, further unraveling the unifying politics of citizenship that matured within the national framework. In short, all these changes have profound political consequences because they threaten the liberal underpinnings of Western democracy.

If employment patterns and living standards have become tenuous in the First World, their status is even more fragile in the former Second and Third Worlds. No country is immune to the vicissitudes of a global labor market. Export zones may attract jobs, but can they survive when other zones come on line? In order to compete, some of these zones, noted for their absence of labor protections, include child labor.

Also in Chapter 6 we noted the growing migration of Southern labor in search of jobs across the world. But these migrants face very uncertain and often hostile situations. The expulsion of "foreign" labor appeals to nationalist rhetoric in a time of economic uncertainty. An example is Gabon, a small oil-producing nation in Central Africa. Faced with a declining economy in 1994, it enacted nationalist legislation that effectively expelled thousands of West Africans.[5]

Ultimately, the fortunes of labor across the world are intertwined. The development project promised a parallel national movement toward First World–style regulation of national wage levels in an increasingly prosperous consumer society. It now appears that as the project has unraveled, with governments surrendering the social achievements of labor in the name of efficiency, the very institution of wage-labor—its organization, its rights, and its social entitlements—is also being transformed. The process is truly global.

Under these circumstances, where the future is unpredictable, development itself is becoming an *uncertain paradigm*. It is not surprising to find the local and the global sides of the development debate reformulating the meaning of development. One example is the common use of the term *sustainable development*, although it has different meanings on each side. These unintended fruits of the development project are another reason to put it in historical context.

Environmental Deterioration

The third observation has to do with the deterioration of the environment. Not only is the future unpredictable, but to a growing number of people around the world it is becoming increasingly uncertain. If the unraveling of the development project has unleashed expressions of diverse identities and local needs, it has at the same time confronted us with the certainty of global environmental degradation. We do have a common future in that we all face growing environmental limits.

In Chapter 7 we saw the wide differences that exist in strategies of sustainability, distribution, and democracy, dividing along global and local lines. Of course, there is a need to attend to global *and* local questions of sustainability, given that diverse cultures inhabit a single planet. Neither can now exist without the viability of the other. The pressing issue now is whether the social and physical world can sustain current economic growth trends with current forms of energy. This problem must be addressed at all levels of organization, under conditions of adequate political representation.

Cumulative deterioration. We can examine the issue from two angles. The first is *cumulative.* We face astounding problems in the depletion of our physical environment. In the United States, for example, 1 million acres disappear annually to urbanization, industrial development, and road building. About 2 million acres of farmland are lost annually to erosion, soil salinization, and flooding or soil saturation, much of which is caused by intensive agriculture. Agriculture is also responsible for serious depletion of groundwater reserves; this water is being consumed up to 160 percent faster than it can be replenished. By 2050, according to some estimates, the United States will be able to supply only the domestic market with food crops.[6]

From a global perspective, estimates of this type cause deep concern. The United States currently provides 50 percent of the world's grain exports, but overall the world has crossed the threshold to declining rates of agricultural productivity. In 1990, less food was produced per person globally than in 1970, and during the 1980s food production lagged behind population growth in 75 poor countries. Plant breeders, addressing these trends, are hard at work developing new seed varieties, such as super-high-yield rice, blight-resistant potatoes, higher-yielding cassava varieties, and tropical corn. But they are in a race against social trends stemming from the development project.

Looking across the Pacific Ocean to China, we find a veritable economic revolution under way that has serious long-term implications. Factories spring up overnight in the roughly 3,000 development zones displacing rice paddies and farmlands.[7] Foreign investors have been taking advantage of the $2- to $4-a-day wage rates for literate, healthy employees, pouring in $11 billion of foreign investment in 1992 alone. This amount was greater than the total investment for the preceding 15 years. Automobile production by companies such as Volkswagen and Ford Motor Company increased 52 percent between 1991 and 1992 in China.[8] Despite China's remarkable gains in industrial efficiency since the early 1980s, however, it also ranks third in carbon dioxide emissions, behind the United States and the former Soviet Union. By some predictions, China could pass the United States in carbon dioxide emissions by 2025.

Meanwhile, intensive agriculture has accelerated since 1949, when the Chinese Communist party assumed state power. Chinese soils are deteriorating from reduced crop rotation, erosion, over-fertilization, and the loss of organic content of soils once nourished by manure-based farming. In

1993 alone, 50 million Chinese farmers abandoned farming for higher-paying urban jobs.[9] Cropland is shrinking at the rate of 1 percent a year, and slowing farm productivity rates suggest a potential 20 percent decline in China's grain production between 1990 and 2030. Even if consumption of animal protein holds constant, China will probably experience a short-fall in grain supplies *in excess of* current world grain exports. Officials at the Chinese National People's Congress in March 1995 acknowledged China's looming grain crisis. Given the projections for shrinking American grain exports, Lester Brown concludes that "the vast deficit projected for China will set up a fierce competition for limited exportable supplies, driving world grain prices far above familiar levels."[10] This is one cumulative scenario—using China as the "wild card" given its sheer size, a population increase of 14 million a year, and its evident industrial trajectory.

Another cumulative scenario is the unpredictability associated with global environmental changes. The United Nations World Commission on Environment and Development noted in 1987 that "major, unintended changes are occurring in the atmosphere, in soils, in waters, among plants and animals, and in relationships among these. . . . The rate of change is outstripping the ability of scientific disciplines and our capabilities to assess and advise." According to epidemiologist A. J. McMichael, these changes foretell threats to global public health arising from "planetary overload, entailing circumstances that are qualitatively different from the familiar, localised problem of environmental pollution." McMichael identifies threats such as immune suppression from ultraviolet radiation, indirect health consequences of climate change on food production and the spread of infections, and loss of biological and genetic resources for producing medicines. He observes:

> This is not to deny the health gains associated with agrarian and industrial settlement, but it emphasizes that human cultural evolution has produced distortions of ecological relationships, causing four main types of health hazard. First came infectious diseases. Then came diseases of industrialisation and environmental pollution by toxic chemicals. Simultaneously, in rich populations, various "lifestyle" diseases of affluence (heart disease, assorted cancers, diabetes, etc.) emerged. Today we face the health consequences of disruption of the world's natural systems.[11]

We cannot pin these cumulative trends on the development project itself; they have had a longer cultural gestation stemming from a long-held belief in the West in the subordination of the natural world to human progress. But industrial development hastened these changes, and the development project acted as midwife to their universalization.

Maldistribution of wealth. The other angle on the sustainability question is a *relational* one, concerning the distribution of global wealth. In the early 1990s, roughly 80 percent of the world's income was produced and consumed by 15 percent of the world's population.[12] Meanwhile, despite positive indices of economic growth, living standards are lower for many in the South. Juan de Dias Parra, leader of the Latin American Association for Human Rights, stated in 1993:

> In Latin America today, there are 70 million more hungry, 30 million more illiterate, 10 million more families without homes and 40 million more unemployed persons than there were 20 years ago. . . . [T]here are 240 million human beings who lack the necessities of life and this when the region is richer and more stable than ever, according to the way the world sees it.[13]

Global resources are disproportionately controlled and consumed by a small minority of the world's population, residing mainly in the First World. For example, grains fed to U.S. livestock equal as much food consumed by the combined populations of India and China.[14] Northern nations account for 75 percent of the world's energy use and have produced two-thirds of the greenhouse gases altering the earth's climate. Since 1950, the world's population has consumed as many goods and services, and the U.S. population has used as many mineral resources, as those consumed by all previous generations of people.[15] In short, the practice of development under the development project has brought us up sharply against growing environmental, resource, and health limits. It is too early to know whether humans are the ultimate "endangered species."

Replicating Western Growth Patterns?

There are many moves afoot, often undertaken by NGOs, to rethink scales and styles of development. These are typically associated with the multitude of grassroots and community-based movements advocating and practicing a scaled-down lifestyle. One success story is that of the Grameen Bank, begun by Muhammad Yunus in 1976 in a village near Chittagong, Bangladesh. With a loan volume of $500 million in 1995, this bank has rapidly become known as the champion of poor women across the former Third World. It extends small amounts of commercial credit for microenterprise to cells of five women, each of whom receives a loan and guarantees that all members of the cell will repay their own loans.[16]

There are also voices espousing perhaps more powerful countertrends, including those who advocate a global vision, arguing that liberal economic reform and globalization stand to revitalize the world economy. Globalists use the metaphor that a rising tide raises all boats. But they do not consider the alternative possibility that economic growth is a rising tide that is less likely to lift all boats than to swamp or overwhelm us all. It is by no means clear that new biotechnologies to raise agricultural productivity or new energy technologies, even with more equitable distribution of the outputs, can enable us to keep our heads above water as global environmental changes unfold.

Another group of these globalists includes those elites in the former Third World who insist that their countries should have the same right to develop as the First World had historically. For example, the Malaysian Prime Minister Mahathir Mohamad plans to catch up to the North by 2020. Part of his plan includes a proposed hydro-electric dam in Sarawak that will require clearing tens of thousands of acres of rain forest and displacing native populations. Mahathir claimed that it was inappropriate for the West, which long ago cut down its own forests and subdued native populations, to protest a repetition in Malaysia in this century.[17] Advocates of this position suggest in addition that the First World offer compensatory financial assistance for the implementation of environmental protections.

This argument reveals the twofold historical dimensions of the development question. First, the new industrializers want to realize the terms of the development project. We have seen that these terms apply less and less in a global marketplace, where impermanence of production complexes, markets, and social entitlements is a governing principle. But this realization does not fulfill the political terms of the development project—that all countries should have the same opportunity.

The promise of equal opportunity highlights another historical dimension of the development question concerning the terms of the globalization project—that opportunity is no longer a national property in a global market, if it ever was. Globalization does not have the universalist consequence that the development project proclaimed. The development project proposed *replication* of the model of national economic growth across the system of states. By contrast, the globalization project *differentiates* states and their producing regions. It assigns communities, regions, and states new niches or specialized roles—including marginalization—in the global economy. So the demand to repeat the Western experience appears to be unrealizable.

Rethinking Development

Where does this leave "development," then? I think its status as an organizing myth has become clearer. By framing this book around the idea of the development project, I have tried to show that development ultimately is a strategy of organizing social change. It occurs within a field of power—national, international, or both. It also occurs within a cultural field—in this case, the Western enterprise of endless capital accumulation. As an organizing myth it mobilized all societies, justifying the cultural frame in the appeals to universalistic economic rationality. In the post–World War II world, this appeal was anchored in the substantive idea of national self-determination. And it was a powerful idea, with some tangible benefits across the world, and in retrospect seems progressive compared to the globalization project. But listen to the words of the South Commission—a think tank of Southern intellectuals and political leaders. In their 1990 report, *The Challenge to the South*, they wrote:

> In the period following the end of the Second World War until the end of the 1970s, a great many of the countries of the South registered impressive social and economic gains. This gave rise to the expectation that the North-South divide in wealth and power could be bridged. The 1980s belied that expectation. They have been rightly described as a lost decade for development.[18]

This was a clear expression of growing skepticism in the development project.

Public disillusionment with the development project echoes across the world. The Alternative Forum: The Other Voices of the Planet is a group representing the growing networks of nongovernmental organizations (NGOs) that now challenge developmentalism. Its 1994 proclamation is worth quoting in full because of how it is framed:

> To overcome the myth of development, to develop more locally self-sufficient economic systems and to disassociate from traditional techno-cratic and economic indicators, does not imply perpetuating the status quo between the supposedly developed North and the supposedly underdeveloped South. Obviously, the production of goods and services in the South has to increase and must be directed primarily towards meeting the enormous number of basic needs that are not being covered. With or without the permission of the North, the countries of the South have to use up the world natural resources needed for this increase in production. However, out of pure self interest they should try to adapt their productive systems as far as possible to local ecological conditions, rather than copying the irresponsible and unsustainable models of the North. This, above all, means generating and using as much of production locally as possible because this is the level at which real human needs are most clearly expressed. . . . The end of the Development Era will be harder for the North than for the South. In fact, if we take the level of social conflict, the fear of the future and the social fulfill-ment of people, as general indicators, the North is probably already starting to experience this process.[19]

The sentiments expressed here speak to several issues in the process by which development is being reconceived. The essential point is that groups with this perspective are proposing a departure from the Western model and a reinvigoration of alternative and/or local systems. Of course, local systems do not have a monopoly on virtue—they are often the site of patriarchy and authoritarianism undiluted by individual rights. Human and individual rights are a fundamental part of the new equation. They are in fact the discourse of a potential world civil society. However, under the globalization project their rising advocacy also signals their fragility, as powerful interests make the key decisions about restructuring and civil wars proliferate.

Market Fetishism and the Question of Representation

The shift in thinking expressed by the Alternative Forum is not simply of scale—from global to local—but also of substance. It speaks to reversing the tendency to make a fetish of the market as the key instrument of social organization and subordinating the economy to community and ecological requirements. Once we address the issue of why we presently surrender our social and natural resources to market disciplines, we can raise the question of who benefits. If countries are indeed racing to the bottom by submitting to the logic of lower labor costs and stripping away social protections, where is it taking us, and who stands to gain?

The absence of representative institutions of a world civil society to match the global market is even more clear when we look at how the global market is managed. At present, only the institutions of national civil societies exist, and they are under siege in various ways that we have discussed. Social institutions have only a limited shelf life, but in the absence of representative forums at the global level, the nation-state still has an important contribution to the protection of social rights. At present, this function is subordinated to more powerful forces, where nationalism takes a rightward turn as threatened groups and labor forces embrace ethnic politics. This brand of politics divides rather than unites, leading nation-states to strengthen their *ideological* grip by functioning as population containment zones or regulators of what groups count as first-class citizens and which as second-class citizens (for example, guest workers).[20] But in doing so, they relinquish their historic function of establishing uniform citizenship.

Demythologizing Development

An interesting observation is that the members of the Alternative Forum perceive Westerners as being at a comparative disadvantage because they are much more thoroughly incorporated into, and therefore more thoroughly affected by the reversals of, the development myth. One reversal that is currently redefining First World politics is the perceived threat of formerly colonized peoples migrating into the First World. This movement has the air of historical chickens coming home to roost:

> For the first time the Northern countries themselves are exposed to the bitter results of Westernizing the world. Immigration, population pressure, tribalism with mega-arms, and above all, the environmental consequences of worldwide industrialization threaten to destabilize the Northern way of life. It is as if the cycle which had been opened by Columbus is about to be closed at the end of this century.[21]

These are admittedly alarming notions, but it is necessary to remember that the first rule in responding to gloomy predictions is to recognize that the more we can understand the process, the better we can respond to it. Most important, it allows us to see that the history of development wove together the fate of people on opposite sides of the world.

I have argued that the development project was an organizing myth that had broad appeal for some time. Much less clear is whether globalization has an equivalent appeal as it subordinates social life to more abstract market principles. The growing uncertainty of unemployment patterns is a palpable experience for more and more of the world's population. In other words, it is hard to imagine people across the world continuing to subscribe to a higher, less representative, or more abstract authority than the nation. Being a global consumer appears to work only for a small minority. We continue to obtain our athletic shoes and CDs from foreign production zones, but how long can that continue if civil institutions around us fail and unemployment begins to bite larger and larger portions of an already subsiding middle class? And being a global worker is an increasingly tenuous condition for labor forces—unskilled and skilled—across the world. Accordingly, I would expect the development debate between global and local visions to occupy citizens, labor organizations, consumers, and political systems at large for some time. In this debate there is perhaps space to make a difference.

Development and Governance

Meanwhile, the institutions of the original development project will continue devising measures to improve or ameliorate the conditions of the world's populations. In March 1995, for example, the United Nations held a World Summit for Social Development in Denmark. The agenda was articulated in former U.N. Secretary General Boutros Boutros-Ghali's call for "a new social contract," a recognition that global poverty has world-wide consequences. Although no funds were forthcoming, the argument was made that agencies like the United Nations have a responsibility to address global conditions of poverty and to fight discrimination. Programmatically, the Social Summit attempted to redefine aid, rejecting the term *foreign aid* and promoting the idea of reallocating money and other resources globally. Under this redefinition, social conditions within former Third World countries will enter into decisions about international financial assistance, including the ability of wealthy elites to help.

In an idea resembling the 1980s debt-for-nature swap, the suggestion was made to insist that every dollar of canceled debt should be spent on social services, and forgiven debt should be matched by reductions in arms expenditure. Sub-Saharan Africa was named as the major development challenge.[22] In an era when foreign aid faces growing skepticism, the prime minister of Denmark, Poul Nyrup Rasmussen, explained the rationale for continuing aid: "We have a good argument now, a very concrete one, for ordinary people, which is, if you don't help the third world, if you don't help northern Africa, if you don't help eastern and central Europe with a little part of your welfare, then you will have these poor people in our society."[23]

If the globalization project has any appeal to people in the First World beyond the idea of efficiency—which may not remain credible over time—it is this notion of *Northern security.* This involves the belief that Southern needs must be taken into account if only to stem the tide of migration. Since economic conditions are hardly robust in the First World, freedom of movement for labor is an unlikely political platform—even though under the terms of the globalization project freedom is extended to money, capital, and goods. The security question, then, compels the global managers to focus on a *new form of loan conditionality*: assistance when governments attend to stabilizing their populations. This factor has been included in the World Bank's new lending criteria. Early 1990s Bank president Lewis Preston declared that "sustainable poverty reduction is the benchmark by which our performance as a development institution will be measured"; and the Bank's 1992 report stated: "Good governance, for the World Bank, is synonymous with sound development management." [24]

It appears, then, that in the immediate future, global management will focus on stabilizing the system of states across the world. This will involve two levels of action. First is elaborating the vision of a global community. In 1995, the Commission on Global Governance, including leaders from North and South, published its report *Our Global Neighborhood*, in which it called for the development of a "global civic ethic." The Commission argues that this is a necessary social cement involving nongovernmental political associations in a time when "groups of many kinds are reaching out and establishing links with counterparts in other parts of the world."[25] How effective this will be without a framework for institutionalizing representation is another, but urgent, matter.

Second, under conditions in which not only the North/South gap commands attention but also the widening gap within countries, states are the ultimate gatekeepers for destabilized populations. Short of military intervention, which we saw in December 1992 when a multinational military force entered Somalia to open relief-supply routes and attempt—unsuccessfully—to build democratic institutions, attaching governance conditions to financial assistance is a new chapter in the continuing story of management of the global order. It is perhaps a measure of the failure of economism in development thinking.

Development or Empowerment?

Where does this leave development theory, then? Let us retrace its steps. Initially, development theory was formalized as part of the foundation of the development project. It took its cues from nineteenth-century social thought, which was concerned primarily with different aspects of the rise of capitalism and industrialism. The grand sociological trio (or the great white fathers) Karl Marx, Max Weber, and Emile Durkheim addressed quite distinct problems, respectively: How can we account for the transition between distinct forms of social organization (feudalism, capitalism, and socialism)? How can we account for the fact that capitalism developed in the West and not the Orient? And how is it possible to retain social cohesion as the division of labor advances?

If there was any common ground among these theorists and others, it was in their identification of *contradictions* attending development in the capitalist era. Marx saw class inequality as the major contradiction, and the market as a new religion that obscures inequality. Weber distrusted the rationalizing thrust that displaced wonder and cultural mythmaking. Durkheim worried about social disorder as the scale and complexity of society grew. These social theorists have recently been criticized as proclaiming a Eurocentric "grand narrative" of history and social change. Whether they did or not, their interpreters in the earlier part of this century reproduced the progressivism of the Eurocentric narrative. Such progressivism in turn shaped and formalized development theory in the mid-twentieth century, giving rise to the development project.

The most powerful theoretical critique of developmentalism came in Immanuel Wallerstein's formulation of **world-system theory** in the early 1970s. The argument he made was twofold. First, since the rise of the sixteenth-century European capitalist world economy under colonialism, the world has been hierarchically organized as a systemic whole divided into unequal zones of specialization—with Europe in the center, and the colonial and postcolonial world in the periphery. Like the middle classes of industrial society, there is also a buffer zone between the poles: the semi-periphery, comprising the middle-income states. In the postwar world, the newly industrializing countries joined other semi-peripheral states like Australia, New Zealand, and Canada; the Southern European states; and the Soviet bloc countries. Second, Wallerstein has produced a sustained critique of the character of developmentalism as an organizing myth, both because of its misapplication as a national strategy in a hierarchical world where only some states can "succeed," and because it has displaced other, more equitable, notions of social organization.[26]

As the development project proceeded, we have seen that revised conceptions of development emerged in response to changing conditions. Growing Third World poverty provoked the "basic needs" approach, new socialist interpretations of underdevelopment as a historical condition, and redefinitions of human development indexes. The industrial growth in the newly industrializing countries in the 1970s produced the World Bank's notion of development as participation in the world market.

Third, the 1980s debt crisis punctured illusions of development, and debt management became the new orthodoxy. The debt regime, I have argued, was the dress rehearsal for a reformulation of the development enterprise as a global project. This project embeds global regulatory mechanisms in global institutions as well as in restructured states acting on behalf of the global economic managers.

And fourth, alongside and often in response to these developments, new social movements have emerged with alternatives that we have identified as expressive (noneconomistic) and rooted in notions of reducing the scale of resource use and revitalizing communities.

If one were to offer a comparative sketch of the two sides of the development debate, it would look something like this. Globalists believe in the rationality of an open world economy, but the level playing field that is supposed to drive this operation is a fiction at best and an assertion of power at worst. Globalists deploy free trade arguments to "open" national economies to privileged investors and transnational corporations; they propose deregulated money markets that encourage financial speculation and huge, destabilizing capital flight as wealthy nationals shift their—and sometimes the public's—money to more inviting regions of the global economy.

By contrast, localists begin from the position of advocating local knowledge and the virtue of small-scale communities. The growing **participatory action research (PAR)** movement is a key example of this kind of localism, where communities achieve self-empowerment through active participation in self-knowledge, such as recovery of local ways of interpreting and being in the world. But communities are historical products and must come to terms with the national states and market institutions within which they currently exist. A dramatic and successful example of empowerment was the victory for all aboriginal people in Australia that was won by the Murray Islander people of the Torres Strait in June 1992. At that time the High Court of Australia, after years of pressure from aboriginal people, discarded the legal fiction of Australia as *terra nullius* (land belonging to no one) established at the moment of British colonization in 1788. The ongoing task now is for aboriginal negotiators to clarify "the indissoluble tie of Aboriginal and Islander people to their land in contrast to the conception of land as a tradeable item."[27] The problem in drawing distinctions, and thereby protecting a way of life, is that there are two basic languages in this case—one economic and one cultural. To the extent that the cultural language succeeds, it subverts the discourse of development.

Elsewhere, communities must negotiate the complexity of class, gender, and cultural relations that shape those communities and connect them to their broader national and global contexts. Whether or not it has endured as a local, grassroots initiative, the Chiapas revolt, discussed in the previous chapter, offers some answers to this complexity in signaling a new form of political action. It successfully linked the struggle for local rights to history—history in the long term in the sense that this region of Mayan ancestry has experienced waves of foreign intervention and exploitation of its natural and human resources; history in the present in the sense that in pursuing structural adjustment, the Mexican state steadily withdrew social subsidies and was on the brink of withdrawing final protections from overwhelming global forces with the implementation of the North American Free Trade Agreement. The Chiapas revolt was rooted in local empowerment demands, but it resonated across communities in similar predicaments in Mexico, and indeed the world.

From this perspective, the question "Whither development?" finds an answer in the notion of cosmopolitan localism. To be sustainable, a global community must situate its constituent community needs within their world-historical context. That means understanding not only how the community has come to be within the context of global processes and relations (such as instituted markets), but also how its members can empower themselves through that context. And that includes ensuring that community empowerment means also empowering the individuals and minorities in those communities. It also means realizing that there are other communities with similar needs precisely because they are woven from similar world-historical threads. It is the genius of the Chiapas rebels to articulate this. It is also the mark of our times that these historical connections are now being made as the currency of development is devalued.

Conclusion

This concluding chapter brings some closure to the story of the rise and demise of the development project. Development was a powerful organizing ideal that was institutionalized on a world scale. In this text, we focused on the changing patterns of development as a world-historical project—citing individual case histories as instances of global trends. We examined developmentalist assumptions, practices, and social legacies. These legacies continue, even as global development overwhelms the historic project of national development. While states endure, their public capacities—those geared to comprehensive citizenship—are under threat across the world in varying degrees. Many international agencies, governments, non-governmental organizations, and populations still pursue national development despite its reformulation and its eroding infrastructures. However, economic growth strategies tend to privilege global rather than national economic relations. A protective global social movement is still quite immature even though ideas of "sustainable development" gain currency.

Human sustainability, however, will depend on more than environmental conservation and less on economic growth. It requires preservation of community in inclusive terms rather than the exclusive or specialized terms of economic globalization. The moral of this story—of the development project's demise—is that the world is at a critical juncture in these respects. A powerful reorganizing myth of globalization would further weaken social protections in the name of economic efficiency. Public capacity to care for disadvantaged populations and to protect human and environmental futures is threatened. The globalization project is not just a successor to the development project. Its prescriptions are double edged because its conception of the future erases the past—a past created by movements for social protection. As the development project has subsided a *general* reversal of thinking has emerged. The present is no longer the logical development of the past, rather it is increasingly the hostage of the future. Those who define the future will frame this new postdevelopmentalist debate.

Endnotes

Development and the Global Marketplace

1. Norberg-Hodge, 1994–1995, p. 2.
2. Korzeniewicz, 1994.
3. Collins, 1995.
4. Barnet & Cavanagh, 1955, p. 383.
5. McMichael, 1990, 1992.

Chapter 1: The Rise of the Development Project

1. Davidson, 1992, pp. 83, 99–101.
2. Bujra, 1992, p. 147.
3. Bujra, 1992, p. 146.
4. Quoted in Stavrianos, 1981, p. 247.
5. Chirot, 1977, p. 124.
6. Wolf, 1882, pp. 369, 377.
7. Wacker, 1994, pp. 132–134.
8. James, 1963.
9. Quoted in Davidson, 1992, p. 164.
10. Memmi, 1967, p. 74.
11. Fanon, 1967, pp. 254–255.
12. Stavrianos, 1981, p. 624.
13. Adams, 1993, pp. 2–3, 6–7.
14. Quoted in Esteva, 1992, p. 6.
15. Quoted in Davidson, 1992, p. 167.
16. Esteva, 1992, p. 7.
17. Quoted in Davidson, 1992, p. 203.
18. Davidson, 1992, pp. 183–184.
19. Dube, 1988, p. 1.
20. Rostow, 1960.
21. Quoted in Hettne, 1990, p. 53.

22. Latouche, 1993, p. 201.
23. Shiva, 1992, p. 215.
24. Quoted in Hettne, 1990, p. 3.
25. Kaldor, 1990, pp. 62, 67.
26. Quoted in Dube, 1988, p. 16.
27. Lehman, 1990, pp. 5–6.
28. Lehman, 1990, pp. 5-6.
29. Harris, 1987, p. 17.
30. Cardoso & Faletto, 1979, pp. 129–131.
31. Kemp, 1989, pp. 162–165.

Chapter 2: The Development Project in Action

1. Block, 1977, pp. 76–77.
2. Quoted in Brett, 1985, pp. 106–107.
3. Quoted in Kolko, 1988, p. 17.
4. Cleaver, 1977, p. 16.
5. Wood, 1986, pp. 38–61.
6. Ideas and quotes from Rich, 1994, pp. 55, 56.
7. Quoted in Adams, 1993, p. 32.
8. Rich, 1994, p. 72.
9. Rich, 1994, p. 58; George & Sabelli, 1994, p. 15.
10. Rich, 1994, p. 73.
11. The examples in the next four paragraphs are from Rich, 1994, pp. 10–13, 39, 41, 94.
12. Rich, 1994, p. 75.
13. Adams, 1993, pp. 68–69.
14. Quoted in Magdoff, 1969, p. 54.
15. Magdoff, 1969, p. 124; Chirot, 1977, pp. 164–165.
16. Quoted in Williams, 1981, pp. 56–57.
17. Brett, 1985, p. 209; Wood, 1986, p. 73.
18. Brett, 1985, p. 209; Wood, 1986, p. 73.
19. Adams, 1993, p. 73.
20. Rich, 1994, p. 84.
21. Harris, 1987, p. 28.
22. Harris, 1987, p. 102.
23. Grigg, 1993, p. 251.
24. Revel & Riboud, 1986, pp. 43–44.
25. Grigg, 1993, pp. 243–244; Bradley & Carter, 1989, p. 104. Self-sufficiency measures do not necessarily reveal the state of nutrition in a country or

region, as a country—for example, Japan—may have a low self-sufficiency because its population eats an affluent diet, which depends on imports.

26. For an extended discussion of food regimes, see Friedmann, 1990; for a discussion of the international monetary regime associated with Bretton Woods, see Ruggie, 1982.
27. Quoted in Magdoff, 1969, p. 135.
28. Quoted in George, 1977, p. 170.
29. Raikes, 1988, pp. 175, 178.
30. Harriet Friedmann, 1992, p. 373.
31. Wessel, 1983, p. 173.
32. Chung, 1990, p. 143.
33. To be sure, Korean farmers protested and in the 1970s the state modernized rice-farming regions to raise rural incomes, but this policy ran out of steam as rice consumption continued to decline with the changing Korean diet (McMichael & Kim, 1994).
34. Dudley & Sandilands, 1975; Friedmann, 1990, p. 20.
35. Morgan, 1980, p. 301.
36. Quoted in George, 1977, p. 170.
37. Friedmann, 1990, p. 20.
38. Harriet Friedmann, 1992, p. 373.
39. McMichael & Raynolds, 1994, p. 322. The terms *peasant foods* and *wage foods* are from de Janvry, 1981.
40. Hathaway, 1987, p. 13.
41. Revel & Riboud, 1986, p. 62.
42. de Janvry, 1981, p. 179.
43. Middleton, O'Keefe, & Moyo, 1993, p. 129.
44. Wessel, 1983, p. 158.
45. Berlan, 1991, pp. 126–127.
46. Burbach & Flynn, 1980, p. 66; George, 1977, p. 171.
47. Quoted in George, 1977, pp. 171–172.
48. Harriet Friedmann, 1992, p. 377.
49. Dalrymple, 1985, p. 1069; Andrae & Beckman, 1985; Raikes, 1988.
50. George, 1977, pp. 174–175.
51. Agarwal, 1994, p. 312.
52. Griffin, 1974; Pearse, 1980; Byres, 1981; Sanderson, 1986a; Dhanagare, 1988; Raikes, 1988; Llambi, 1990.
53. Griffin, 1974; Athreya, Djurfeldt, & Lindberg, 1990.
54. Shiva, 1991, pp. 175–176.
55. Lipton, 1977.
56. McMichael & Kim, 1994; Araghi, 1995.
57. Grigg, 1993, pp. 103–104, 185; Araghi, 1995.

58. Rich, 1994, pp. 95, 155.

59. Rich, 1994, pp. 91, 97; Feder, 1983, p. 222.

60. de Janvry, 1981; Araghi, 1995.

Chapter 3: A Global Production System

1. Arrighi, 1994, p. 68.

2. Bello, 1994, p. 7.

3. Hoogvelt, 1987, pp. 43–45.

4. Harris, 1987, p. 75.

5. Hoogvelt, 1987, p. 40.

6. Knox & Agnew, 1994, p. 340.

7. The term *newly industrializing countries* (NICs) was coined by the Organization for Economic Cooperation and Development in 1979 and included four other Southern European countries: Spain, Portugal, Yugoslavia, and Greece. The common attributes of NICs were (1) rapid penetration of the world market with manufactured exports, (2) a rising share of industrial employment, and (3) an increase in real GDP per capita relative to the First World (Hoogvelt, 1987, p. 25).

8. Brett, 1985, pp. 185–186.

9. Hoogvelt, 1987, p. 28.

10. Brett, 1985, p. 188.

11. Knox & Agnew, 1994, p. 347.

12. Hoogvelt, 1987, p. 64.

13. Knox & Agnew, 1994, p. 331. (Between 1975 and 1989, this group enlarged to include China, South Africa, Thailand, and Taiwan; Argentina dropped out.)

14. Knox & Agnew, 1994, p. 331.

15. Quoted in Brett, 1985, p. 188.

16. The following two paragraphs draw on Gereffi, 1989.

17. Quoted in Hill & Fujita, 1995, p. 95.

18. Nayyar, 1976, p. 25.

19. Hoogvelt, 1987, pp. 26–31. At the same time, as a consequence of import-substitution industrialization and the buoyancy of the export-oriented industrialization strategy in the 1970s, the composition of imports mainly from the First World moved from manufactured consumer goods to capital goods.

20. Landsberg, 1979, pp. 52, 54.

21. See Gereffi, 1994.

22. Baird & McCaughan, 1979, pp. 130–132. For an excellent and detailed study of the *maquiladora* industry, see Sklair, 1989.

23. Henderson, 1991, p. 3.

24. Sivanandan, 1989, pp. 2, 8.

25. Brown, 1993, p. 46.

26. See Harris, 1987. See also Gereffi and Korzeniewicz, 1994, for an alternative formulation of the world product as a series of commodity chains.

27. Brown, 1993, p. 46.

28. Barnet & Cavanagh, 1994, p. 300.

29. For an extended account of the gendered restructuring of the world labor force, see Mies, 1991, and Benería and Feldman, 1992.

30. Baird & McCaughan, 1979, pp. 135–136.

31. Baird & McCaughan, 1979, p. 135.

32. Brown, 1993, p. 47.

33. Ellwood, 1993, p. 5.

34. Daly & Logan, 1989, p. 67.

35. *The Economist*, July 16, 1994, p. 56.

36. *The New Internationalist*, August 1993, p. 18.

37. Hobsbawm, 1992, p. 56.

38. Henderson, 1991.

39. *Pacific Basin Reports*, August 1973, p. 171.

40. Fröbel, Heinrichs, & Kreye, 1979, pp. 34–36.

41. Henderson, 1991, p. 54.

42. Henderson, 1991, pp. 57–58, 61.

43. Korzeniewicz, 1994, p. 261.

44. *The Economist*, June 3, 1995, p. 59.

45. Heffernan & Constance, 1994, pp. 42–45.

46. Friedmann, 1991.

47. Sanderson, 1986b; Raynolds, Myhre, McMichael, Carro-Figueroa, & Buttel, 1993; Raynolds, 1994.

48. DeWalt, 1985.

49. DeWalt, 1985.

50. Friedland, 1994.

51. Rama, 1992, p. 269.

52. Schoenberger, 1994, p. 59.

53. Quoted in Appelbaum & Gereffi, 1994, p. 54.

54. Daly & Logan, 1989, p. 13; Schoenberger, 1994, pp. 59–61.

55. Templin, 1994, p. A10.

56. Schwedel & Haley, 1992, p. 49; Kuenzler, 1992, p. 47.

57. Carlsen, 1991, p. 15.

58. Crook, 1993, p. 16.

59. Uchitelle, 1994, p. D2.

Chapter 4. A Global Infrastructure

1. Hoogvelt, 1987, p. 58.
2. Hoogvelt, 1987, p. 58.
3. Reich, 1992, p. 114 (emphasis in original).
4. George, 1988, p. 12.
5. Strange, 1994, p. 112.
6. Crook, 1992, p. 10.
7. Strange, 1994, p. 107.
8. Quoted in Brecher & Costello, 1994, p. 30.
9. *The New Internationalist,* August 1993, p. 18; Kolko, 1988, p. 24.
10. *Debt Crisis Network,* 1986, p. 25.
11. Kolko, 1988, p. 26.
12. Lissakers, 1993, p. 59.
13. George, 1988, p. 36.
14. George, 1988, p. 33.
15. Lissakers, 1993, p. 66.
16. Lissakers, 1993, p. 56.
17. Lissakers, 1993, pp. 69–73.
18. Wood, 1986, pp. 247, 253, 255; Evans, 1979.
19. George, 1988, p. 6.
20. Quoted in Wood, 1986, p. 197.
21. See, for example, Cardoso & Faletto, 1979.
22. Hoogvelt, 1987, p. 77.
23. Seers, 1979, p. 12.
24. Rich, 1994, p. 84.
25. Rich, 1994, p. 85.
26. Wood, 1986, pp. 210–212; Hoogvelt, 1987, p. 102.
27. Quoted in Adams, 1993, p. 123.
28. Hoogvelt, 1987, pp. 80–87.
29. Adams, 1993, p. 127.
30. Hoogvelt, 1987, pp. 87–95.
31. George, 1988, p. 6.
32. Walton & Seddon, 1994, pp. 13–14.
33. George, 1988, pp. 28–29.
34. Lissakers, 1993, p. 67.
35. Singh, 1992, p. 141.
36. George, 1988, pp. 12, 73.
37. Singh, 1992, p. 144.

38. George, 1988, p. 60.
39. Economic Commission for Latin America and the Caribbean, 1989, p. 123.
40. Strange, 1994, p. 112.
41. George, 1988, pp. 41, 49.
42. Barkin, 1990, pp. 104–105.
43. Cheru, 1989, pp. 24, 27–28, 41–42.
44. George, 1988, p. 95.
45. Rich, 1994, pp. 186–187.
46. Singh, 1992, pp. 138–139, 147–148.
47. Bello, 1994.
48. George, 1992, p. xvi.
49. George, 1992, p. 97.
50. Cox, 1987, p. 301.
51. Corbridge, 1993, pp. 129, 131–132.
52. Calculated from Crook, 1993, p. 16.
53. George, 1988, p. 97.
54. Crook, 1992, p. 9.
55. Crook, 1993. p. 16.
56. Arrighi, 1990.
57. Payer, 1974.
58. Canak, 1989.
59. Bangura & Gibbon, 1992, p. 19.
60. Gibbon, 1992, p. 137.
61. Bernstein, 1990, p. 17.
62. Beckman, 1992, p. 99.
63. Gibbon, 1992, p. 141.
64. Stephany Griffith-Jones, quoted in Crook, 1991, p. 19.
65. Cahn, 1993, p. 179.
66. Quoted in Cahn, 1993, p. 180.
67. Cahn, 1993, pp. 161, 163; Rich, 1994; Corbridge, 1993, p. 127.
68. Cahn, 1993, pp. 168, 172.
69. Gill, 1992.
70. World Bank, 1990, pp. 10–11.

Chapter 5: The Rise of the Globalization Project

1. Giddens, 1990, p. 65.
2. Quoted in Bello, 1994, p. 72.
3. Bello, 1994, p. 35.

4. Acharya, 1995, p. 22.

5. George, 1992, p. 11.

6. Nash, 1994, p. C4.

7. Bello, 1994, p. 59.

8. Rich, 1994, p. 188.

9. Quoted in Bello, 1994, p. 63.

10. Rich, 1994, p. 188.

11. Hathaway, 1987, pp. 40–41.

12. Ricardo, 1821.

13. Kolko, 1988, pp. 271–272.

14. Bello, 1994, p. 68.

15. The South Centre, 1993, p. 13.

16. Quoted in Bradsher, 1995, p. D6.

17. Quoted in Golden, 1995, p. 5.

18. McMichael, 1993a.

19. Adams, 1993, pp. 196–197.

20. Quoted in Watkins, 1991, p. 44.

21. McMichael, 1993a.

22. Middleton, O'Keefe, & Moyo, 1993, pp. 127–129.

23. Watkins, 1991, p. 43.

24. Kolko, 1988, p. 215.

25. Quoted in Ritchie, 1994.

26. Harvey, 1994, p. 14.

27. Quoted in Chomsky, 1994, p. 180.

28. Watkins, 1991, p. 47.

29. Watkins, 1991, p. 50.

30. Quoted in Ritchie, 1993, p. 11.

31. Quoted in Ritchie, 1993, footnote 25.

32. Quoted in Schaeffer, 1995, p. 268.

33. See Raghavan, 1990.

34. McMichael & Kim, 1994.

35. Lang & Hines, 1993, p. 55.

36. Madden & Madeley, 1993, p. 17.

37. Quoted in Weissman, 1991, p. 337.

38. Brecher & Costello, 1994, p. 59.

39. Brecher & Costello, 1994, p. 59.

40. *NAFTA Fact Sheet*, conference trade library, 9/23/93.

41. Dicken, 1992, p. 45.

42. Baer, 1991, p. 132.
43. Baer, 1991, p. 146.
44. Drozdiak, 1995.
45. Goldsmith, 1994, pp. 66, 67, 77.
46. See, for example, Wallerstein, 1983; Arrighi, 1990.
47. George & Sabelli, 1994, p. 147.
48. Rueschemeyer, Stephans & Stephans, 1992.
49. Bacon, 1994, p. A1.
50. Arrighi, 1994.
51. Bacon, 1994, p. A1.
52. Sanger, 1995.

Chapter 6: The Globalization Project in Action

1. Goldsmith, 1994, p. 18. (The official French figure for current unemployment is 3.3 million, but according to Goldsmith, the government's own statistics show the omission of categories consisting of an additional 1.8 million people.)
2. Quoted in Lang & Hines, 1993, p. 77.
3. Kolko, 1988, p. 339.
4. See, for example, Brecher & Costello, 1994.
5. Quoted in Rocher, 1993, p. 143.
6. Lewin, 1995, p. A5.
7. *The Nation*, November 8, 1993, p. 3.
8. Kolko, 1988, pp. 337–338.
9. Lang & Hines, 1993, p. 81.
10. Sassen, 1991, p. 219.
11. *The Economist*, March 19, 1994, p. 92.
12. Woodall, 1994, p. 24.
13. *The Economist*, March 19, 1994, p. 91.
14. George, 1992, p. 103.
15. Milbank, 1994, pp. A1, 6.
16. Sassen, 1991.
17. Whitney, 1995, p. 3.
18. Kolko, 1988, p. 341.
19. Brecher & Costello, 1994, p. 27.
20. Quoted in Bonacich & Waller, 1994, p. 90.
21. Attali, 1991, pp. 5, 14.
22. Cited in Keatley, 1993.

23. Sanger, 1994, p. A3.

24. Enzenburger, 1994, p. 112.

25. *Los Angeles Times*, October 1, 1991.

26. Montalbano, 1991, p. F1; Tan, 1991a.

27. Ball, 1990.

28. Tan, 1991b.

29. MacShane, 1991.

30. Andreas, 1994, p. 53.

31. Andreas, 1994, p. 52.

32. Goldsmith, 1994, pp. 64–65.

33. Andreas, 1994, p. 45.

34. Anderson, 1994.

35. De Soto, 1990, p. 11.

36. King & Schneider, 1991, p. 164; Harrison, 1993, p. 170.

37. Reich, 1991, p. 42.

38. Quoted in Ritchie, 1994.

39. Cited in Ritchie, 1994.

40. Goldsmith, 1994, pp. 38–39.

41. Escobar, 1995, Chapter 2.

42. LaTouche, 1993, p. 130.

43. Cheru, 1989, pp. 8, 19.

44. LaTouche, 1993, pp. 133–134.

45. Quoted in LaTouche, 1993, p. 158.

46. Harrison, 1993, p. 174.

47. de la Rocha, 1994.

48. Esteva, 1992, p. 21.

49. Darnton, 1994b, p. A8.

50. Bello, 1994, p. 52.

51. Quoted in Lang & Hines, 1993, p. 84.

52. Woodall, 1994, p. 23.

53. Enzenburger, 1994, p. 35.

54. Attali, 1991, p. 73.

55. Brown & Tiffen, 1992, p. 140.

56. Schaeffer, 1995, p. 267.

57. Quoted in King & Schneider, 1991, p. 185.

58. Rothchild & Lawson, 1994, pp. 257–258.

59. Ul-Haq, 1995, p. 9.

60. Cumings, 1987.

61. *The Economist*, August 27, 1995, p. 15.
62. Koo, 1987, p. 33.
63. Edwards, 1992, pp. 123–124.
64. Kagarlitsky, 1995, p. 217.
65. Walton & Seddon, 1994, p. 42.
66. Beckman, 1992, p. 97.
67. Lorch, 1995, p. A3.
68. Darnton, 1994c, p. A8.
69. Noble, 1994a, p. A3.
70. Quoted in Darnton, 1994c, p. A9.
71. Noble, 1994b, pp. A1, 6.
72. Darnton, 1994a, p. A1.
73. Darnton, 1994d, p. A1.
74. Crossette, 1994a, p. A3.
75. Johnson, 1993, p. 22.
76. Quoted in Richburg, 1994, p. 25.
77. Darnton, 1994b, p. A1.

Chapter 7: Social Responses to Globalization

1. See Williams, 1990.
2. Stavrianos, 1981, p. 657.
3. Stavrianos, 1981, pp. 657–659.
4. Stavrianos, 1981, p. 657; Araghi, 1989.
5. Watts, 1992.
6. Stavrianos, 1981, p. 660.
7. Cowell, 1994, p. A14.
8. Ibrahim, 1994, pp. A1, 10.
9. Swamy, 1995.
10. McMichael, 1993, p. 51.
11. Harrison, 1993, p. 54.
12. See McMichael, 1993.
13. Amin, Arrighi, Frank, & Wallerstein, 1990.
14. Quoted in Sachs, 1992, p. 107.
15. Stewart, 1994, pp. 108–109.
16. Quoted in Rich, 1994, p. 197.
17. Quoted in Middleton et al., 1993, p. 19.
18. Agarwal & Nurain, cited in Rich, 1994, p. 262.

19. Quoted in John Friedmann, 1992, p. 123.
20. Rich, 1994, pp. 244–245.
21. Middleton et al., 1993, p. 25.
22. Hildyard, 1993, pp. 32–34.
23. Colchester, 1994, pp. 71–72.
24. Quoted in Colchester, 1994, p. 72.
25. Fried, forthcoming.
26. Rich, 1994, pp. 160–165.
27. Rich, 1994, p. 167.
28. Rich, 1994, pp. 168–169.
29. Rich, 1994, pp. 34–37.
30. Quoted in Colchester, 1994, p. 78.
31. Colchester, 1994, pp. 83, 88.
32. Lohmann, 1993, p. 10.
33. Colchester, 1994, p. 88.
34. Colchester, 1994, p. 89.
35. Rau, 1991, pp. 156–157, 160.
36. Amanor, 1994, p. 64.
37. Quoted in George & Sabelli, 1994, p. 170.
38. Jahan, 1995, p. 13.
39. Harcourt, 1994, p. 4.
40. Harcourt, 1994, p. 5.
41. Apffel-Marglin & Simon, 1994.
42. Harcourt, 1994, p. 19.
43. Apffel-Marglin & Simon, 1994, p. 33.
44. Häusler, 1994, pp. 149–150.
45. Rocheleau, 1991.
46. Abramovitz, 1994, p. 201.
47. "Battle of the Bulge," 1994, p. 25.
48. Bryant Robey, Shea O. Rutstein, & Leo Morris, quoted in Stevens, 1994, p. A8.
49. Chira, 1994, p. A12.
50. Sen, 1994, p. 221.
51. Quoted in Hedges, 1994, p. A10.
52. Benería, 1992.
53. Quoted in Jahan, 1995, p. 77.
54. Jahan, 1995, p. 109.
55. Quoted in Jahan, 1995, p. 109.
56. Sachs, 1992, p. 112.

57. Fox, 1994.
58. Communiqués No. 1, 22, quoted in *AVA* 42, 31, 1994, p. 1.
59. Harvey, 1994, p. 14.
60. Hernández, 1994, p. 51; Harvey, 1994, p. 20.
61. Harvey, 1994, pp. 36–37; Fox, 1994, p. 18.
62. Wallerstein, 1992.
63. Cleaver, 1994, p. 150.
64. Cleaver, 1994, pp. 154–155.
65. Walton & Seddon, 1994, p. 335.
66. Ross & Trachte, 1990, Chapter 9.
67. Brecher & Costello, 1994, pp. 153–154.
68. Benería, 1995, p. 48.

Chapter 8: Whither Development?

1. Hobsbawm, 1994, p. 353.
2. Ewert, 1992, pp. 86–88. Includes account of Tanzanian scheme.
3. Davidson, 1992.
4. Uchitelle, 1993a; Chase, 1995, p. 16.
5. French, 1995, p. 4.
6. Segelken, 1995, p. 5.
7. Lappin, 1994, p. 193.
8. WuDunn, 1993.
9. Tyler, 1994, p. 8.
10. Brown, 1994, p. 19.
11. McMichael, 1993, p. 336.
12. Ihonvbere, 1993, p. 8.
13. Quoted in Press, 1993, p. 20.
14. Hildyard, 1993, p. 30.
15. Durning, 1993, pp. 14–15.
16. Tyler, 1995, p. A6.
17. *The Economist*, April 8, 1995, p. 34.
18. Quoted in The South Centre, 1993, p. 3.
19. Borrador Conclusiones, Madrid, May 1994.
20. This notion comes from personal correspondence with Peter Znoj.
21. Sachs, 1993, p. 20.
22. Crossette, 1995a.
23. Quoted in Crossette, 1995b.

24. Quoted in George & Sabelli, 1994, pp. 148, 150.

25. Commission on Global Governance, 1995, p. 55.

26. Wallerstein, 1983. See also Sklair, 1991, for a global sociology of the current world economy.

27. Sharp, 1994, pp. 116, 126.

References

Abramovitz, Janet N. 1994. "Biodiversity and Gender Issues." In Wendy Harcourt (Ed.), *Feminist Perspectives on Sustainable Development*. London: Zed Books.

Acharya, Anjali. 1995. "Plundering the Boreal Forests." *World Watch* 8, 3:2–29.

Adams, Nassau A. 1993. *Worlds Apart. The North-South Divide and the International System*. London: Zed Books.

Agarwal, Bina. 1994. *A Field of One's Own. Gender and Land Rights in South Asia*. Cambridge: Cambridge University Press.

Amanor, Kojo. 1994. "Ecological Knowledge and the Regional Economy: Environmental Management in the Asesewa District of Ghana." In Dharam Ghai (Ed.), *Environment & Development: Sustaining People and Nature*. Oxford: Blackwell.

Amin, Samir, Giovanni Arrighi, Andre Gunder Frank, and Immanuel Wallerstein. 1990. *Transforming the Revolution: Social Movements and the World System*. New York: Monthly Review Press.

Anderson, Benedict. 1994. "Exodus." *Critical Inquiry*, Winter.

Andrae, Gunilla, and Björn Beckman. 1985. *The Wheat Trap*. London: Zed Books.

Andreas, Peter. 1994. "The Making of Amerexico." *World Policy Journal*, Summer:45–56.

Apffel-Marglin, Fréderique, and Suzanne L. Simon. 1994. "Feminist Orientalism and Development." In Wendy Harcourt (Ed.), *Feminist Perspectives on Sustainable Development*. London: Zed Books.

Appelbaum, Richard P., and Gary Gereffi. 1994. "Power and Profits in the Apparel Commodity Chain." In Edna Bonacich, Lucie Cheng, Norma Chinchilla, Nora Hamilton, and Paul Ong (Eds.), *Global Production. The Apparel Industry in the Pacific Rim*. Philadelphia: Temple University Press.

Araghi, Farshad. 1989. "Land Reform Policies in Iran: A Comment." *American Journal of Agricultural Economics* 74, 4:1046–1049.

———. 1995. "Global Depeasantization, 1945–1990." *The Sociological Quarterly* 36, 2:337–368.

Arrighi, Giovanni. 1990. "The Developmentalist Illusion: A Reconceptualization of the Semiperiphery." In William G. Martin (Ed.), *Semiperipheral States in the World Economy*. Westport, CT: Greenwood.

———. 1994. *The Long Twentieth Century. Money, Power, and the Origins of Our Times.* London: Verso.

Athreya, Venkatesh B., Göran Djurfeldt, and Staffan Lindberg. 1990. *Barriers Broken. Production Relations and Agrarian Change in Tamil Nadu.* Newbury Park, CA: Sage.

Attali, Jacques. 1991. *Millenium. Winners and Losers in the Coming World Order.* New York: Times Books.

Bacon, Kenneth M. 1994. "Politics Could Doom a New Currency Plan." *The Wall Street Journal,* May 9:A1.

Baer, M. Delal. 1991. "North American Free Trade." *Foreign Affairs* 70, 4:132–149.

Baird, Peter, and Ed McCaughan. 1979. *Beyond the Border: Mexico & the U.S. Today.* New York: North American Congress on Latin America.

Ball, Rochelle. 1990. *The Process of International Contract Labor Migration from the Philippines: The Case of Filipino Nurses.* Unpublished doctoral dissertation. Sydney: Department of Geography, University of Sydney.

Bangura, Yusuf, and Peter Gibbon. 1992. "Adjustment, Authoritarianism and Democracy in Sub-Saharan Africa: An Introduction to Some Conceptual and Empirical Issues." In Peter Gibbon, Yusuf Bangura, & Arve Ofstad (Eds.), *Authoritarianism, Democracy and Adjustment. The Politics of Economic Reform in Africa.* Uppsala: Nordiska Afrikainstitutet.

Barkin, David. 1990. *Distorted Development. Mexico in the World Economy.* Boulder, CO: Westview Press.

———. 1991. "About Face." *North American Congress on Latin America (NACLA)* 24, 6:35.

Barnet, Richard J., and John Cavanagh. 1994. *Global Dreams. Imperial Corporations and the New World Order.* New York: Touchstone.

Barry, Tom. 1995. *Zapata's Revenge: Free Trade and the Farm Crisis in Mexico.* Boston: South End Press.

"Battle of the Bulge." 1994. *The Economist,* September 3:25.

Beckman, Björn. 1992. "Empowerment or Repression? The World Bank and the Politics of African Adjustment." In Peter Gibbon, Yusuf Bangura, & Arve Ofstad (Eds.), *Authoritarianism, Democracy and Adjustment. The Politics of Economic Reform in Sub-Saharan Africa.* Uppsala: Nordiska Afrikainstitutet.

Bello, Walden. 1992–1993. "Population and the Environment." *Food First Action Alert,* Winter:5.

———. 1994. *Dark Victory. The United States, Structural Adjustment and Global Poverty.* With Shea Cunningham and Bill Rau. London: Pluto Press, with Food First and Transnational Institute.

Benería, Lourdes. 1992. "Accounting for Women's Work: The Progress of Two Decades." *World Development* 20, 11:1547–1560.

———. 1995. "Response: The Dynamics of Globalization" (Scholarly Controversy: Global Flows of Labor and Capital). *International Labor and Working-Class History* 47:45–52.

Benería, Lourdes, and Shelley Feldman (Eds.). 1992. *Unequal Burden. Economic Crises, Persistent Poverty, and Women's Work.* Boulder, CO: Westview Press.

Berlan, Jean-Pierre. 1991. "The Historical Roots of the Present Agricultural Crisis." In W. Friedland, L. Busch, F. Buttel, and A. Rudy (Eds.), *Towards a New Political Economy of Agriculture.* Boulder, CO: Westview Press.

Bernstein, Henry. 1990. "Agricultural 'Modernization' and the Era of Structural Adjustment: Observations on Sub-Saharan Africa." *Journal of Peasant Studies* 18, 1:3–35.

Block, Fred L. 1977. *The Origins of International Economic Disorder. A Study of United States International Monetary Policy from World War II to the Present.* Berkeley: University of California Press.

Bonacich, Edna, and David V. Waller. 1994. "The Role of U.S. Apparel Manufacturers in the Globalization of the Industry in the Pacific Rim." In Edna Bonacich, Lucie Cheng, Norma Chinchilla, Nora Hamilton, and Paul Ong (Eds.), *Global Production: The Apparel Industry in the Pacific Rim.* Philadelphia: Temple University Press.

Borthwick, Mark. 1992. *Pacific Century. The Emergence of Modern Pacific Asia.* Boulder, CO: Westview Press.

Bradley, P. N., and S. E. Carter. 1989. "Food Production and Distribution—and Hunger." In R. J. Johnston and P. J. Taylor (Eds.), *A World in Crisis? Geographical Perspectives.* Oxford: Blackwell.

Bradsher, Keith. 1995. "White House Moves to Increase Aid to Mexico." *The New York Times,* January 12:D6.

Brandt Commission (Independent Commission on International Development Issues). 1983. *Common Crisis: North, South & Cooperation for World Recovery.* London: Pan Books.

Brecher, Jeremy, and Tim Costello. 1994. *Global Village or Global Pillage? Economic Reconstruction from the Bottom Up.* Boston: South End Press.

Brett, E. A. 1985. *The World Economy Since the War: The Politics of Uneven Development.* London: Macmillan.

Brown, Lester R. 1994. "Who Will Feed China?" *World Watch* 7, 5:10–19.

———. 1995. "China's Food Problem: The Massive Imports Begin." *World Watch* 8, 5:38.

Brown, Michael Barratt. 1993. *Fair Trade.* London: Zed Books.

Brown, Michael Barratt, and Pauline Tiffen. 1992. *Short Changed. Africa and World Trade.* Boulder, CO: Pluto Press with the Transnational Institute.

Bujra, Janet. 1992. "Diversity in Pre-capitalist Societies." In Tim Allen and Allan Thomas (Eds.), *Poverty and Development in the 1990s.* Oxford: Oxford University Press.

Burbach, Roger, and Patricia Flynn. 1980. *Agribusiness in the Americas.* New York: Monthly Review Press.

Buttel, Frederick H. 1992. "Environmentalization: Origins, Processes, and Implications for Rural Social Change." *Rural Sociology* 57, 1:1–28.

Byres, Terry J. 1981. "The New Technology, Class Formation and Class Action in the Indian Countryside." *Journal of Peasant Studies* 8, 4:405–454.

Cahn, Jonathan. 1993. "Challenging the New Imperial Authority: The World Bank and the Democratization of Development." *Harvard Human Rights Journal* 6:159–194.

Canak, William L. 1989. "Debt, Austerity, and Latin America in the New International Division of Labor." In William L. Canak (Ed.), *Lost Promises: Debt, Austerity, and Development in Latin America*. Boulder, CO: Westview Press.

Cardoso, Fernando H., and Enzo Faletto. 1979. *Dependency and Development in Latin America*. Berkeley: University of California Press.

Carlsen, L. 1991. "Reaping Winter's Harvest." *Business Mexico*, May:20–23.

Chase, Edward T. 1995. "Down and Out in London, Paris and New York." *The Bookpress* (Ithaca), March:16.

Cheru, Fantu. 1989. *The Silent Revolution in Africa: Debt, Development and Democracy*. London: Zed Books.

Chira, Susan. 1994. "Women Campaign for New Plan to Curb the World's Population." *The New York Times*, April 13:A12.

Chirot, Daniel. 1977. *Social Change in the Twentieth Century*. New York: Harcourt Brace Jovanovich.

Chomsky, Noam. 1994. *World Orders Old and New*. New York: Columbia University Press.

Chung, Youg-Il. 1990. "The Agricultural Foundation for Korean Industrial Development." In Chung Lee and Ippei Yamazawa (Eds.), *The Economic Development of Japan and Korea*. New York: Praeger.

Cleaver, Harry. 1977. "Food, Famine and the International Crisis." *Zerowork* 2: 7–70.

———. 1994. "The Chiapas Uprising." *Studies in Political Economy* 44:141–157.

Colchester, Marcus. 1994. "Sustaining the Forests: The Community-based Approach in South and Southeast Asia." In Dharam Ghai (Ed.), *Development & Environment. Sustaining People and Nature*. Oxford: Blackwell.

Collins, Jane. 1995. "Gender and Cheap Labor in Agriculture." In Philip McMichael (Ed.), *Food and Agrarian Orders in the World-Economy*. Westport, CT: Praeger.

Commission on Global Governance. 1995. *Our Global Neighborhood*. Oxford: Oxford University Press.

Corbridge, Stuart. 1993. "Ethics in Development Studies: The Example of Debt." In Frans J. Schuurman (Ed.), *Beyond the Impasse: New Directions in Development Theory*. London: Zed Books.

Cowell, Alan. 1994. "Muslim Party Threatens Turk's Secular Heritage." *The New York Times*, November 30:A14.

Cox, Robert W. 1987. *Production, Power, and World Order. Social Forces in the Making of History*. New York: Columbia University Press.

Crook, Clive. 1991. "Sisters in the Wood. A Survey of the IMF and the World Bank." *The Economist*, Special Supplement, October 12.

———. 1992. "Fear of Finance. A Survey of the World Economy." *The Economist*, Special Supplement, September 19.

———. 1993. "New Ways to Grow. A Survey of World Finance." *The Economist*, Special Supplement, September 25.

Crossette, Barbara. 1994a. "U.N. Chief Chides Security Council on Military Missions." *The New York Times*, January 6:A3.

———. 1994b. "A Third-World Effort on Family Planning." *The New York Times*, September 7: A8.

———. 1995a. "U.N. Parley Puts Focus on Africa." *The New York Times*, March 9:A10.

———. 1995b. "Talks in Denmark Redefine 'Foreign Aid' in Post–Cold-War Era." *The New York Times*, March 10:A5.

Cumings, Bruce. 1987. "The Origin and Development of the Northeast Asian Political Economy: Industrial Sectors, Product Cycles, and Political Consequences." In Frederic C. Deyo (Ed.), *The Political Economy of the New Asian Industrialism*. Ithaca, NY: Cornell University Press.

Dalrymple, D. 1985. "The Development and Adoption of High-Yielding Varieties of Wheat and Rice in Developing Countries." *American Journal of Agricultural Economics* 67:1067–1073.

Daly, M. T., and M. I. Logan. 1989. *The Brittle Rim. Finance, Business and the Pacific Region*. Ringwood, Victoria: Penguin.

Darnton, John. 1994a. "Crisis-torn Africa Becomes Continent of Refugees." *The New York Times*, May 23:A2.

———. 1994b. "In Poor, Decolonized Africa Bankers Are New Overlords." *The New York Times*, June 20:A1.

———. 1994c. "Africa Tries Democracy, Finding Hope and Peril." *The New York Times*, June 21:A9.

———. 1994d. "U.N. Faces Refugee Crisis That Never Ends." *The New York Times*, August 8:A1.

Davidson, Basil. 1992. *The Black Man's Burden. Africa and the Curse of the Nation-State*. New York: Times Books.

de Janvry, Alain. 1981. *The Agrarian Question and Reformism in Latin America*. Baltimore: Johns Hopkins University Press.

de la Rocha, Mercedes Gonzaléz. 1994. *The Resources of Poverty. Women and Survival in a Mexican City*. Cambridge, MA: Blackwell.

DePalma, Anthony. 1993. "Mexico Unloads State Companies, Pocketing Billions, but Hits Snags." *The New York Times*, October 27:A1, 8.

DeWalt, Billie. 1985. "Mexico's Second Green Revolution: Food for Feed." *Mexican Studies/Estudios Mexicanos* 1:29–60.

Deyo, Frederic C. 1989. *Beneath the Miracle: Labor Subordination in the New Asian Industrialism*. Berkeley: University of California Press.

———. 1991. "Singapore: Developmental Paternalism." In Steven M. Goldstein (Ed.), *Mini-Dragons: Fragile Economic Miracles in the Pacific*. Boulder, CO: Westview Press.

Dhanagare, D. N. 1988. "The Green Revolution and Social Inequalities in Rural India." *Bulletin of Concerned Asian Scholars* 20, 2:2–13.

Dicken, Peter. 1992. "International Production in a Volatile Regulatory Environment: The Influence of National Regulatory Policies on the Spatial Strategies of Transnational Corporations." *Geoforum* 23:303-316.

Drozdiak, William. 1995. "Trade Zone Plan Intrigues Leaders on Both Sides of Atlantic." *The Washington Post,* May 28:A39.

Dube, S. C. 1988. *Modernization and Development—The Search for Alternative Paradigms.* London: Zed Books.

Dudley, Leonard, and Roger Sandilands. 1975. "The Side Effects of Foreign Aid: The Case of Public Law 480 Wheat in Colombia." *Economic Development and Cultural Change* 23, 2:325-336.

Durning, Alan Thein. 1993. "Supporting Indigenous Peoples." In Lester Brown (Ed.), *State of the World.* New York: Norton.

Economic Commission for Latin America and the Caribbean (ECLAC). 1989. *Transnational Bank Behaviour and the International Debt Crisis.* Santiago, Chile: ECLAC/UN Center on Transnational Corporations.

Edwards, Chris. 1992. "Industrialization in South Korea." In Tom Hewitt, Hazel Johnson, and Dave Wield (Eds.), *Industrialization and Development.* Oxford: Oxford University Press.

Ellwood, Wayne. 1993. "Multinationals and the Subversion of Sovereignty." *New Internationalist* 246:4–7.

Enzenburger, Hans Magnus. 1994. *Civil Wars: From L.A. to Bosnia.* New York: The New Press.

Escobar, Arturo. 1995. *Encountering Development: The Making and Unmaking of the Third World.* Princeton, NJ: Princeton University Press.

Esteva, Gustavo. 1992. "Development." In Wolfgang Sachs (Ed.), *The Development Dictionary.* London: Zed Books.

Evans, Peter. 1979. *Dependent Development.* Princeton, NJ: Princeton University Press.

Ewert, Merril. 1992. "Adult Education and International Development." In S. B. Merriam and P. M. Cunningham (Eds.), *Handbook of Adult Education.* San Francisco: Jossey-Bass.

Fanon, Frantz. 1967. *The Wretched of the Earth.* Harmondsworth: Penguin.

Feder, Ernst. 1983. *Perverse Development.* Quezon City, Philippines: Foundation for Nationalist Studies.

Fenley, Lindajoy. 1991. "Promoting the Pacific Rim." *Business Mexico,* June:41.

Fidler, Stephen, and Lisa Bransten. 1995. "Mexican Sell-Offs to Help Solve the Debt Crisis." *Financial Times,* August 1:1.

Fox, Jonathan. 1994. "The Challenge of Democracy: Rebellion as Catalyst." *Akwe:kon* 11, 2:13–19.

French, Howard W. 1995. "Migrants' Sad Cries Now Echo Through Africa." *The New York Times,* February 6:4.

Fried, Stephanie. Forthcoming. "Writing for Their Lives: Bentian Dyak Authors and Indonesian Development Discourse." In C. Zerner (Ed.), *Forests, Coasts, and Seas: Culture and the Question of Rights to Southeast Asian Environmental Resources.*

Friedland, William H. 1994. "The Global Fresh Fruit and Vegetable System: An Industrial Organization Analysis." In Philip McMichael (Ed.), *The Global Restructuring of Agro-Food Systems.* Ithaca, NY: Cornell University Press.

Friedmann, Harriet. 1990. "The Origins of Third World Food Dependence." In Henry Bernstein, Ben Crow, Maureen Mackintosh, and Charlotte Martin (Eds.), *The Food Question: Profits Versus People?* New York: Monthly Review Press.

———. 1991. "Changes in the International Division of Labor: Agri-food Complexes and Export Agriculture." In William Friedland, Lawrence Busch, Frederick H. Buttel, and Alan P. Rudy (Eds.), *Towards a New Political Economy of Agriculture.* Boulder, CO: Westview Press.

———. 1992. "Distance and Durability: Shaky Foundations of the World Food Economy." *Third World Quarterly* 13, 2:371–383.

Friedmann, Harriet, and Philip McMichael. 1989. "Agriculture and the State System: The Rise and Fall of National Agricultures, 1870 to the Present." *Sociologia Ruralis* 29, 2: 93–117.

Friedmann, John. 1992. *Empowerment. The Politics of Alternative Development.* Cambridge: Blackwell.

Fröbel, Folker, Jürgen Heinrichs, and Otto Kreye. 1979. *The New International Division of Labor.* New York: Cambridge University Press.

George, Susan. 1977. *How the Other Half Dies. The Real Reasons for World Hunger.* Montclair, NJ: Allenheld, Osmun and Co.

———. 1988. *A Fate Worse Than Debt. The World Financial Crisis and the Poor.* New York: Grove Press.

———. 1992. *The Debt Boomerang. How Third World Debt Harms Us All.* Boulder, CO: Westview Press.

George, Susan, and Fabrizio Sabelli. 1994. *Faith and Credit. The World Bank's Secular Empire.* Boulder, CO: Westview Press.

Gereffi, Gary. 1989. "Rethinking Development Theory: Insights from East Asia and Latin America." *Sociological Forum* 4, 4:505–533.

———. 1994. "The Organization of Buyer-Driven Global Commodity Chains: How U.S. Retailers Shape Overseas Production Networks." In Gary Gereffi and Miguel Korzeniewicz (Eds.), *Commodity Chains and Global Capitalism.* Westport, CT: Praeger.

Gibbon, Peter. 1992. "Structural Adjustment and Pressures Toward Multipartyism in Sub-Saharan Africa." In Peter Gibbon, Yusuf Bangura, & Arve Ofstad (Eds.), *Authoritarianism, Democracy and Adjustment. The Politics of Economic Reform in Sub-Saharan Africa.* Uppsala: Nordiska Afrikainstitutet.

Giddens, Anthony. 1990. *The Consequences of Modernity.* Stanford: Stanford University Press.

Gill, Stephen. 1992. "Economic Globalization and the Internationalization of Authority: Limits and Contradictions." *Geoforum* 23, 3:269–283.

Golden, Tim. 1995. "Mexicans Find Dream Devalued." *The New York Times* The Week in Review, January 8:5.

Goldsmith, James. 1994. *The Trap.* New York: Carroll & Graf.

Griffin, K. B. 1974. *The Political Economy of Agrarian Change: An Essay on the Green Revolution.* Cambridge: Harvard University Press.

Grigg, David. 1993. *The World Food Problem.* Oxford: Blackwell.

Harcourt, Wendy. 1994. "Introduction." In Wendy Harcourt (Ed.), *Feminist Perspectives on Sustainable Development.* London: Zed Books.

Harper, Doug. 1994. "Auto Imports Jump in Mexico." *The New York Times,* July 7:D1.

Harris, Nigel. 1987. *The End of the Third World. Newly Industrializing Countries and the Decline of an Ideology.* Harmondsworth: Penguin.

Harrison, Paul. 1993. *The Third Revolution. Population, Environment and a Sustainable World.* Harmondsworth: Penguin.

Harvey, Neil. 1994. *Rebellion in Chiapas. Rural Reforms, Campesino Radicalism, and the Limits to Salinismo.* San Diego: Center for U.S.-Mexican Studies.

Hathaway, Dale E. 1987. *Agriculture and the GATT. Rewriting the Rules.* Washington, DC: Institute for International Economics.

Häusler, Sabine. 1994. "Women and the Politics of Sustainable Development." In Wendy Harcourt (Ed.), *Feminist Perspectives on Sustainable Development.* London: Zed Books.

Hedges, Chris. 1994. "Key Panel at Cairo Talks Agrees on Population Plan." *The New York Times,* September 13:A10.

Heffernan, William D., and Douglas H. Constance. 1994. "Transnational Corporations and the Globalization of the Food System." In Alessandro Bonanno, Lawrence Busch, William Friedland, Lourdes Gouveia, and Enzo Mingione (Eds.), *From Columbus to ConAgra. The Globalization of Agriculture and Food.* Lawrence: University Press of Kansas.

Henderson, Jeffrey. 1991. *The Globalisation of High Technology Production.* London: Routledge.

Hernández, Luis Navarro. 1994. "The Chiapas Uprising." In Neil Harvey (Ed.), *Rebellion in Chiapas.* University of California–San Diego: Center for U.S./Mexican Studies.

Hettne, Björn. 1990. *Development Theory and the Three Worlds.* White Plains, NY: Longman.

Hewitt, Tom. 1992. "Brazilian Industrialization." In Tom Hewitt, Hazel Johnson, and Dave Wield (Eds.), *Industrialization and Development.* Oxford: Oxford University Press.

Hildyard, Nicholas. 1993. "Foxes in Charge of Chickens." In Wolfgang Sachs (Ed.), *Global Ecology. A New Arena of Political Conflict.* London: Zed Books.

Hill, Richard Child, and Kuniko Fujita. 1995. "Product Cycles and International Divisions of Labor: Contrasts Between the United States and Japan." In

David A. Smith and József Böröcz (Eds.), *A New World Order? Global Transformations in the Late Twentieth Century.* Westport, CT: Praeger.

Hobsbawm, Eric J. 1992. "The Crisis of Today's Ideologies." *New Left Review* 192: 55–64.

———. 1994. *The Age of Extremes. A History of the World from 1914 to 1991.* New York: Pantheon.

Hoogvelt, Ankie M. M. 1987. *The Third World in Global Development.* London: Macmillan.

Ibrahim, Youssef M. 1994. "Fundamentalists Impose Culture on Egypt." *The New York Times,* February 3:A1, 10.

Ihonvbere, Julius O. 1993–1994. "The Third World and the New World Order in the 1990s." In Robert J. Griffiths (Ed.), *Third World 94/95. Annual Editions.* Guildford, CT: Dushkin.

Jahan, Rounaq. 1995. *The Elusive Agenda. Mainstreaming Women in Development.* London: Zed Books.

James, C. L. R. 1963. *The Black Jacobins. Toussaint L'Ouverture and the San Domingo Revolution.* New York: Vintage.

Jenkins, Rhys. 1992. "Industrialization and the Global Economy." In Tom Hewitt, Hazel Johnson, and Dave Wield (Eds.), *Industrialization and Development.* Oxford: Oxford University Press.

Johnson, Paul. 1993. "Colonialism's Back—and Not a Moment Too Soon." *The New York Times* Magazine, April 18:22.

Kagarlitsky, Boris. 1995. *The Mirage of Modernization.* New York: Monthly Review Press.

Kaldor, Mary. 1990. *The Imaginary War. Understanding the East-West Conflict.* Oxford: Blackwell.

Keatley, Robert. 1993. "If Free-Trade Accord Fails, the Impact on Mexico Could Quickly Spread North." *Wall Street Journal,* May 28:A1.

Kemp, Tom. 1989. *Industrialization in the Non-Western World.* London: Longman.

King, Alexander, and Bertrand Schneider. 1991. *The First Global Revolution. A Report by the Council to the Club of Rome.* New York: Pantheon.

Knox, Paul, and John Agnew. 1994. *The Geography of the World Economy.* London: Edward Arnold.

Kolko, Joyce. 1988. *Restructuring the World Economy.* New York: Pantheon.

Koo, Hagen. 1987. "The Interplay of State, Class, and World System in East Asian Development: The Cases of South Korea and Taiwan." In Federic C. Deyo (Ed.), *The Political Economy of the New Asian Industrialism.* Ithaca, NY: Cornell University Press.

Korzeniewicz, Miguel. 1994. "Commodity Chains and Marketing Strategies: Nike and the Global Athletic Footwear Industry." In Gary Gereffi and Miguel Korzeniewicz (Eds.), *Commodity Chains and Global Capitalism.* Westport, CT: Praeger.

Kothari, Smitu, and Pramod Parajuli. 1993. "No Nature Without Social Justice: A Plea for Cultural and Ecological Pluralism in India." In Wolfgang Sachs (Ed.), *Global Ecology. A New Arena of Political Conflict.* London: Zed Books.

Kuenzler, L. T. 1992. "Foreign Investment Opportunities in the Mexican Agricultural Sector." *Business Mexico* Special Edition:44–47.

Landsberg, Martin. 1979. "Export-led Industrialization in the Third World: Manufacturing Imperialism." *Review of Radical Political Economics* 2, 4:50–63.

Lang, Tim, and Colin Hines. 1993. *The New Protectionism. Protecting the Future Against Free Trade.* New York: The New Press.

Lappin, Todd. 1994. "Can Green Mix with Red?" *The Nation*, February 14:193.

LaTouche, Serge. 1993. *In the Wake of the Affluent Society. An Exploration of Post-Development.* London: Zed Books.

Lehman, David. 1990. *Democracy and Development in Latin America.* Philadelphia: Temple University Press.

Lewin, Tamar. 1995. "Family Decay Global, Study Says." *The New York Times*, May 30: A5.

Lewis, W. Arthur. 1950. "Industrialization of the British West Indies." *Caribbean Economic Review* 2, 1:1–62.

Lipton, Michael. 1977. *Why Poor People Stay Poor: Urban Bias in World Development.* London: Temple Smith.

Lissakers, Karin. 1993. *Banks, Borrowers, and the Establishment. A Revisionist Account of the International Debt Crisis.* New York: Basic Books.

Llambi, Luis. 1990. "Transitions to and Within Capitalism: Agrarian Transitions in Latin America." *Sociologia Ruralis* 30, 2:174–196.

Lohmann, Larry. 1993. "Resisting Green Globalism." In Wolfgang Sachs (Ed.), *Global Ecology. A New Arena of Political Conflict.* London: Zed Books.

London, Christopher. 1993. *The Cultural Policies of Technical Change in Colombian Coffee Production.* Unpublished master's thesis. Ithaca, NY: Development Sociology, Cornell University.

Lorch, Donatella. 1995. "Ugandan Strongman a Favorite of World Lenders." *The New York Times*, January 29:A3.

MacShane, Denis. 1991. "Working in Virtual Slavery: Gulf Migrant Labor." *The Nation*, March 18:325, 343–344.

Madden, Peter, and John Madeley. 1993. "Winners and Losers: The Impact of the GATT Uruguay Round in Developing Countries." *Christian Aid*, December: 17.

Magdoff, Harry. 1969. *The Age of Imperialism.* New York: Monthly Review Press.

McMichael, A. J. 1993. *Planetary Overload: Global Environmental Change and the Health of the Human Species.* Cambridge: Cambridge University Press.

McMichael, Philip. 1990. "Incorporating Comparison Within a World-Historical Perspective: An Alternative Comparative Method." *American Sociological Review* 55, 2:385–397.

————. 1992. "Rethinking Comparative Analysis in a Post-Developmentalist Context." *International Social Science Journal* 133:351–365.

————. 1993a. "World Food System Restructuring Under a GATT Regime." *Political Geography* 12, 3:198–214.

————. 1993b. "Agro-Food Restructuring in the Pacific Rim: A Comparative-International Perspective on Japan, South Korea, the United States, Australia, and Thailand." In Ravi Palat (Ed.), *Pacific-Asia and the Future of the World-System*. Westport, CT: Greenwood.

McMichael, Philip, and Chul-Kyoo Kim. 1994. "Japanese and South Korean Agricultural Restructuring in Comparative and Global Perspective." In Philip McMichael (Ed.), *The Global Restructuring of Agro-Food Systems*. Ithaca, NY: Cornell University Press.

McMichael, Philip, and David Myhre. 1991. "Global Regulation versus the Nation-State: Agro-Food Systems and the New Politics of Capital." *Capital & Class* 43, 2:83-106.

McMichael, Philip, and Laura T. Raynolds. 1994. "Capitalism, Agriculture, and World Economy." In Leslie Sklair (Ed.), *Capitalism and Development*. London: Routledge.

Memmi, Albert. 1967. *The Colonizer and the Colonized*. Boston: Beacon Press.

Middleton, Neil, Phil O'Keefe, and Sam Moyo. 1993. *Tears of the Crocodile. From Rio to Reality in the Developing World*. Boulder, CO: Pluto.

Mies, Maria. 1991. *Patriarchy and Accumulation on a World Scale: Women in the International Division of Labor*. London: Zed Books.

Milbank, Dana. 1994. "Unlike Rest of Europe, Britain Is Creating Jobs but They Pay Poorly." *Wall Street Journal*, March 28:A1, 6.

Montalbano, William D. 1991. "A Global Pursuit of Happiness." *Los Angeles Times*, October 1:F1.

Moore, Barrington, Jr. 1967. *Social Origins of Dictatorship and Democracy. Lord and Peasant in the Making of the Modern World*. Boston: Beacon Press.

Morgan, Dan. 1980. *Merchants of Grain*. Harmondsworth: Penguin.

Myers, Norman. 1981. "The Hamburger Connection: How Central America's Forests Became North America's Hamburgers." *Ambio* 10, 1: 3–8.

Myhre, David. 1994. "The Politics of Globalization in Rural Mexico: Campesino Initiatives to Restructure the Agricultural Credit System." In Philip McMichael (Ed.), *The Global Restructuring of Agro-Food Systems*. Ithaca, NY: Cornell University Press.

Nash, Nathaniel C. 1994. "Vast Areas of Rain Forest Are Being Destroyed in Chile." *The New York Times*, May 31: C4.

Nayyar, D. 1976. "Transnational Corporations and Manufactured Exports from Poor Countries." *University of Sussex Economic Seminar Paper Series* 76, 17.

Noble, Kenneth B. 1994a. "Democracy Brings Turmoil in Congo." *The New York Times*, January 31:A3.

————. 1994b. "French Devaluation of African Currency Brings Wide Unrest." *The New York Times*, February 23:A1, 6.

Norberg-Hodge, Helena. 1994–95. "Globalization Versus Community." *ISEC/ Ladakh Project* 14: 1–2.

Payer, Cheryl. 1974. *The Debt Trap.* New York: Monthly Review Press.

Pearse, A. 1980. *Seeds of Plenty, Seeds of Want.* Oxford: Clarendon Press.

Pepper, Suzanne. 1988. "China's Special Economic Zones." *Bulletin of Concerned Asian Scholars* 20, 3:2–21.

Phillips, Anne. 1977. "The Concept of 'Development.' " *Review of African Political Economy* 8:7–20.

Place, Susan E. 1985. "Export Beef Production and Development Contradictions in Costa Rica." *Tijdschrift voor Econ. en Soc. Geografie* 76, 4:288–297.

Press, Eyal. 1993. "Free-Market Misery for Latin America." *The New York Times* This Week in Review, Letters to the Editor, December 5:20.

Raghavan, Chakravarthi. 1990. *Recolonization: GATT, the Uruguay Round and the Third World.* Penang, Malaysia: Third World Network.

Raikes, Philip. 1988. *Modernising Hunger. Famine, Food Surplus & Farm Policy in the EC and Africa.* London: Catholic Institute for International Affairs.

Rama, Ruth. 1985. "Some Effects of the Internationalization of Agriculture on the Mexican Agricultural Crisis." In Steven Sanderson (Ed.), *The Americas in the New International Division of Labor.* New York: Holmes & Meier.

———. 1992. *Investing in Food.* Paris: Organization for Economic Cooperation and Development.

Rau, Bill. 1991. *From Feast to Famine: Official Cures and Grassroots Remedies to Africa's Food Crisis.* London: Zed Books.

Raynolds, Laura T. 1994. "The Restructuring of Export Agriculture in the Dominican Republic: Changing Agrarian Relations and the State." In Philip McMichael (Ed.), *The Global Restructuring of Agro-Food Systems.* Ithaca: Cornell University Press.

Raynolds, Laura T., David Myhre, Philip McMichael, Viviana Carro-Figueroa, and Frederick H. Buttel. 1993. "The 'New' Internationalization of Agriculture: A Reformulation." *World Development* 21, 7:1101–1121.

Reich, Robert B. 1991. "Secession of the Successful." *The New York Times Magazine,* January 20:42.

———. 1992. *The Work of Nations: Preparing Ourselves for 21st Century Capitalism.* New York: Vintage Press.

Resource Center Bulletin. 1993. "Free Trade: the ifs, ands and buts." 31–32.

Revel, Alain, and Christophe Riboud. 1986. *American Green Power.* Baltimore: Johns Hopkins University Press.

Ricardo, David. 1821. *On the Principles of Political Economy and Taxation.* 3rd ed., reprinted in *The Works and Correspondence of David Ricardo,* Vol. 1, ed. P. Sraffe with the collaboration of M. M. Dobb. Cambridge: Cambridge University Press, 1951.

Rich, Bruce. 1994. *Mortgaging the Earth. The World Bank, Environmental Impoverishment and the Crisis of Development.* Boston: Beacon Press.

Richburg, Keith B. 1994. "Looking Back to Colonial Past for Clues to Future." *The Washington Post,* July 10:A25.

Riding, Alan. 1993. "France, Reversing Course, Fights Immigrants' Refusal to Be French." *The New York Times,* December 5:A1, 14.

Rifkin, Jeremy. 1992. *Beyond Beef. The Rise and Fall of the Cattle Culture.* New York: Penguin.

Ritchie, Mark. 1993. *Breaking the Deadlock: The United States and Agriculture Policy in the Uruguay Round.* Minneapolis: Institute for Agriculture and Trade Policy.

———. 1994. "GATT Facts: Africa Loses Under GATT." Working paper. Minneapolis: Institute for Agriculture and Trade Policy.

Rocheleau, Dianne E. 1991. "Gender, Ecology, and the Science of Survival: Stories and Lessons from Kenya." In Wendy Harcourt (Ed.), *Feminist Perspectives on Sustainable Development.* London: Zed Books.

Rocher, Francis. 1993. "Canadian Business, Free Trade and the Rhetoric of Economic Continentalization." *Studies in Political Economy* 35:143.

Ross, Robert J. S., and Kent C. Trachte. 1990. *Global Capitalism: The New Leviathan.* Albany: State University of New York Press.

Rostow, Walt W. 1960. *The Stages of Economic Growth. A Non-Communist Manifesto.* Cambridge: Cambridge University Press.

Rothchild, Donald, and Letitia Lawson. 1994. "The Interactions Between State and Civil Society in Africa: From Deadlock to New Routines." In John W. Harbeson, Donald Rothchild, and Naomi Chazan (Eds.), *Civil Society and the State in Africa.* Boulder, CO: Lynne Reinner.

Rowley, C. D. 1974. *The Destruction of Aboriginal Society.* Ringwood, Victoria: Penguin.

Rueschemeyer, Dietrich, Evelyne Huber Stephens, and John Stephens. 1992. *Capitalist Development and Democracy.* Chicago: University of Chicago Press.

Ruggie, John G. 1982. "International Regimes, Transactions and Change: Embedded Liberalism in the Postwar Economic Order." *International Organization* 36:397–415.

Sachs, Wolfgang. 1992. "One World." In Wolfgang Sachs (Ed.), *The Development Dictionary.* London: Zed Books.

———. 1993. "Global Ecology and the Shadow of 'Development.' " In Wolfgang Sachs (Ed.), *Global Ecology: A New Arena of Political Conflict.* London: Zed Books.

Salinger, Lynn, and Jean-Jacques Dethier. 1989. "Policy-Based Lending in Agriculture: Agricultural Sector Adjustment in Mexico." Paper presented at World Bank Seminar on Policy-Based Lending in Agriculture, Baltimore, May 17–19.

Sanderson, Steven. 1986a. *The Transformation of Mexican Agriculture. International Structure and the Politics of Rural Change.* Princeton, NJ: Princeton University Press.

———. 1986b. "The Emergence of the 'World Steer': Internationalization and Foreign Domination in Latin American Cattle Production." In F. L. Tullis and W. L. Hollist (Eds.), *Food, the State and International Political Economy.* Lincoln: University of Nebraska Press.

Sanger, David E. 1994. "Mexico Crisis Seen Spurring Flow of Aliens." *The New York Times,* January 18: A3.

———. 1995. "Big Powers Plan a World Economic Bailout Fund." *The New York Times,* June 8:A1, D8.

Sassen, Saskia. 1991. *The Global City.* Princeton, NJ: Princeton University Press.

Schaeffer, Robert. 1995. "Free Trade Agreements: Their Impact on Agriculture and the Environment." In Philip McMichael (Ed.), *Food and Agrarian Orders in the World-Economy.* Westport, CT: Praeger.

Schoenberger, Erica. 1994. "Competition, Time, and Space in Industrial Change." In Gary Gereffi and Miguel Korzeniewicz (Eds.), *Commodity Chains and Global Capitalism.* Westport, CT: Praeger.

Schwartz, Sara J., and Douglas Brooks. 1990. *Thailand's Feed and Livestock Industry to the Year 2000.* Washington, DC: U.S. Department of Agriculture, Economic Research Service.

Schwedel, Kenneth. 1991. "Will the Countryside Modernize?" *Business Mexico,* July:25.

Schwedel, S., and K. Haley. 1992. "Foreign Investment in the Mexican Food System." *Business Mexico* Special Edition:48–55.

Seers, Dudley. 1979. "The Meaning of Development." In David Lehman (Ed.), *Development Theory: Four Critical Studies.* London: Frank Cass.

Segelken, Roger. 1995. "Fewer Foods Predicted for Crowded Future Meals." *Cornell Chronicle,* February 23:5.

Seidman, Gay. 1994. *Manufacturing Militance. Workers' Movements in Brazil and South Africa, 1970–1985.* Berkeley: University of California Press.

Selden, Mark. 1994. "Russia, China, and the Transformation of Collective Agriculture." *Contention* 3, 3:73–93.

Selwyn, Michael. 1991. "The New Food Chain." *Asian Business,* December:26–34.

Sen, Gita. 1994. "Women, Poverty, and Population: Issues for the Concerned Environmentalist." In Wendy Harcourt (Ed.), *Feminist Perspectives on Sustainable Development.* London: Zed Books.

Shaiken, Harley. 1993. "Two Myths about Mexico." *The New York Times,* August 22:Op-Ed.

Sharp, Nonie. 1994. "Native Title in the Reshaping of Australian Identity." *Arena Journal* 3:115–148.

Shenon, Philip. 1993. "Saipan Sweatshops Are No American Dream." *The New York Times,* July 18:A1, 10.

Shiva, Vandana. 1991. *The Violence of the Green Revolution*. London: Zed Books.

Singh, Ajit. 1992. "The Lost Decade: The Economic Crisis of the Third World in the 1980s: How the North Caused the South's Crisis." *Contention* 2:58–80.

Sivanandan, A. 1989. "New Circuits of Imperialism." *Race & Class* 30, 4:1–19.

Sklair, Leslie. 1989. *Assembling for Development. The Maquila Industry in Mexico and the United States*. Boston: Unwin Hyman.

———. 1991. *The Sociology of the Global System*. Baltimore: Johns Hopkins University Press.

Soto, Hernando de. 1990. *The Other Path. The Invisible Revolution in the Third World*. New York: Harper & Row.

The South Centre. 1993. *Facing the Challenge. Responses to the Report of the South Commission*. London: Zed Books.

Stavrianos, L. S. 1981. *Global Rift. The Third World Comes of Age*. New York: William Morrow & Co.

Stevens, William K. 1994. "Poor Lands' Success in Cutting Birth Rate Upsets Old Theories." *The New York Times*, January 2: A8.

Stevenson, Richard W. 1993. "Ford Sets Its Sights on a 'World Car.'" *The New York Times*, October 27:D1, 4.

Stewart, Douglas Ian. 1994. *After the Trees. Living on the Amazon Highway*. Austin: University of Texas Press.

Strange, Susan. 1994. *States and Markets*. London: Pinter.

Swamy, M. R. Narayan. 1995. "Hindu Groups Step Up 'Buy Indian' Campaign." *IA News*, January 10.

Tan, Abby. 1991a. "Paychecks Sent Home May Not Cover Human Losses." *Los Angeles Times*, October 1:H2–3.

———. 1991b. "The Labor Brokers: For a Price, There's a Job Abroad—Maybe." *Los Angeles Times*, October 1:H1.

Templin, Neal. 1994. "Mexican Industrial Belt Is Beginning to Form as Car Makers Expand." *The Wall Street Journal*, June 29:A1, 10.

Tyler, Patrick E. 1994. "China Planning People's Car to Put Masses Behind Wheel." *The New York Times*, September 22: A1, D8.

———. 1995. "Star at Conference on Women: Banker Who Lends to the Poor." *The New York Times*, September 14:A6.

Uchitelle, Louis. 1993a. "Stanching the Loss of Good Jobs." *The New York Times*, January 31, Section 3:1, 6.

———. 1993b. "America's Newest Industrial Belt." *The New York Times*, March 21, Business Section:1.

———. 1994. "U.S. Corporations Expanding Abroad at a Quicker Pace." *The New York Times*, July 25:A1, D2.

Udesky, Laurie. 1994. "Sweatshops Behind the Labels." *The Nation*, May 16:665–668.

Ufkes, Fran. 1995. "Industrial Restructuring and Agrarian Change: The Greening of Singapore." In Philip McMichael (Ed.), *Food and Agrarian Orders in the World Economy.* Westport, CT: Praeger.

Ul Haq, Mahbub. 1995. "Whatever Happened to the Peace Dividend?" *Our Planet* 7, 1:8–10.

Vernon, Raymond. 1971. *Sovereignty at Bay: The Multinational Spread of U.S. Enterprises.* New York: Basic Books.

Vieille, P. 1988. "The World's Chaos and the New Paradigms of the Social Movement." In Lelio Basso International Foundation for the Rights and Liberation of Peoples (Ed.), *Theory and Practice of Liberation at the End of the 20th Century.* Brussels: Bruylant.

Wacker, Corinne. 1993. "Sustainable Development Through Women's Groups: A Cultural Approach to Sustainable Development." In Wendy Harcourt (Ed.), *Feminist Perspectives on Sustainable Development.* London: Zed Books.

Wallerstein, Immanuel. 1983. *Historical Capitalism.* London: Verso.

———. 1992. "The Collapse of Liberalism." In Ralph Miliband and Leo Panitch (Eds.), *Socialist Register.* London: Merlin.

Walton, John, and David Seddon. 1994. *Free Markets & Food Riots. The Politics of Global Adjustment.* Oxford: Blackwell.

Watkins, Kevin. 1991. "Agriculture and Food Security in the GATT Uruguay Round." *Review of African Political Economy* 50:38–50.

Watts, Michael. 1992. "The Shock of Modernity: Petroleum, Protest, and Fast Capitalism in an Industrializing Society." In Allan Pred and Michael Watts (Eds.), *Reworking Modernity.* New Brunswick: Rutgers University Press.

———. 1994. "Life Under Contract: Contract Farming, Agrarian Restructuring and Flexible Accumulation." In Peter D. Little and Michael J. Watts (Eds.), *Living Under Contract. Contract Farming and Agrarian Transformation in Sub-Saharan Africa.* Madison: University of Wisconsin Press.

Weissman, Robert. 1991. "Prelude to a New Colonialism: The Real Purpose of GATT." *The Nation,* March 18:337.

Wessel, James. 1983. *Trading the Future. Farm Exports and the Concentration of Economic Power in Our Food System.* San Francisco: Institute for Food and Development Policy.

Whitney, Craig R. 1995. "Jobless Legions Rattle Europe's Welfare States." *The New York Times,* June 14: 3.

Williams, Gwyneth. 1981. *Third-World Political Organizations. A Review of Developments.* Montclair, NJ: Allenheld, Osmun & Co.

Williams, Richard. 1990. *Hierarchical Structures and Social Value. The Creation of Black and Irish Identities in the United States.* New York: Cambridge University Press.

Williams, Robert G. 1986. *Export Agriculture and the Crisis in Central America.* Chapel Hill: University of North Carolina Press.

Wolf, Eric. 1982. *Europe and the People Without History.* Berkeley: University of California Press.

Wood, Robert E. 1986. *From Marshall Plan to Debt Crisis: Foreign Aid and Development Choices in the World Economy.* Berkeley: University of California Press.

Woodall, Pam. 1994. "War of the Worlds. A Survey of the Global Economy." *The Economist* Special Supplement, October 1:24.

World Bank. 1990. *World Development Report.* Washington, DC: World Bank.

WuDunn, Sheryl. 1993. "Booming China Is Dream Market for West." *The New York Times,* February 15:A1–6.

Recommended Supplements to This Text

Detailed case studies complement this globally oriented text. I particularly recommend Helena Norberg-Hodge's text *Ancient Futures: Learning from Ladakh* (Sierra Club Books, 1992) and its companion film "Ancient Futures," distributed by The Ladakh Project/International Society for Ecology and Culture, Box 9475, Berkeley, CA 94709. This study presents strikingly clear and comprehensive images of life in Ladakh before and after its very recent modernization, and it evaluates our assumptions about development and raises questions about global social trends. It offers a human-scale version of development to complement the global story of the development project. Other case studies include a proliferating literature on grassroots projects (see the references in this book) and various communities, such as Borneo's forest dwellers depicted in Wade Davis et al., *Nomads of the Dawn* (Pomegranate Artbooks, 1995). Additional case studies include various treatments of the debt crisis, studies of the international financial world such as Bruce Rich's *Mortgaging the Earth,* and studies of transnational firms such as Dan Morgan's *Merchants of Grain,* Richard Barnet and John Cavanagh's *Global Dreams* (see the references in this book), Brewster Kneen's study of Cargill, *Invisible Giant* (Pluto, 1995), and Bryan D. Palmer's *Goodyear Invades the Backcountry* (Monthly Review, 1994) about a corporate takeover of a rural town in Ontario.

Recent films that depict aspects of developmentalism and globalism addressed in this text include PBS documentaries such as "The Politics of Food" (global agribusiness and food aid programs); "Local Heroes: Global Change" (case studies introduced by Southern intellectuals of structural adjustment programs, export processing zones, and so forth); series such as "The Africans," narrated by Ali Mazrui, and East Asia's "Minidragons"; "The Global Economy: Four Weeks in the Life of the Earth" (global corporate and communication networks and the dilemma of unemployment); and "The Decade of Destruction" (of the Amazon forest in the 1980s). "Jungleburger" (Filmkraft Production, 1986) is a graphic portrayal of the U.S./Costa Rica hamburger connection.

Publications such as the U.N. Development Program's (UNDP) annual *Human Development Report* and the World Bank's annual *Development Report* are useful databases, with up-to-date development agency interpretation. Visually striking geopolitical data sources are Alan Thomas's *Third World Atlas* (Taylor & Francis, 1994) and Michael Kidron and Ronald Segal's *The State of the World Atlas* (Penguin, 1995).

Glossary/Index

Cheru, Fantu, 194, 199

Chiapas rebellion, 234–237

Chile, 151–152

China, 154–155, 246–247, 248

Chinese entrepreneurial networks, 83

Chipko movement, 224

Chopsticks, 1, 152

CIMMYT Spanish acronym for the International Wheat and Maize Improvement Center, founded in Mexico in 1943 by the Rockefeller Foundation, 147

Civil war

Africa, 204–206

Congo, 204

Ethiopia, 33

Nigeria, 33

Rwanda, 33, 204

Somalia, 33, 207

United States, 26

Class politics, 200–202

Clausen, A. W., 159

Clayton, Will, 46

Clinton, President Bill, 161, 186

Coca-colonization, 197

Codex Alimentarius, 168

Coffee, Colombian, 27

Cold War

and Asian NICs, 87

bloc rivalry, 36, 53–55

blocs, 35

containment strategy of U.S., 46–48, 79

and development project, 54

free enterprise strategy, 47

geopolitics of, 55

Colombia

coffee culture, 27

food dependency, 63

parastatals, 52

Colonial division of labor specialization between a colony and its metropolitan, colonizing country exchanging primary products for manufactured goods, respectively, 18, 21, 40

Colonialism, 15

in Africa, 32

British, 19–21

East India Company, 19

forms of, 22–23

and gender roles, 23, 226–227

in Ghana, 226

and migration, 188

racist legacy of, 24

settler, 23

social-psychology of, 24–25

systems of rule in, 22

Colonization, 16–23

of Africa, 32–33

frontier, 72–73

of India, 19–21

Columbus, Christopher, 252

Commission on Global Governance, 253

Commodity chain a series of linkages between sites involved in producing part of an overall product for sale on the market, 1, 2, 4, 6, 9

global assembly lines, 89–91

global livestock complex, 66

hierarchical, 92

intra-firm transfers, 112–113

Commodity prices, 127, 129

Commons, 153

Comparative advantage a theorem about how countries specialize in producing and trading what they excel in by virtue of their human and natural resources, 156, 158, 236

Conditionality, IMF, 51, 127–128, 134–135, 138, 154

Confucianism, 60, 157

Congo, 205

Contract labor, 4, 103–104

Corn syrup, 127, 153

Corporatism a method of political incorporation of workers and capitalists into a state-guided project of capitalist development, 120, 121

Cosmopolitan localism a concept describing social action at the local level that takes into account its

Time
market, 106–107
social, 7, 8
Toyota Company, 107
Trade
feed-grain, 67–68
grain, 65
Transmigration scheme, 223
Transnational banks, 113–114, 117, 118
Transnational communities, 189
Transnational corporation (TNC)
a firm, dispersed among several
countries, whose economic activity
is global, 67, 88, 93, 94–95, 96, 99,
101, 102, 105, 107, 108
agribusiness, 67, 101–102, 103, 105,
108, 137
and beef, 100–101
in China, 246
and GATT, 163
and genetic patents, 167
global diversification, 105, 107, 117,
137
joint ventures, 90
markets, 94–95, 105–109
and Mexican BIP, 88, 107, 181
regionalism, 108–109
scale of, 94, 113
subcontracting, 185
Treaty of Maastricht, 170
Triad, 196
Tropical Forest Action Plan, 222
Truman, President Harry S., 30
Trusteeship, 142, 207
Tunisia, 233
Turkey, 214

U

Uganda, 19, 204
Underdevelopment a concept referring to the active retardation of
development as a consequence of
colonialism or modern imperialism,
22, 122
discourse of, 30–31

United Nations
Charter, 33
Codex Alimentarius, 168
Development Decades, 45
new states, 25
policing, 206–207
relief organizations, 47
Social Summit, 252–253
UNCTAD, 123
**United Nations Conference on Eco-
nomic Development (UNCED)**
the 1992 Earth Summit, 220–221
**United Nations Conference on Trade
and Development (UNCTAD)** the
arm and voice of the Third World
in matters of international trade,
established in 1964, 56
**United Nations Development Program
(UNDP)** organization of the
United Nations that enters into
joint ventures with Third World
governments to fund training and
other development programs, 222
United Nations Education, Scientific,
and Cultural Organization
(UNESCO), 242
United Nations Environment Program
(UNEP), 220
United States
debt, 126, 174
deindustrialization, 244
dollar, 174–175
environmental deterioration, 246
as First World leader, 29
fundamentalism, 212
immigration, 187, 189
as initiator of Uruguay Round, 162,
166
military superiority, 175
NAFTA, 180–183
regional trade patterns, 170
resource consumption, 248
trade war, 166, 175
**United States Agency for Interna-
tional Development (USAID)**
a U.S. government agency responsible for financing development
initiatives on a bilateral basis, 70